CAMBRIDGE STUDIES IN
CHINESE HISTORY, LITERATURE AND INSTITUTIONS

General Editors
PATRICK HANAN & DENIS TWITCHETT

The Han Rhapsody

Other books in the series

GLEN DUDBRIDGE: The *Hsi-yu chi*: A study of Antecedents
to the Sixteenth-Century Chinese Novel

STEPHEN FITZGERALD: China and the Overseas Chinese: A
study of Peking's Changing Policy, 1949–1970

CHRISTOPHER HOWE: Wage Patterns and Wage Policy in
Modern China, 1919–1972

RAY HUANG: Taxation and Governmental Finance in Sixteenth-
Century Ming China

DIANA LARY: Region and Nation: The Kwangsi Clique in
Chinese Politics, 1925–1937

CHI-YUN CHEN: Hsün Yüeh (A.D. 148–209): The Life and
Reflections of an Early Medieval Confucian

The Han Rhapsody

A study of the *Fu* of Yang Hsiung
(53 B.C.–A.D. 18)

DAVID R. KNECHTGES

Department of Asian Languages and Literature
University of Washington

CAMBRIDGE UNIVERSITY PRESS

CAMBRIDGE

LONDON · NEW YORK · MELBOURNE

Published by the Syndics of the Cambridge University Press
The Pitt Building, Trumpington Street, Cambridge CB2 1RP
Bentley House, 200 Euston Road, London NW1 2DB
32 East 57th Street, New York, NY 10022, USA
296 Beaconsfield Parade, Middle Park, Melbourne 3206, Australia

ISBN: 0 521 20458 5

First published 1976

Printed in Great Britain
at the University Printing House, Cambridge
(Euan Phillips, University Printer)

To my respected teacher

HELLMUT WILHELM

Professor Emeritus
University of Washington

Contents

Preface   *page* ix

List of Abbreviations   xi

Foreword, by Hans H. Frankel   xiii

1 Introduction   1

2 The Rhapsody before Yang Hsiung   12

3 The 'Sweet Springs' and 'Ho-tung' Rhapsodies   44

4 The 'Barricade Hunt' and 'Ch'ang-yang' Rhapsodies   63

5 The Rhapsody Criticized and Reformed   89

6 Epilogue   109

Appendix I: The Dates of Yang Hsiung's Imperial Rhapsodies   113

Appendix II: Rhapsodies of Doubtful Authenticity   117

Appendix III: Chronology   119

Notes to the text   120

Bibliography   140

Character Glossary   148

Index   152

Preface

This study of Yang Hsiung began in the autumn of 1963 while I was still an undergraduate at the University of Washington. I was introduced to the Han *fu* in Professor Hellmut Wilhelm's course in the history of Chinese literature. Discovering that the only translations of Yang Hsiung's major writings were the German renderings of Erwin von Zach,[1] I was bold enough to make my own clumsy translations. Encouraged by Professor Wilhelm, I continued to study more *fu*, and in my reading of these poems I became increasingly convinced that the key to understanding this perplexing literary genre lay in an examination of early Chinese rhetoric. While studying Chinese literature at Harvard University under James Robert Hightower in 1965, I began a study of Han rhetoric, and I was helped immensely by the timely appearance of Professor James I. Crump's study on the rhetorical features of the *Chan-kuo ts'e*.[2]

When I returned to Seattle in the summer of 1965 I resumed my study of Han literature. Already by this time two important monographs on the *fu* had been published: Yves Hervouet's study of Ssu-ma Hsiang-ju,[3] and Nakashima Chiaki's extensive monograph on the *fu* of the Former and Later Han dynasties.[4] It was particularly gratifying to find that Professor Nakashima devoted much of his volume to the relationship between the *fu* and the rhetorical tradition. During 1966 I was fortunate enough to study for a brief period with Professor Robert O. Payne of the University of Washington's department of English. Professor Payne had just completed a study of Chaucer and medieval rhetoric,[5] and I learned much about Western rhetoric from him.

The present study is a substantially revised version of my doctoral dissertation 'Yang Shyong, the *Fuh*, and Han Rhetoric' (University of Washington, 1968). This work contained a detailed biography of Yang Hsiung followed by an examination of the rhetorical features and conventions of the Han *fu*, particularly as reflected in the writings of the Yang Hsiung.

It should be noted that I use the word rhetoric in two senses: one, in the primary sense of persuasive speech; and secondarily, as ornamental speech. The single term 'rhetoric' generally designates the primary meaning of the word. The secondary sense is normally indicated by the qualified terms 'ornamental rhetoric', 'decorative rhetoric', etc.

Another term that may be somewhat confusing to the Sinologist is the use of the word 'poem' to refer to a composition in the *fu* genre. The use of this term implies no judgment on the prose or verse character of the *fu*, and simply means 'a composition, whether in prose or verse, having beauty of thought or language'.[6]

There are many who have been helpful to me in my studies. My first expression of gratitude must go to Hellmut Wilhelm, who introduced me to Yang Hsiung. I hope some of his enthusiasm for Yang's writing has been imparted to me. I owe a special debt to another of my respected teachers, Professor Hsiao Kung-ch'üan, whose encyclopedic knowledge of Chinese literature and language is always astounding. He was kind enough to carefully read my manuscript, and thanks to his critical eye, the errors are less than they would have been. Also helpful on crucial problems of classical language was Professor Paul L-M. Serruys, who has had a long-term interest in Yang Hsiung. I am especially grateful to Professor Vincent Yu-chung Shih, who gave me much aid in unravelling the abstruse philosophical problems of Yang Hsiung's *Model Sayings* and *The Great Dark*. My colleague C. H. Wang and my former colleague, Hans Frankel of Yale University, have both read my manuscript and offered constructive criticism. I especially want to thank Professor Frankel for writing the Foreword.

Others who helped me in ways impossible to specify here include: Jack L. Dull, Roy Andrew Miller, Robert O. Payne, and the late Hsü Dau-lin of the University of Washington; Li Fang-kuei of the University of Hawaii; Maureen Robertson of Rochester University; James Robert Hightower of Harvard University; Chow Tse-tsung and Francis A. Westbrook of the University of Wisconsin; Jerry Swanson of the University of Vermont; Stephen Owen and Hugh M. Stimson of Yale University; Yves Hervouet of the University of Versailles; Timoteus Pokora, Prague; and J. T. Wixted, Oxford.

D. R. K.

Bothell, Washington
August 1973

Abbreviations

AM: *Asia Major*
AO: *Archiv Orientální*
AS: *Asiatische Studien*
BD: *A Chinese Biographical Dictionary*
BMFEA: *Bulletin of the Museum of Far Eastern Antiquities*
BSOAS: *Bulletin of the School of Oriental and African Studies*
CHC: *Ch'u hsüeh chi*
CHW: *Ch'üan Han wen*
CKT: *Chan-kuo t'se*
FYYS: *Fa-yen yi-shu*
HCTC: *Hsi-ching tsa-chi*
HFHD: *History of the Former Han Dynasty*
HJAS: *Harvard Journal of Asiatic Studies*
HNT: *Huai-nan tzu*
HS: *Han shu*
JA: *Journal asiatique*
JAS: *Journal of Asian Studies*
JAOS: *Journal of the American Oriental Society*
JNCBRAS: *Journal of the North China Branch of the Royal Asiatic Society*
KWY-A: *Ku-wen yüan, Tai-nan ko ts'ung-shu* ed.
KWY-B: *Ku-wen yüan, SPTK* ed.
LSCC: *Lü-shih ch'un-ch'iu*
Mh: *Les Mémoires historiques de Se-ma Ts'ien*
MS: *Monumenta Serica*
MTB: *Memoirs of the Research Department of the Toyo Bunko*
PTSC: *Pei-t'ang shu-ch'ao*
SC: *Shih chi*
SPPY: *Ssu-pu pei-yao*
SPTK: *Ssu-pu ts'ung-k'an*
TP: *T'oung Pao*
WH: *Wen hsüan*
YWLC: *Yi-wen lei-chü*

Foreword

A sort of divine justice guides ultimate judgments in literary history. No matter how badly and how long great writers, movements, and art forms are downgraded or ignored, eventually their true worth will be recognized. For centuries, *gongorismo* was considered a symptom of decadence in the development of Spanish literature, but since 1927 Góngora has been celebrated as one of Spain's finest poets. In France, the unique beauty of that country's baroque literature has been appreciated only since the late 1940s. In our own time, too, we have witnessed the rehabilitation of Li Ho as one of the great Chinese poets, after nearly a thousand years of neglect. Now we have a book which establishes the rightful positions in Chinese literature for a brilliant writer and an important poetic genre.

True, Yang Hsiung has had other scholarly champions before, as Professor Knechtges points out, but the full range of his literary qualities and his particular contributions to the *fu* genre have never been as thoroughly explored and as fairly assessed as in this book. And though Knechtges benefits by earlier investigations of the *fu*, he breaks new ground in reaching a broader and deeper understanding of this literary genre and in demolishing the prejudices that are still widely held against it. Typical of what many specialists in Chinese literature have thought of the *fu* down to modern times is the following statement: '...even the best *fu* has become difficult to understand, let alone to appreciate' (Lai Ming, *A History of Chinese Literature* [first published 1964], New York: Capricorn Books, 1966, p. 107).

Despite his youth, David R. Knechtges has already had a distinguished academic career, and mastered several diverse fields of study, all of which come into play in the present work. He has become an expert on the literature of the Han period (he is currently collaborating with Hellmut Wilhelm on a literary history of that period), on the *fu* genre, on the rhetorical tradition in China and Europe, and on Yang Hsiung. It is no accident that he has been attracted to this particular writer, for the two men have much in common. Yang Hsiung, like David Knechtges and his teacher Hellmut Wilhelm (to whom this book is dedicated), was a polyhistor with wide-ranging interests and extraordinary literary sensibility. What makes the study of Yang Hsiung's works especially rewarding is that he was not only a brilliant writer but also a literary critic, graced with the rare gift of self-criticism. On the other hand, he is one of the most difficult authors in the Chinese language, and a lesser scholar would be unable to translate and interpret him as accurately, lucidly, and profoundly as David Knechtges does in this volume. Nor would a lesser scholar be able to muster so much secondary literature – in many languages – on the complex subject, and to adduce so many illuminating parallels from Western civilization to the phenomena being studied.

It is interesting to reflect on the different developments of the rhetorical tradition in China and the West. In China, as this book shows, it arose among itinerant political theorists and promoters of specific political programs. It soon became a literary tradition, in marked contrast to ancient Greece and Rome, where oratory played an important role. Aside from the arguments put forward at court, seeking to persuade the ruler to adopt the viewpoint of an individual or a group, there was little demand in early China for the art of elocution. Conspicuously absent in China were the Western legal tradition where lawyers pleaded their clients' or the state's case, and the tradition of public political debate in a popular assembly, forum, parliament, or mass meeting. At the same time, the high value which the Chinese have always placed on the written word, and the extraordinary literacy of Chinese civilization, may help to explain why rhetoric ceased to be an oral function and became instead a genre of poetry. The astounding popularity of this genre in Han times may also have been a reaction against the prevailing trend toward brevity, conciseness, and understatement in Chinese poetry and prose. Admirable though these qualities are, there can be too much of a good thing, and the opposite tendencies, long suppressed, burst forth with tremendous vigor in the Han *fu*. The special qualities of this unique Chinese art form, so long deprecated and misunderstood, will be appreciated by the readers of this book.

HANS H. FRANKEL
Yale University

1

Introduction

In Chinese literary history the name of the poet Yang Hsiung (53 B.C.–A.D. 18) has figured prominently, although not as prominently as one might expect considering the bulk and variety of his literary production. He is generally better known for his non-poetic writings. He is the author of two important philosophical works, *The Great Dark Classic* (*T'ai-hsüan ching*), which is constructed around eighty-one four-line figures (tetragrams) in the manner of the *Book of Changes*,[1] and the *Model Sayings* (*Fa yen*), a collection of aphorisms and short dialogues concerning miscellaneous historical and philosophical questions.[2] Yang is also credited with two philological studies, the *Annotations on the Ts'ang Chieh*, which was a recension of the most important dictionaries of the Former Han period,[3] and the *Regional Words* (*Fang yen*), a collection of dialect expressions.[4] In addition to these works, Yang has a large and respectable literary corpus.[5] This corpus includes a group of writings called *fu* or 'rhapsodies', a poetic genre that Yang mastered at an early age and that brought him recognition and honours at the imperial court.

The rhapsody was the most popular poetic type of the Han dynasty. Among most Chinese critics, Yang generally has taken second place to an earlier poet, Ssu-ma Hsiang-ju (179–117 B.C.), who customarily is credited with shaping the genre into the florid display of verbal virtuosity that is usually associated with the Han rhapsody. Whether Ssu-ma Hsiang-ju was the originator of this type of rhapsody, which I term the epideictic rhapsody, is difficult to prove, mainly because there are few extant genuine specimens of the form that ante-date Ssu-ma Hsiang-ju. There is no denying, however, that his influence on the development of the genre was considerable. The shadow cast by Ssu-ma Hsiang-ju in Chinese literary history is so immense that it even eclipses a genuine creative genius like Yang Hsiung.

In many respects, Yang Hsiung is as important in the development of the rhapsody as Ssu-ma Hsiang-ju. Yang lived at the end of the Former Han dynasty (206 B.C.–A.D. 8), which was the period in which the conventions of the rhapsody became firmly established. These conventions, which slowly emerged throughout the Former Han, are clearly discernible in Yang Hsiung's rhapsodies, for Yang was a most tradition-conscious poet, and he

[1]

made a concerted effort to adhere to the traditions of the genre. In addition to writing poetry, Yang wrote about poetry, and he is the first poet to espouse his own theory of the rhapsody, which is something that Ssu-ma Hsiang-ju probably never did.[6] It is clear from Yang's theoretical writings, and even in the rhapsodies themselves, that Yang was somewhat uneasy about the way in which the rhapsody had developed since Ssu-ma Hsiang-ju. Yang believed that writing poetry was essentially a moral act, and that the proper function of all literature was to promote ethical conduct. The rhapsody, in Yang Hsiung's eyes at least, seemed to be doing just the opposite. The epideictic rhapsodies, written to eulogize the extravagance and indulgences of the imperial court, were failing in their fundamental task of conveying effective moral reprimands, and this failure led Yang Hsiung eventually to repudiate the rhapsody.

Yang Hsiung's discussion of the rhapsody is instructive, for he is no mere armchair critic, but a practicing poet who was the premier Chinese poet at the end of the Former Han. One can follow what almost appear to be experiments by Yang in attempting to make a moral statement in his rhapsodies. He is more successful in some pieces than others, but his attempts at using the genre for persuasion are always evident. Yang was constantly changing, and his later works are not the same as his earlier ones. The change in style and focus could be cited as partial evidence to belie the notion that Yang lacked a creative imagination and that he only wrote in imitation of his predecessors.

In addition to the widely held belief that Yang is a mere hack, there is a tendency to condemn him for his personal conduct. Yang Hsiung in his later life served at the court of Wang Mang (43 B.C.–A.D. 23), who is one of the few Chinese statesmen to earn the odious designation of 'usurper'. Wang Mang seized the throne and declared himself emperor of the short-lived Hsin dynasty (A.D. 8–23). Although Yang held an extremely low position in the Wang Mang regime, later Chinese scholars, particularly in the Sung (960–1279), found the act of serving a usurper tantamount to treason.[7] Yang did have his defenders, but the charges by his detractors certainly did not enhance his reputation, and even today, one often hears the words 'traitor' and 'Yang Hsiung' uttered in the same breath.

The attacks on his personal behavior undoubtedly are partially responsible for the negative evaluation of Yang's writing. 'There is a purported scandal, ergo his poetry is worthless.' One need not elaborate on the fallacy of this type of criticism. Rimbaud is not a bad poet simply because he may have been a despicable person. Similarly, Yang Hsiung deserves to be evaluated in terms of his literary achievement, and not on the basis of non-literary criteria.

Yang Hsiung's literary career must have begun relatively early, and while he was still residing in his home province of Shu (modern Szechwan), which lay in the extreme southwestern reaches of the Han empire. Although Shu was considered a somewhat uncivilized place during the Han period, it produced excellent scholars and poets. Government schools established to educate the local youth in the proper moral teachings contributed greatly to the high level of learning in this isolated area.[8] Geography can occasionally be an important influence on literary development, and in the case of the rhapsody, it is not pure coincidence that the most prominent writers prior to Yang Hsiung, Ssu-ma Hsiang-ju and Wang Pao (fl. 58 B.C.), were from Shu, and it is highly probable that young scholars, particularly in Ch'eng-tu, the provincial capital, were schooled in rhapsody composition. Yang Hsiung, in fact, is credited with a rhapsody describing this city, and if it is from his hand, most likely it was written as a practice composition.[9]

Yang Hsiung was nurtured on the rhapsodies of Ssu-ma Hsiang-ju, and it was because of his ability to write in the style of Ssu-ma Hsiang-ju that he was summoned to the imperial capital in Ch'ang-an. Unfortunately, none of these imitation pieces survives, and the only work from his early corpus still extant is the 'Contra Sao' (*Fan Sao*), a poeticized criticism of the poet Ch'ü Yüan (ca. 340–278).[10] Ch'ü Yüan, a poet-statesman of the southern state of Ch'u, had become almost a saint through the legend of his reputed suicide by drowning after being maltreated by the rulers of the Ch'u house. The 'Encountering Sorrow' (*Li sao*), in which Ch'ü Yüan purportedly states his complaint and anticipates eventual suicide, was at that time one of the most respected poems in the Chinese language. The 'Contra Sao' is a direct attack on the idealization of Ch'ü Yüan. It is a poem using the meter and diction of 'Encountering Sorrow' to strongly condemn Ch'ü Yüan's suicide. Apparently Yang followed 'Contra Sao' with several other poems on the same subject, but none of these pieces survives.[11]

Around 20 B.C. Yang left his native province to take up residence as an official at the imperial court in Ch'ang-an.[12] During the Han, it was not uncommon for distinguished poets to be given government posts on the basis of their poetical ability alone.[13] Although poets were given regular administrative titles, one of their primary tasks was to compose poems and other pieces, including rhapsodies, on behalf of the emperor. This activity made such officials the equivalent of a 'court poet', although there was no official designation of this kind. Yang's official title was initially Candidate for Appointment (tai-chao), which was not an official post but a designation commonly given to those under consideration for a government position.[14] It was while he was a 'candidate' during the reign of Emperor Ch'eng (reg. 32–7 B.C.) that Yang wrote his first rhapsodies for the emperor. The first of these pieces was the 'Sweet Springs Rhapsody' (*Kan-ch'üan fu*), which was written on the occasion of the celebration of the sacrifices to Heaven at the Sweet Springs Palace north of Ch'ang-an. Yang's poem evidently pleased the emperor, for he was asked to accompany the imperial party to Fen-yin in Ho-tung Commandery where sacrifices to Sovereign Earth (Hou-t'u), the chief earth deity, were performed. Yang was asked to produce another rhapsody on this occasion. This piece he titled 'Ho-tung Rhapsody' (*Ho-tung fu*).[15] Later, perhaps in that same year, Yang was invited to view the great imperial hunt held in the Shang-lin Park. He wrote two rhapsodies about this event: 'Barricade Hunt Rhapsody' (*Chiao-lieh fu*) and 'Ch'ang-yang Rhapsody' (*Ch'ang-yang fu*).[16] It was probably after presenting these poems that Yang was given his first regular appointment: Gentleman (*lang*) or Attendant Gentleman (*shih-lang*), and concurrently Servitor at the Yellow Gate (*chi-shih huang-men*).[17]

As a court poet, and as a candidate for an imperial appointment, Yang was expected to praise the emperor's greatness and the magnificence of the spectacles he was so privileged to attend. Thus, all of these rhapsodies are in varying degree panegyrical. Nevertheless, Yang was obviously appalled by the extravagance and waste of these activities, and one can detect in the poems subtle moral reprimands to the emperor reminding him that such indulgences are improper for the supreme sovereign. Yang shows great skill in the technique known as *feng* or 'indirect criticism', and by his use of it shows that he was intent on using the rhapsody for moral suasion.

Yang Hsiung soon found, however, that his subtle hints were going unheeded. It was at this point that he decided that the technique of indirect criticism simply did not work, and that he would have to give up writing rhapsodies. In his 'Autobiography' Yang describes what he felt were the inadequacies of the rhapsody:

I believe the rhapsody is for the purpose of criticizing by indirection, and a writer is required to speak by adducing examples, use ornate language to the extreme, grossly exaggerate, greatly amplify, and strive to make it such that another person cannot add to it. Thus, by the time he returns to the rectifying message, the reader has already erred. In former times Emperor Wu was interested in immortals. Hsiang-ju presented the 'Great Man Rhapsody' in order to criticize him by indirection. The emperor, on the contrary, had the intention of airily floating on the clouds.[18] From this it is clear that the rhapsody only encourages and does not restrain. It is rather like an entertainer such as Ch'un-yü K'un or Jester Meng.[19] It is nothing sustained by rules and measures, nor does it rectify behavior like the poems and rhapsodies of nobles and gentlemen. Therefore, I have stopped and will no longer write any.[20]

Yang's renunciation of the rhapsody seems to have been in name only, for he continued to write poems, which, although not titled 'rhapsody', clearly belonged to that tradition. One of these poems, the 'Dissolving Ridicule' (*Chieh ch'ao*), written in defense of his decision to remain aloof from court affairs, shows Yang writing more forthrightly and directly.[21] In another piece, perhaps from this same period, Yang not too subtly compares life of a court official to the precarious position of a water pitcher that is about to topple into a well and be smashed on the bricks below.[22] Yang continues to theorize about the rhapsody, and he eventually postulates what he considered to be the ideal rhapsody: a poem that stresses content over form, directness over obliqueness, plain language over floridity. Yang may have even written a rhapsody that conforms to this ideal.[23]

Yang's significance thus lies in both his theory and practice, and he clearly holds an important position in the history of the Han rhapsody. His importance cannot be understood, however, unless one first understands the nature and development of the Han rhapsody. Unfortunately, the rhapsody today is held in low repute in China, both on the mainland and Taiwan. Few if any writers deign to write in this form, and except for two works published in the 1930s, virtually nothing of substance on the rhapsody has been published in recent years.[24] Those studies that have been done are mostly handbooks or chronicles, which are somewhat useful, but really do not attempt to provide a clear definition of the genre. Even the history of the rhapsody given in these works lacks coherence.

The most extensive research on the rhapsody has been done by the Japanese, notably Suzuki Torao and Nakashima Chiaki. Suzuki's monumental work, published in 1936, is still the most comprehensive study of the rhapsody.[25] Suzuki traces the genre from its beginnings in the fourth century B.C. all the way through the Ch'ing dynasty. Although his discussion of the Han rhapsody occupies only some fifty pages, it was for many years the definitive statement about the formative period of the genre. Recently, Suzuki's study of the Han has been superceded by his compatriot, Nakashima Chiaki. Nakashima has devoted a monograph of almost six hundred pages to the Han rhapsody.[26] Nakashima's work is important, for he is the first to document in detail the relationship of the rhapsody to the early Chinese rhetorical tradition. Early Chinese rhetoric, as in ancient Greece, was concerned primarily with persuasion, and many of the techniques used by the Chinese persuaders found their way into the rhapsody.

Work on the rhapsody in Western languages is mainly limited to translation, and in fact the rhapsody has enjoyed somewhat more popularity in translation than in the original during the past fifty years. Many of Arthur

Waley's first translations from the Chinese were rhapsodies.[27] In the 1930s, Erwin von Zach, working in isolation from academia in Batavia, produced good, literal translations of rhapsodies in German.[28] Recently, Burton Watson has translated a modest number of rhapsodies which have appeared in a volume intended for the general reader.[29]

Studies of the rhapsody in Western languages are not especially numerous or noteworthy. Probably the best general discussion of the genre is the succinct description given by James Robert Hightower in his survey of Chinese literature.[30] On the Han rhapsody, most studies provide only vague generalities. Yves Hervouet's work on Ssu-ma Hsiang-ju, which touches on the development of the rhapsody during the period prior to Ssu-ma Hsiang-ju, is encyclopedic rather than analytical.[31] Burton Watson's account of the genre, which is given in several places, offers occasional insights but it is not thorough.[32]

One of the most significant and groundbreaking studies of the rhapsody is a short article published by Hellmut Wilhelm in 1957.[33] In this article, prepared for a conference on Chinese thought and institutions, Dr Wilhelm proposed the novel idea that contrary to the commonly held notion the rhapsody did not develop from the so-called Ch'u school of literature, but 'was a legacy of the School of Politicians and of their art of conveying things by indirection'.[34] The main concern of the School of Politicians was political rhetoric, and if the connection between this school and the rhapsody can be established, one can easily show that the rhapsody is essentially a rhetorical genre. Following Dr Wilhelm's theory, my own studies have proceeded to investigate the rhetorical character of the rhapsody, and my research tends to corroborate Wilhelm's thesis.[35]

On Yang Hsiung, most research has been concentrated on subjects other than his rhapsodies. Yang has no less than three *nien-p'u* or 'chronological biographies', which summarize year by year the main events of his life.[36] In the 1930s, the German Sinologist Alfred Forke devoted several short articles and a major part of his history of early Chinese philosophy to Yang Hsiung.[37] Forke's work led to further studies, including an important article by Forke's student, Fritz Jäger, on Yang Hsiung's relationship with Wang Mang.[38] Forke's studies unfortunately were marred by numerous errors, which Erwin von Zach was quick to point out in an article titled 'In Defense of the Philosopher Yang Hsiung'.[39] Zach then proceeded to translate a number of Yang's works including several rhapsodies and the long philosophical treatise *Model Sayings*.[40] The *Model Sayings* is a thirteen chapter work patterned on the *Analects* (*Lun yü*). Like the *Analects*, the *Model Sayings* consists of a series of dialogues in which an anonymous questioner poses a query to Yang Hsiung, which he answers in a highly terse fashion. It was written sometime during the Wang Mang period, and thus it has been one of Yang's more controversial works. Some scholars have viewed it as an apology for Wang Mang's usurpation, while others have examined it for what they claim is a veiled attack on Wang. Several Ch'ing and early Republican period scholars in particular rose to Yang Hsiung's defense, including the eminent philologist Yü Yüeh (1821–1907)[41] and the diplomat Wang Jung-pao (1878–1933). Wang wrote an extensive commentary to the *Model Sayings* which is exhaustive if not always reliable.[42]

Regardless of the political purport of the *Model Sayings*, its major focus is the defense and justification of the Confucian tradition as Yang Hsiung understood it. Yang strongly desired to see a return to classical precepts or what he called the 'teachings of the sages', of whom the Duke of Chou and Confucius were considered the leading lights. He acutely felt the apparent lack of interest in classical learning, which he considered in a state of decline. At one point in the *Model Sayings* he declares to his questioner: 'I have seldom seen people who favor the works of the remote past. They read instead contemporary literature and listen to contemporary sayings. They ignore the remote past!'[43]

Much of the *Model Sayings* is thus directed toward disputing notions of many pre-Ch'in and Han thinkers. In addition to attacking earlier philosophers, Yang also makes critical remarks on intellectual currents of his time. Yang expresses particularly strong opposition to the prevailing interest in immortality quests and the astrological and numerological speculation that was growing in popularity during this period.[44] It was in this context that Yang Hsiung speaks about literature, and its proper function of combatting deleterious influences and pernicious doctrines. In the *Model Sayings* Yang makes a series of remarks about the rhapsody, giving his reasons for repudiating the genre as it was currently written. His statements, although formulated long after he had purportedly given up writing the rhapsody, offer an important insight into what he conceived to be the generic ideal of the rhapsody and its proper function.

Another work important for an understanding of Yang Hsiung's ideas, and these include his literary theory, is *The Great Dark*, which is commonly called *The Great Dark Classic*. Since I shall have occasion to refer to it, a short description of this difficult work is necessary. *The Great Dark* was written before the Wang Mang period, perhaps around 2 B.C. Like its prototype, the *Book of Changes*, it is based on a series of linear complexes. Instead of the hexagram (a six-line figure), Yang uses a four-line complex or tetragram, but unlike the *Changes*, each line can be divided not only once but twice. Thus, in

Yang's system there are eighty-one (3^4) possible combinations instead of the sixty-four (2^6) possibilities of the *Changes*. Each line of the tetragram has been co-ordinated with administrative and social institutions. Thus, the lines from top to bottom are titled 'region' (*fang*), 'province' (*chou*), 'department' (*pu*), and 'family' (*chia*). This hierarchy and the various combinations of the lines represent the basic process of development in Yang's cosmography.

The number three plays an important role in this system. Yang conceives of a universe guided by the force he calls the Dark (*hsüan*), which governs a hierarchy of tri-partite divisions in the cosmos. The Dark occupies the center of the universe and embraces three 'regions'. Each of the three 'regions' is divided into three parts known as 'provinces', yielding a total of nine 'provinces'. Similarly, each 'province' divides into three 'departments' (totalling twenty-seven), and each department in turn separates into three 'families' (totalling eighty-one). The symbolic representation of this process is the tetragram. The top line represents the 'region'; the second line, the 'province'; the third line, the 'department'; and the lowest line, the 'family'.

————	Region
————	Province
————	Department
————	Family

By dividing each line once or twice in an orderly sequence the eighty-one possibilities are exhausted. Each line also is symbolic: a solid line represents Heaven; a once-divided line, Earth; and a twice divided line, Man. The individual tetragrams that are formed in this manner represent the fundamental concepts of the universe, and like the *Changes*, each has a special name.

A similar trinary process governs the production of things in the universe. Yang conceived of three stages of growth, culmination, and decline which he termed 'thought' (*ssu*), 'fortune' (*fu*), and 'disaster' (*huo*). Each of these stages is further divisible by three. In each tetragram there are nine texts called 'judgments' or 'appraisals' (*tsan*), which like the 'line texts' of the *Changes* are short verse oracles giving an interpretation of the situation represented by each stage of the tetragram. (Unlike the *Changes*, the 'judgments' are not keyed on the lines of the tetragram.) Each judgment is then followed by a 'commentary' or 'probe' (*ts'e*), which further elaborates on the significance of the oracle given in the judgment. The first through the third judgments depict the stages of progressive growth; the middle judgments (four to six) represent the apex of development; and the seventh through the ninth judgments portray the process of decline. The system is also coordinated with numbers, constellations, time, colors, animals, and other objects so that it can represent virtually everything in the universe.[45]

The Great Dark has always been considered a highly perplexing book, and few scholars have had the courage to try to read it, let alone to understand it.[46] The same principle would seem to apply to Yang's rhapsodies. A common opinion of Yang Hsiung is that he contributed nothing original. Even if one granted credence to this view, this does not mean that what he wrote is dull and without interest. A major reason for the appeal of Yang Hsiung's works may be credited in large part to his skill with words, a feature that even seems to characterize his purely philosophical writings. His philosophical works are in fact so 'poetic' that a modern philosopher would probably disqualify them as philosophy. Although this book is confined to a treatment of Yang Hsiung as a writer of rhapsodies, it is proper to keep in mind that Yang was more than a good poet. He was a profound thinker, and his intellectual interests extended into widely diverse areas, including history, mathematics, philology, lexicography, music, astronomy, and politics. It would probably distress Yang to find in the twentieth century a scholar writing on the narrow subject of his rhapsodies, but the narrowness is mine and not his.

Sources. The primary source of information about Yang Hsiung is the long two-chapter biography (87A–B) in the *History of the Former Han* (*Han shu*). The *History of the Former Han* was compiled by Pan Ku (A.D. 32–92) and members of his family around A.D. 70. Yang's biography follows the general pattern of most biographies (*lieh-chuan*) in the *History*. It contains a genealogy of the Yang family, a sketch of Yang Hsiung's character and personality, the texts of seven rhapsodies and essays, a description of the cosmography contained in *The Great Dark*, a brief section giving Yang's criticisms of the rhapsody, a chapter outline of the *Model Sayings*, and finally an 'Appraisal' (*Tsan*) by Pan Ku, which details Yang Hsiung's career at court, particularly under Wang Mang. The 'Appraisal' also contains remarks about Yang Hsiung by such contemporaries as the scholar Liu Hsin (?–A.D. 23) and the philosopher Huan T'an (ca. 43 B.C.–A.D. 28).[47]

What is particularly valuable about this biography is that it is most probably based on an 'Autobiography' written by Yang Hsiung himself.[48] Thus, the information it contains is potentially more reliable than what one ordinarily finds in the standard dynastic history biography. Particularly useful for the literary historian are the detailed introductions to Yang Hsiung's rhapsodies, which appear to come from the 'Autobiography'. These introductions give an account of the circumstances of the composition of the poem, in several cases the date, and an explanation of the poem's purpose.

Relatively speaking the amount of rhapsodies from the Former Han dynasty still surviving is small. At the end of the Former Han one catalogue listed around 1000 rhapsodies, while today approximately 40 pieces attributed to Former Han writers survive.[49] The best Han source for texts of rhapsodies is the *History of the Former Han*. Also useful for the early part of the Han dynasty is the *Records of the Historian (Shih chi)* compiled by Ssu-ma Ch'ien (ca. 145–90 B.C.). However, these two sources contain only about a half of the extant rhapsodies, and one must go to later, less reliable works to find texts of other pieces.

During the Six Dynasties period (A.D. 222–589) a large number of anthologies was compiled, including special collections of rhapsodies. The only extant collection containing rhapsodies is *The Literary Selections (Wen hsüan)*.[50] This work was compiled by Hsiao T'ung (501–531). Originally in thirty *chüan*, it was rearranged into sixty *chüan* by Li Shan (?–689), who also wrote an important commentary on the text. In spite of its importance in Chinese literary studies, *The Literary Selections* contains only two Former Han rhapsodies not in the *History of the Former Han*. Its main use lies in its commentary, including that by Li Shan and the later commentary known as the *Five Subjects Commentary (Wu ch'en chu)*.[51]

Somewhat useful, but not altogether reliable, are the T'ang dynasty compendia. The earliest of these is the *Documents of the Northern Hall (Pei-t'ang shu-ch'ao)* compiled by Yü Shih-nan (558–638).[52] It contains only short excerpts of rhapsodies, and because it was drastically altered in the Ming dynasty, the *Documents* must be used with great care. The best of the T'ang compendia is the *Compendium of Arts and Letters (Yi-wen lei-chü)*, compiled by an imperial commission under the direction of Ou-yang Hsün (557–641) in A.D. 624.[53] The *Compendium* contains at least thirty-five Former Han rhapsodies, and about half of these do not occur earlier. Unfortunately, most of them are fragments, and the compilers do not indicate the provenance of the text. A smaller companion volume to the *Compendium* is the *Student's Primer (Ch'u hsüeh chi)*, another imperially sponsored compilation presented to the throne in 727.[54] The *Primer* contains fewer rhapsodies than the *Compendium*, and those it does cite are virtually identical to those in the *Compendium*.

In addition to the compendia, there are two sources of questionable reliability. The first of these is the *Western Capital Miscellany (Hsi-ching tsa chi)*, a collection of anecdotes purportedly relating events of the Former Han period. The exact date of its compilation is unknown although it most likely was compiled around the fifth century A.D.[55] The rhapsodies and remarks about the rhapsody it contains must be used with extreme care. The same warning should be heeded for the *Garden of Ancient Literature (Ku-wen yüan)*, an anthology attributed to the T'ang dynasty but most likely compiled in the eleventh century.[56] This collection is the earliest source for several Former Han rhapsodies including ones by Yang Hsiung. Again, the compiler does not indicate the provenance of his texts, and in some cases the text is in poor condition.

Later collections important for a study of the rhapsody include the *Complete Han Prose* (*Ch'üan Han wen*) compiled by Yen K'o-chün (1762–1843).[57] This work contains texts of all rhapsodies attributed to Former Han writers, including fragments. Yen was careful to supply information on the sources for his texts, and occasionally provides collation notes. A more limited anthology is the *Collection of One Hundred Three Writers of the Han, Wei and Six Dynasties* (*Han Wei Liu-ch'ao yi-pai-san chia chi*) by Chang P'u (1602–1641).[58] Chang selected only major writers for this collection, which contains the complete extant works of each writer. Chang was somewhat uncritical of his material, and he fails to provide the sources of the texts. An extremely useful, but somewhat rare collection, is the *Rhapsodies throughout the Ages Classified* (*Li-tai fu hui*) compiled under imperial auspices by Ch'en Yüan-lung (1652–1736) *et al.* Compiled in 1706, this anthology contains rhapsodies that date from the pre-Han period to the end of the Ming dynasty. It is the most complete collection of rhapsodies ever produced (they number something over 4000).[59]

2

The Rhapsody before Yang Hsiung

The Meaning of the Word Fu. The word *fu*, which I have chosen to call 'rhapsody', has been rendered into English by various expressions, including 'rhyme-prose', 'prose poetry', 'poetical description', and 'verse essay'. *Fu* (Old Chinese *p_iwo*) was in use long before it became the name of a literary genre, and it is not entirely clear how its earliest sense of 'tax' or 'to tax'[1] is related to its later meaning as the name of a type of poetry. The best explanation seems to be that the meaning of 'to tax' became extended to the general sense of 'to contribute' (presumably taxes), 'to give', and 'to distribute'.[2] In early usage it was a loan for a phonetically similar word, also pronounced *fu* (Old Chinese *p'_iwo*), meaning 'to extend', 'to spread out', 'to display'.[3] *Fu* is further considered semantically related to words of the same phonetic series also meaning 'to spread out/display': *pu* (Old Chinese *pwo*) and *p'u* (Old Chinese *$p'wo$*).[4]

In the sense of 'to display', 'to present', or 'to express', *fu* (and words with meanings similar to *fu*) came to be applied in the pre-Han period to the 'presentation' of poems at the courts of kings and lords. In the *Tso Commentary (Tso chuan)*, which may be a work of the fourth century B.C., there are numerous examples of the practice known as *fu shih*, which generally signifies two things. The most common meaning was to present or recite (chant) an existing poem (*shih*), usually from the *Book of Songs*.[5] The phrase in its secondary sense refers to the actual composition or extemporization of an original poem.[6] The ability to recite and extemporize became the mark of a good official and even was a theoretical requirement for holding office. The importance of this skill was reportedly emphasized by Confucius, who declared to his son: 'If you do not learn the *Songs*, you will have nothing to use in your speech'[7]

One of the most informative statements on the early use of the term *fu* is contained in the 'Summary on Songs and Rhapsodies' (*Shih fu lüeh*) of the 'Treatise on Bibliography' in the *History of the Former Han*.

The commentary says,[8] *'To recite/chant* (sung) *without singing is called* fu. *Upon climbing high, if one can recite/chant* (fu), *he may become a great officer.'* *This means that he is aroused by the circumstances and creates his theme. When his talent and wisdom are profound and excellent, it is possible to consult with him on state affairs. Therefore, he can be ranked with the great officers. Anciently, when the lords, ministers, and great officers had contact with a neighbouring state they tried to exert their influence with subtle words. When the time came to present themselves they invariably recited a poem in order to express their intention. Generally, in this way they could distinguish between the worthy and unworthy and perceive whether a state would prosper or decay.*[9]

This account is instructive on a number of points. The first thing it tells us is that *fu* was applied to a special type of recitation that differed from singing proper (*ke*). This type of recitation was known as *sung*, which in pre-Han texts generally designates a chant or declamation unaccompanied by music.[10] According to Suzuki Torao, chanting (*rôdoku*) was most commonly used for oral presentation of political advice or criticism at court.[11]

The political function of chanting and recitation is also reflected in the dictum expressed in the 'Summary': *teng kao neng fu, k'o wei ta-fu* ('upon climbing high, if one can recite/chant, he may become a great officer'). There is some confusion about the exact meaning of the phrase *teng kao* (climbing high), mainly because in Han times and thereafter *teng kao* referred to climbing a high place such as a mountain or tower, where a poem would be composed or recited.[12] It has been suggested that in pre-Han times 'climbing high' had nothing to do with climbing a mountain or tower and designated instead the ascent of the hall, platform, or stairs in the court where affairs of state were conducted.[13] Certainly, the 'Summary' passage, which refers to ministers and diplomats reciting poems at court, should be understood in this way.

Throughout the pre-Han period *fu* was used almost exclusively as a verb that designated the recitation of a poem, usually at court. Then, at a date impossible to specify exactly, *fu* became the name of a type of declamatory poem commonly characterized by a mixture of prose and verse, relatively long lines (usually six or seven syllables), parallelism, elaborate description, dialogue, extensive cataloguing, and difficult language. In the Han dynasty poets began writing pieces with the word *fu* in the title, and apparently the reason these poems were called *fu* is that they were often chanted. Thus, one could translate *fu* as 'declamation', but declamation is not a literary term. For this reason I have chosen to translate *fu* as 'rhapsody'. The rhapsody in ancient Greece was an epic poem recited or extemporized by a minstrel or court poet, known as a rhapsode. The *fu*, of course, was not exclusively an epic poem, although some *fu* exhibit epic features, but its medium of presentation makes it akin to the rhapsody. The *fu* poet in many ways is a kind of rhapsode, and the poems he composed often display the ecstasy, grandeur, and emotional intensity associated with the rhapsody.

Calling the *fu* rhapsody, however, does not completely define the genre that existed in the Han dynasty. The *fu* is somewhat illusory in that it existed in many different forms, and was constantly changing throughout the Former Han period. For this reason, it is virtually impossible to provide a succinct definition of the genre that would apply to all specimens of *fu*. Thus, rather than trying to give a vague, general characterization of the *fu* I prefer to present a brief history of the *fu* prior to Yang Hsiung. Through an historical approach one can more easily understand how the *fu* developed, what types of *fu* were written, what their function was, and what conventions existed. This history further provides a context in which one can place the *fu* of Yang Hsiung, who wrote at the end of the Former Han period. Yang not only wrote *fu* of several different kinds, but he was the first thinker to postulate literary theories about the *fu*. The historical background enables us to better comprehend what Yang Hsiung was trying to do in his *fu*, and what the purpose of his theoretical discussions was.

The ' Li Sao' and Ch'u tz'u. Although the word *fu* in the pre-Han period was not the name of a literary genre,[14] later classifications and histories of the *fu* have labelled certain pre-Han poets as the originators of the genre.[15] The earliest poet included in these schemes is Ch'ü Yüan, whose traditional dates are ca. 340–278 B.C. According to Han sources, which are not altogether reliable, Ch'ü Yüan was a minister to King Huai of Ch'u (328–299 B.C.). He was slandered at court by rival ministers who encouraged the king to have him banished. To vent his sorrow and frustration Ch'ü Yüan wrote a long poem titled 'Li Sao' (Encountering Sorrow). Shortly after writing the 'Li Sao' Ch'ü Yüan reportedly committed suicide by drowning himself in the Mi-lo River.[16] Many scholars believe that the traditional story about Ch'ü Yüan is pure myth, and some have even doubted that he wrote the 'Li Sao'.[17] Others maintain that this account is historically accurate; they accept Ch'ü Yüan as the author of the 'Li Sao' and credit him with other poems as well. Regardless of the historicity of the man, there is no denying the literary significance of the poems that surround Ch'ü Yüan's name, for the 'Li Sao' and other poems attributed to him inspired the creation of an important poetic tradition. This tradition is now preserved in the anthology titled *Ch'u tz'u* (Songs of Ch'u or Literature of Ch'u), which was put together in its present form by the Later Han scholar Wang Yi (ca. A.D. 89–ca. 158).[18]

The oldest poems in the anthology are most likely the 'Nine Songs' (*Chiu ke*). As the title indicates, these poems, actually eleven in number, were intended to be sung to music. It is now generally agreed that they are literary reworkings of shamanistic hymns.[19] Except for the final two songs in the series, the hymns portray a mystical religious rite in which a shaman attempts to consumate a union with a god or goddess. In some of these songs, notably 'The Hsiang Princess' (*Hsiang chün*) and 'The Hsiang Lady' (*Hsiang fu-jen*), the 'shaman's relationship with the spirit is represented as a kind of love-affair'.[20] The shaman's aim is to make a tryst with the deity, and he is often depicted as a suitor who tries to win the hand of the elusive, fickle goddess.[21] He makes elaborate preparations, dressing himself in sumptuous clothing, particularly garments made of fragrant flowers and plants. He sings, dances, and attempts to entice the deity to join him. Usually he must undertake a long journey in order to locate the spirit. The meeting with the deity is always ephemeral, if it is completed at all, and the shaman invariably is left alone, waiting in vain for the spirit's return.

If we now turn to the 'Li Sao', we can see that it is a poem of a completely different type. Although it exhibits many of the religious features of the 'Nine Songs', including the magical journey motif, the frustrated quest for a 'Fair One', and even a kind of liturgical language, the 'Li Sao' is primarily a secular poem. The 'Li Sao' is difficult to classify generically because its radical of presentation is not clearly identifiable. The poem is essentially an objective first-person narration of the poet-hero's action, which makes it neither epic nor lyric. For this reason, the Hungarian scholar, Ferenc Tökei, defines the 'Li Sao' as a synthesis of epic and lyric, and this genre he calls the elegy.[22] While this might be a slight misapplication of the term elegy as known in Western literature, Tökei's description of the 'Li Sao' as an epic-lyric poem is essentially correct.

The agent of the 'Li Sao' is the poet himself, or more correctly his persona. He describes himself as a man of noble birth descended from the Ch'u royal house. Although possessed of loyalty and integrity, he finds himself fallen on evil times. He says that a person named the Fair One failed to heed his advice and listened instead to slanderers. Thus, like the shaman in the 'Nine Songs', the poet-hero dresses in garments of fragrant plants, takes a meal of dew and chrysanthemums (which increase longevity), and embarks on a long journey in search of a 'Beauty' who understands him. He travels far south to Ts'ang-wu, where he consults with the legendary sage-king Ch'ung-hua (Shun) and goes from there to the K'un-lun Mountains where he is denied admission into Heaven. He tries to woo Fu-fei, goddess of the Lo River, but finds her fickle and arrogant. His attempts at using matchmakers to court the maiden Chien Ti and the daughters of the Lord of Yü are also unsuccessful. A shaman named Ling Fen then performs a divination, which advises him to continue his search for a mate. A shaman-god called Wu Hsien (Shaman Hsien) descends from the heavens and gives him similar advice. The poet-hero resolves to continue his journey into the remote western regions of the universe. From here he suddenly looks back in the direction of his home and finds that he can go no farther.

The poem closes with a short four-line envoi in which the poet declares that since there is no one in his home state worth serving he will go and join one P'eng Hsien, identified in traditional Chinese commentaries as a Shang dynasty official who drowned himself rather than compromise his principles. This line has been interpreted to mean that the poet is declaring his intention to commit suicide. This identification of P'eng Hsien is most probably based on the legend of Ch'ü Yüan's own suicide, and modern scholars have attempted to show that P'eng Hsien is the name of an ancient shaman (or shamans), and that 'joining P'eng Hsien' actually refers to a desire to became a shaman recluse.[23]

Regardless of how the reference to P'eng Hsien is interpreted, it is impossible to deny that the 'Li Sao' contains political allegory. The allusions to the political situation at court are all too clear.[24] Lines such as the following can have only a political reference (ll. 17–20):

> *The cliquish enjoy a momentary pleasure,*
> *But their road is dark and dangerous.*
> *I do not fear trouble for myself,*
> *But I am afraid my lord's chariot will topple.*
> *I raced about forward and back,*
> *Hoping you would follow the tracks of ancient kings.*

In addition, the personified plants such as Pepper and Orchid can only be understood in terms of political allegory.

The 'Li Sao' does contain many of the same features as the shamanistic hymns, but as David Hawkes has shown, in the 'Li Sao' they have become secularized.[25] Instead of a shaman the suitor is a virtuous minister who had once enjoyed his ruler's favor but is now rejected. The relationship between the minister and the king is described in the same erotic terms that were used in the 'Nine Songs'. The poet pictures himself as the jilted suitor and the ruler who has rejected him is called variously the Divine Beauty (*Ling hsiu*), the Lovely One (*Mei jen*), and the Fragrant One (*Ch'üan*). Like the shaman he embarks on a long journey in search of a more constant lover, but fails to make the tryst, even with the help of matchmakers, and he is forced to wander alone throughout the world.

Prosodically, the 'Li Sao' exhibits features of a chanted recitation. The basic line is a distich consisting of hemistichs divided by the particle *hsi*, which marks the major caesura. Each hemistich includes an A and B member, which are separated by an unstressed mid-particle known as the 'key word'. Represented graphically this would look:

A	key word	B
xxx	o	xxx *hsi*
xxx	o	xxx

(x represents a stressed syllable; o represents an unstressed syllable.) While we do not know exactly how the 'Sao-style', as this prosodic pattern is called, was read in early China, it appears that it was designed for chanting rather than singing to musical accompaniment. This feature is primarily reflected in the contrast between the stressed and unstressed syllables, which give the line its rhythmic effect.[26]

Thus, the 'Li Sao' may be considered a *fu* in the pre-Han sense of the term as a chanted poem of political criticism.[27] Furthermore, the 'Li Sao' is extremely important in the development of a particular type of *fu* which was popular in the Han dynasty. This is what Hellmut Wilhelm calls the 'frustration *fu*', a special variety of the rhapsody that relies on a convention termed by David Hawkes 'tristia'. The *tristia* 'expresses the poet's sorrows, his resentments, his complaints against a deluded prince, a cruel fate, a corrupt and uncomprehending society...'[28] This convention becomes even more firmly established in the later *Ch'u tz'u* pieces, most of which are imitations of the 'Li Sao'. In the 'Nine Declarations' (*Chiu chang*), which is a group of nine (possibly ten) poems modeled after the 'Li Sao', the *tristia* virtually dominates the poem. Also common in these pieces, as in the 'Li Sao', is the 'topos of the world upside down'.[29] This *topos* is almost identical to the examples found in medieval European literature. It is an important ingredient of the *tristia*, and consists of a series of statements that the world is topsy-turvy, disjointed, and that nothing is in its proper place. The 'Nine Declarations' poem 'Embracing the Sand' (*Huai sha*) contains a good example (11. 13–5):

> They have changed white into black,
> Overturned up into down.
> The phoenix lies in a cage,
> While chickens and ducks soar aloft.
> They mix together jade and stones,
> And weigh them on the same balance.

Another convention which found extensive application in the *Ch'u tz'u* and in later rhapsodies is the magical journey, or what David Hawkes called the '*itineraria*'.[30] In its basic form the journey involves a flight through space, usually in a chariot drawn by dragons or a phoenix (*feng-huang*). The traveller has in his retinue gods and spirits whom he commands at will. In the shamanistic hymns of the 'Nine Songs' the magical journey is related to the shaman's quest of the spirit. Another *Ch'u tz'u* poem, the 'Distant Wandering' (*Yüan yu*), describes the mystical wanderings of a Taoist adept.[31] In the 'Li Sao' the *itineraria* has been secularized, and is an 'allegorical representation' of the scholar-poet's 'flight from a corrupt society and a foolish and faithless prince'.[32] This convention thus is another aspect of the poem's political character.

The 'Fu Chapter' of Hsün tzu.[33] Another piece that figures prominently in accounts of the early development of the rhapsody is chapter eighteen in the *Hsün tzu*, a work attributed to the great pre-Ch'in philosopher Hsün Ch'ing (ca. 312–ca. 235 B.C.). Titled '*Fu*', this chapter consists of five rhymed riddles and two additional poems designated 'Poem of Anomalies' (*Kuei shih*) and 'Small Song' (*Hsiao ke*). If this chapter title is genuine, it would be the earliest work to bear the generic name of *fu*. However, it is uncertain whether the title was originally part of the chapter or whether the editor of the text, Liu Hsiang (77–6 B.C.), affixed the title when he compiled the 32 *p'ien* (section) *Hsün tzu* from the 322 *p'ien* of miscellaneous *Hsün tzu* texts held in the imperial archives. It should be noted that the rhymed riddles have no titles, and the word *fu* occurs nowhere in the text.

The first part of the chapter contains the five riddles. Each riddle begins with a person enumerating the attributes of an unnamed object. After the object is sufficiently described, the narrator pretends ignorance and requests a second person to name the object. The second person describes the object further and then comes forth with the answer to the riddle. The five subjects include: (1) 'Ritual' (*Li*), (2) 'Wisdom' (*Chih*), (3) 'Cloud' (*Yün*), (4) 'Silkworm' (*T'san*), and 'Needle' (*Chen*).[34] The 'Poem of Anomalies' and 'Small Song' follow the five riddles. They are both 'poems of frustration' and express resentment at the evil and perverted times in which a man of integrity and uprightness cannot gain acceptance.

It is not clear how these two poems are connected with the five riddles; nor do we know exactly how to interpret the term '*fu*' in the title, assuming it is genuine. Is this chapter one poem (i.e. one *fu*) or is it a collection of miscellaneous poems attributed to Hsün tzu? Professor Hellmut Wilhelm believes that the chapter is a single poem, which consists of five sections (the riddles) plus a coda (the 'Poem of Anomalies' and 'Small Song'). He claims that Hsün tzu 'in the first five sections of his *fu*, displays in a veiled form his personal qualifications for holding office: knowledge of social principles, wisdom, agility, assiduity, and critical faculty... Then, in the coda, he bemoans the times which are not propitious for a man of his qualifications, bringing in historical references to similar situations...'[35]

Professor Wilhelm thus accepts the chapter title as genuine and concludes that this piece is an early example of the 'fu of frustration'. There are several things, however, which makes this interpretation somewhat tenuous. First of all, there is evidence that the piece called 'Small Song' existed in an early text, separate from the 'Fu Chapter',[36] indicating that the 'Fu Chapter' pieces do not necessarily belong together. In addition, it is difficult to construe each of the riddles as representations of the writer's qualifications for holding office, mainly because three of the objects described (Cloud, Silkworm, and Needle) seem to have nothing to do with personal qualities, even in a metaphorical sense.[37]

It is more reasonable to assume that the riddles are independent poems that have no relationship to the 'Poem of Anomalies' and 'Small Song'. If this assumption is correct, one must then answer the question why the term *fu* came to be applied to them, for the riddles do not conform exactly to the prevailing notion of the *fu*. They do contain certain features that occur in later *fu* such as the dialogue and extended description, as well as a certain obliqueness and indirection characteristic of many *fu*. One might also note that the 'Treatise on Bibliography' of the *History of the Former Han* lists in the 'Miscellaneous *Fu*' section eighteen *yin shu* or 'riddles', which indicates that Liu Hsiang and Liu Hsin considered the riddle a legitimate part of the *fu* genre.[38] Unfortunately, we do not know what riddles were listed here. A fragment from Liu Hsiang's 'Separate List' (*Pieh lu*) contains a definition of *yin shu* which is somewhat helpful: '*Yin shu* means to be hesitant with one's words in questioning someone. The one who responds thus ponders and thinks about it. In this way, one can be assured of elucidation.'[39] Implied in this definition is that the riddle was used for moral teaching and persuasion, and that it was considered effective because it led to a spontaneous or voluntary conversion of the person being persuaded. The riddle thus might have been considered a special type of *fu* that never achieved much popularity, and the only surviving specimens of the genre are those in the *Hsün tzu*.

The most original feature of the riddles is their prosody, which represents a departure from pre-Han metrical patterns. The first half of the poem is almost entirely in four-syllable lines, which is the dominant pattern of the *Book of Songs*. The second half, however, uses a much longer line. Each part begins with the words *tz'u fu* ('as for this') and follows with a series of questions. The basic form of these questions somewhat resembles the *Sao*-line, with an A and

B member separated by a particle, usually the subordinative conjunctions *erh* or *tse*. It concludes with an interrogative word (either *yü* or *yeh*), preceded by the particle *che*. Represented graphically this would appear:

A member	key	B member	interrogative
xxx	o	xxx	*che yeh/yü*

Usually these lines form independent rhyming units, but in several cases they actually form *Sao*-style couplets (of course, there is an additional syllable in the B member and no *hsi*):

A member	key	B member	interrogative
xxx	o	xxx	
xxx	o	xxx	*che yeh/yü*

It would appear that this pattern would be particularly well-suited for recitation. Just as with the *Sao*-line, the key word could represent an unstressed syllable or slight pause, while the interrogative particles indicate the major caesura. Judging from the abundance of other oral conventions such as the dialogue and repetition of words it seems probable that these riddles belong to the tradition of the oral court recitation.

The 'Poem of Anomalies' and 'Small Song' are somewhat easier to relate to the *fu* tradition, for both are poems of political criticism. They appear to be two sections of the same piece. The 'Poem of Anomalies', which is about twice as long as the 'Small Song', is the main text, while the much shorter 'Small Song' is thought to be the analogue of the *luan* or coda in the *Ch'u tz'u*.[40] The 'Poem of Anomalies' begins with a statement of the author's purpose in writing the piece: 'The world is in disorder. I beg to present a *kuei shih*.' The word *kuei* in this title is somewhat difficult to interpret. The basic meaning of *kuei* is 'strange', 'perverse', or 'crafty', and here probably refers to the subject of the poem, which is the perverse, anomalous, topsy-turvy condition of the world. The piece is really one long 'topos of the world upside-down' as the following excerpt shows:

> *Heaven and Earth have changed positions;*
> *The four seasons have altered directions.*
> *The constellations have fallen from the sky;*
> *Day and night it is dark.*
> *Deep darkness shines above,*
> *The sun and moon hide below.*

The 'Poem of Anomalies' is properly labelled a *shih*, for it follows almost entirely the four-syllable line which is basic to *shih* verse. It does contain two five-syllable, one eight-syllable, and two ten-syllable lines, which is another indication of the tendency in the Warring States period to break away from the short *shih* structure into more prosaic (but rhymed) patterns.

The poems in the 'Fu Chapter' represent a transition from the chanted *shih* of predominantly four-syllable lines to poems that exhibit features of an embryonic rhyme-prose. The rhymed riddles are the antecedent for the lengthy descriptive *fu* of Han times, while the 'Poem of Anomalies' is one of the ancestors of the frustration *fu*.

The Rhetorical Tradition. Rhetoric in its historical sense means the 'art of persuasion'.[41] The basic function of rhetoric is 'the use of words by human agents to form attitudes or to induce actions in other human agents',[42] and is a basic human phenomenon common to all cultures. To claim that the art of rhetoric was invented in the fifth century B.C. in Sicily would be as absurd as claiming that the Greeks invented sex. In China rhetorical writing was one of the earliest types of literature to develop. As early as the *Book of Documents* (*Shu ching*) one finds examples of speeches, most probably fictional, attributed to early Chinese culture heroes. It is not certain to what extent oratory was practiced in ancient China, mainly because most of the 'orations' contained in pre-Han texts verge on the fictional.[43] Nevertheless, since court business was most frequently conducted orally during this period, one would suppose that a scholar-official required a certain oral eloquence in presenting his views to a ruler or high official. With the development of contending philosophical schools in the sixth and fifth centuries B.C. the art of disputation became even more important.[44]

Most early Chinese rhetoric is primarily concerned with political persuasion and usually involves an official who attempts to influence his ruler. The most sophisticated rhetorical writing of this kind began to emerge in the fifth and fourth centuries B.C. This development is closely related to the appearance of the itinerant persuader or *yu-shui*, a travelling diplomat or politician skilled in the techniques of rhetoric. Eventually, many of these itinerant persuaders became identified with a school known as the *Tsung-heng chia*. It is not known if the *Tsung-heng chia* was a formal school which offered training in oratory and rhetoric or was simply a general designation for writers and thinkers who specialized in 'political thought and political rhetoric'. A good translation of the term, which encompasses both of these activities, is 'School of Politicians'.[45]

Although a large body of writings attributed to members of this school survives,[46] we know almost nothing about their theory of rhetoric. Hellmut Wilhelm has mentioned sources that deal with rhetorical theory,[47] but 'none of them is a work on techniques of presentation; all concentrate on the relation between the already accomplished persuader and the ruler'.[48] It has also been suggested that the *Kuei-ku tzu* (Master of Devil Valley) was the chief rhetorical handbook of the *Tsung-heng* school, but this work is of doubtful authenticity.[49] The main method of determining anything about their technique of persuasion is to examine the existing rhetorical literature. The primary source of these writings is the *Intrigues of the Warring States* (*Chan-kuo ts'e*). The *Intrigues* contains a large number of speeches and stratagems attributed to itinerant persuaders of the Warring States period. The work was edited in the Former Han by Liu Hsiang from a group of works containing material about the Warring States persuaders.

Although there is disagreement about the exact nature of the *Intrigues*, most scholars now agree that it is basically a collection of rhetorical prose. There seems to be little question that the speeches it contains are fictional although based on historical circumstances and attributed to historical figures. They appear to have served as models of suasory writing, and in fact many of the *Intrigues* persuasions found their way into other pre-Han and Han sources.[50] The wide currency of these fictionalized speeches attests to the special status of written oratory, particularly in the fourth century B.C. and later.

In order to understand the nature of early Chinese rhetoric and its relationship to the rhapsody, it might be useful to examine one *Intrigues* persuasion attributed to the master persuader, Su Ch'in. In this account Su Ch'in presents himself at the court of King Hui of Ch'in and offers to serve as his adviser. After listening to Su's preliminary speech the king declares rather pompously that he would prefer to listen another day. Su then replies that even if the king were to heed his plan, he doubts that he could put it to use. Su follows with a long speech outlining his plan:

> In the past Shen-nung attacked the Pu-sui, the Yellow Emperor attacked Cho-lu and captured Ch'ih-yu, Yao attacked Huan-tou, Shun attacked the Three Miao, Yü attacked Kung-kung, T'ang attacked the Hsia, King Wen attacked Ch'ung, King Wu attacked Chou, and Duke Huan of Ch'i employed warfare to become hegemon of the empire. Looking at it from this point of view, one might ask, who has not gone to war?

> > Anciently, chariots raced hub to hub,
> > States were bound by word,
> > The Empire was unified.
> > They made north–south treaties, east–west alliances,
> > But weapons and armor were never stored away.
> > Literary scholars all showed great craft,
> > But the lords became more confused and uncertain.

A myriad troubles arose all at once,
So many they could not all be controlled.
Once laws and statutes were perfected,
The people assumed deceitful airs.
Documents became more numerous and murkier,
But the people were increasingly in want.
Superior and inferior were resentful of each other,
The people had nothing to rely on.
With brilliant words and clear reasoning
Warfare increased more and more.
With specious arguments and elaborate uniforms,
Warfare still did not cease.
In spite of the effusive praise and ornate verbiage,
The empire was still in disorder.
Tongues rotted, ears became deaf,
Yet nothing could be accomplished.
They practiced rightness and swore fidelity,
But the empire was still at odds.

Thereupon, they rejected culture and adopted warfare. They generously supported brave warriors, donned armor, sharpened their weapons in order to achieve victory on the battlefield.[51]

It seems readily apparent that this persuasion is not the text of an actual speech, but is a highly polished piece of written rhetoric. The devices used here are common to most of early Chinese rhetoric. One of the most striking features is the long rhymed tetrasyllabic section, which I have indicated with an indented text. This is a good illustration of the insertion of verse into a prose structure, which forms a proto-rhyme-prose.

One technique favored by the ancient Chinese persuader was the enumeration of historical examples. This mode of persuasion was considered important by the Greek and Roman rhetoricians. Quintilian, in speaking of the modes of proof based on similitude, said: 'The most important of proofs of this class is that which is most properly styled example, that is to say the adducing of some past action real or assumed which may serve to persuade the audience of the truth of the point which we are trying to make.'[52] In ancient China proof by historical example is more common than the logical or syllogistic argument.[53] Most early Chinese rhetoric was concerned with persuading one man, the ruler, and it was impossible to argue in the same way as orators who declaimed before a throng in the Greek or Roman forum.

What distinguishes the Chinese use of the historical example from Western usage is the tendency of the Chinese persuader to string together examples in a series. As in Su Ch'in's speech, in which the persuader cites eight examples of ancient rulers who went to war, the same verb '*fa*' (to attack) is repeated eight times in a scheme of repetition. Another repetition scheme used in the Su Ch'in speech is the figure the Greeks called *synonomia* (Latin, *interpretation*, *expolitio*). The figure is a mode of amplification in which synonymous words are repeated in adjacent clauses. This reads in translation with the synonyms italicized

> The hereditary rulers of the present
> Are *heedless* of the supreme *doctrine*,
> Are *ignorant* of *teachings*,
>
> They are *disordered* in government,
> *Confused* by *words*,
> *Befuddled* by *language*,
> *Inundated* by *discourse*,
> *Drowned* by *speech*.

Techniques of this kind are introduced into a composition not simply for their persuasive effect, but to decorate and embellish. It should be remembered that the term rhetoric, besides persuasion, also means ornamentation. Northrop Frye has lucidly explained the distinction between the two:

Rhetoric has from the beginning meant two things: ornamental speech and persuasive speech. These two things seem psychologically opposed to each other, as the desire to ornament is essentially disinterested, and the desire to persuade is essentially the reverse...Persuasive rhetoric is applied literature, or the use of literary art to reinforce the power of argument. Ornamental rhetoric acts on its hearers statically, leading them to admire its own beauty or wit; persuasive rhetoric tries to lead them kinetically toward a course of action. One articulates emotion, the other manipulates it.[54]

One might add that these two elements, while essentially opposed, usually are inseparable and co-exist in the same poem. It is often difficult to determine where persuasion ends and ornament begins, for verbal embellishment is one of the main methods of enhancing an argument. The classical rhetoricians were well aware of the merits of *ornatus* in persuasive rhetoric. Thus, Quintilian says: 'But rhetorical ornament contributes not a little to the furtherance of our case as well. For when our audience find it a pleasure to listen, their attention and their readiness to believe what they hear are both alike increased, and sometimes even transported by admiration.'[55] The main difficulty of the persuader is to prevent his interest in embellishment from standing in the way of his argument, for often a piece of rhetoric is nine parts *ornatus* and one part *persuasio*.

Since the persuader generally presented his argument before a ruler, an absolute one at that, it was not always possible to openly admonish, lecture, or criticize. Court decorum obliged the persuader to use an oblique and circuitous method of argument, which would lead the ruler to the desired decisions spontaneously, as if he had arrived at it on his own.

The most common form of the indirect argument found in the *Intrigues* perusasions is what J. I. Crump calls the 'doubled persuasion'. It exists in several types, but generally involves the presentation of alternatives that are equally efficacious or convincing. This doubling includes such things as thesis and antithesis (if an action succeeds one will achieve A; if it fails one will achieve B) and arguments for a given action and against its opposite (if one does A the result will be favorable; if one does not do A the result will be unfavorable).[56] Also common is the dilemma in which two equally unacceptable alternatives are proposed. *Intrigues* 205 is a good example:

Four states attacked Ch'u. Ch'u ordered Chao Chü to resist Ch'in. The king of Ch'u wanted to assault Ch'in, but Chao Chü was unwilling. Huan Tsang spoke to the king on his behalf.

'*If Chü were victorious in battle* [1], *the three other states would be jealous of Ch'u's power and would fear that Ch'in might change sides and heed Ch'u. They would invariably attack deep into Ch'u in order to strengthen Ch'in. The king of Ch'in, angry that he had not been victorious in battle, would arouse all his troops and attack Ch'u. This would exhaust both your majesty and Ch'in to the advantage of the other three states. If he is not victorious in battle against Ch'in* [2], *Ch'in will advance its troops in an attack against Ch'u. It would be better to increase Chao Chü's troops, and order him to show Ch'in that we are determined to fight. The king of Ch'in would dislike the possibility of exhausting both Ch'in and Ch'u to the advantage of the empire. Ch'in can cede a small amount of territory to Ch'u to avoid injury. With Ch'in and Ch'u brought together, Yen, Wei, and Chao dare not refuse to comply, and the three states can be settled.*'[57]

The effect of this type of argument is to give the listener the impression that all possibilities have been explored, and that he has a choice between alternatives. Occasionally, the doubling took the form of a debate between two or more persuaders (cf. *Intrigues* 239) in which the pro and con alternatives were argued at great length, until all were overwhelmed by the most eloquent speaker. As we shall see, this framework becomes an important characteristic of the rhapsody, which is often structured around a debate between several imaginary figures.

The Early Han Rhapsody. Although there are poems labelled '*fu*' that are assigned to the pre-Han period, the first reliable and datable pieces with the word '*fu*' in the title appear in the early years of the Former Han dynasty (206 B.C.–A.D. 8).[58] According to the 'Treatise on Bibliography' there were several important rhapsody writers during this period, but information on their literary production is scanty. It is not too surprising that the majority of these early Han poets came from the south, notably Ch'u. Liu Pang, the first Han emperor, was from Ch'u, and many of his supporters were from Liu's home area. In addition, several of these writers distinguished themselves are accomplished persuaders, and are often referred to as the 'remnants' of the Warring States 'School of Politicians'.[59]

The most prominent writer was Lu Chia (228–ca. 140 B.C.), who was born in Ch'u and was an early follower of Liu Pang. His reputation rested mainly on his skill as a debater and rhetor, and like the itinerant persuaders of the Warring States period, he often used his rhetorical skills on his emperor's behalf as an envoy to neighboring states. Lu lived in semi-retirement during the reigns of Emperor Hui and Empress Lü (195–180 B.C.), but was summoned to court when Emperor Wen took the throne in 179 B.C. As an elder statesman he had prestige and influence at court. At this time he was sent on a diplomatic mission to Southern Yüeh (Nam-Viet). He died sometime between 150 and 140 B.C.[60]

The 'Treatise on Bibliography' credits Lu Chia with three rhapsodies, all of which have been lost. Liu Hsieh (ca. A.D. 465–522) mentions the title of one rhapsody, 'Early Spring' (*Meng ch'un*), but later encyclopedias or anthologies fail to preserve it.[61] Even though Lu's poems no longer exist, it is significant that a diplomat and persuader of his ability was at the same time a writer of rhapsodies. Undoubtedly, his pieces must have made use of some of the devices found in Warring States rhetoric.[62] It is also possible that since he was from Ch'u his rhapsodies may have been in the 'Li Sao' style, although if he had written something of this kind, one would think it would have been preserved in the *Ch'u tz'u*.

Another rhapsody writer of approximately the same period, also known for his eloquence, was Chu Chien. A native of Ch'u, Chu served Ch'ing Pu, prince of Huai-nan. After Ch'ing's abortive revolt of 197 B.C. Chu moved to Ch'ang-an where he was given a title. He became involved in a political intrigue in 177 and committed suicide. The 'Treatise on Bibliography' credits him with two rhapsodies, neither of which survives.[63]

The most important poet of early Han times is unquestionably Chia Yi (ca. 200–168 B.C.). Chia's biography is well-known, and need not be retold here.[64] Chia Yi has always been closely identified with Ch'ü Yüan, as evidenced by the fact they share the same chapter in the *Records*. The subject of Chia Yi's earliest extant poem in fact is Ch'ü Yüan. Titled 'Lament for Ch'ü Yüan' (*Tiao Ch'ü Yüan fu*), it was written after Chia had been dismissed from court (ca. 176 B.C.), and while he was on his way to exile in south China.[65] The 'Lament' is divided into two parts, a main text and epilogue, which differ both in prosody and content.[66] The main text contains the lament for Ch'ü Yüan. The poet begins with what amounts to a preface describing the occasion on which he wrote the piece. He prepares to await the emperor's command at Ch'ang-sha, and recalling Ch'ü Yüan's suicide by drowning he is inspired to write a lament and throw it into the Hsiang River. The part of the piece that follows consists almost entirely of the world upside down *topos* and bemoans the unlucky time in which Ch'ü Yüan was born:

> *Oh, how pitiful!*
> *You met such an unlucky time!*
> *The* luan-huang *crawls away and hides,*
> *While the owl soars on high.*
> *The untalented are honored and made illustrious,*
> *And the slanderer and flatterer attain their ambitions,*
> *While the worthy and sage are dragged upside-down,*
> *And the square and upright are topsy-turvey.*[67]

In the epilogue the poet focuses on his own misery and even gently chides Ch'ü Yüan for committing suicide. He declares that it is better to withdraw from an impossible situation than to stubbornly persist in trying to influence a recalcitrant ruler. When the time is again favorable one can resume an active role in the world.

The 'Lament' is the earliest datable example of the subgenre I will term the 'rhapsody of frustration.' This special type of rhapsody is essentially a subjective and personal expression as opposed to the long descriptive rhapsodies which are objective and impersonal. It is the only place in the *fu* form where the 'Self as agent', to borrow James Dickey's term,[68] operates to any degree. Incorporated in the rhapsody of frustration are the conventions already developed in the Ch'ü Yüan poems and the 'Fu Chapter' of *Hsün tzu*. There is above all the *tristia*, which expresses the poet's resentment against the world and society. His complaint is reinforced by the inclusion of the *topoi* of 'time's fate' (the time is unlucky, fate is hostile) and 'the world upside down'. This type of rhapsody, furthermore, uses relatively simple diction, and eschews difficult ornament found in other rhapsodies. Finally, almost always the dominant prosodic pattern is the 'Sao-style'.

Chia Yi's longest and most famous rhapsody was written while he was serving as tutor to the Prince of Ch'ang-sha. This poem, titled 'The Owl Rhapsody' (*Fu-niao fu*), has been termed 'the earliest reliably dated specimen of the genre to bear the label *fu*'.[69] The date is variously given as 175, 174, and 173 B.C., depending on how one interprets the astronomical date given in the first few lines. The poem opens with the poet telling of an owl, a bird of evil auspice in China, who flew into his house. Alarmed, the poet wonders what this omen can forbode, but since the bird cannot speak, he uses the persona of the owl to express his own feelings.

The owl's speech, which is liberally sprinkled with quotations from *Lao tzu* and *Chuang tzu*, reads like a Taoist philosophical essay. Through the owl the poet preaches the familiar Taoist message that everything in the world is in constant flux, and that life and death are simply part of the continuous process of change. This use of verse to expound philosophy is not new with Chia Yi, for we find the same thing in the *Hsün tzu*. What is important in Chia Yi is that for the first time the piece is designated as a *fu*, and his poem is not part of a larger philosophical work. If one were to forget that 'The Owl' is called *fu*, he would probably classify it, along with Pope's *Essay on Man*, as a verse essay on philosophy. However, it is distinguished from the usual philosophical essay by its tight poetic structure and uniform prosodic pattern.[70] Nevertheless, 'The Owl' represents a form of the rhapsody rarely seen in Chinese literature, and is almost an anomaly (another in this class is Lu Chi's 'Rhapsody on Literature'). However, as we have already seen, the notion of *fu* was extremely broad in Han times, and almost any long rhymed composition could be called *fu*.

It is somewhat difficult to assess Chia Yi's contribution to the development of the rhapsody on the basis of two reliable poems.[71] In the 'Lament' he continues the tradition of the rhapsody of frustration, but adds little to the technique of the genre. 'The Owl' is more original, and represents a considerable advance over the philosophical poems of *Hsün tzu*. Nevertheless, Chia Yi's compositions are much closer to the embryonic rhapsody than the long and rhetorically complex rhapsodies that were written shortly after his death. The development of this type of poem was the work of a group of southerners, whose writings will be considered in the following section.

Ssu-ma Hsiang-ju and His Contemporaries. Almost immediately after the death of Chia Yi there was a sudden increase in the writing of rhapsodies. It is in this period that we find what is commonly considered representative of the Han rhapsody. This is the era of Ssu-ma Hsiang-ju (179–117 B.C.), who is generally acknowledged as the greatest rhapsodist of the Han dynasty. During

this relatively brief period the rhapsody became a mature and highly sophisticated genre, with clearly identifiable conventions.

One of the major reasons for the rapid increase in poetic production was the
end to the political instability that beset the early years of the Han empire.
During this time there had been frequent revolts by the princes and feudal
lords who were strong enough to challenge the emperor's authority. After the
suppression of the Revolt of the Seven Kingdoms in 154 B.C., this problem
ceased to exist. All prerogatives were now in the hands of the emperor, and
Ch'ang-an, the imperial capital, became the center of all cultural and political
life. The culmination of this process of centralization occurred with the
accession of Emperor Wu in 140 B.C. This powerful figure was able to solidify
imperial control and at the same time develop a complex of institutions that
would endure for most of the Han dynasty. It was in the shadow of this
institution-building that the rhapsody emerged as a full-fledged literary genre.

However, in the early part of this period not all literary activity was centred
at Ch'ang-an. In 168 B.C., the year of Chia Yi's death, Liu Wu, the second son
of Emperor Wen, was enfeoffed as Prince of Liang. Better known by his
posthumous name of Prince Hsiao (the Filial), Liu Wu was heir to one of the
richest fiefs in China. Liang was a leading munitions manufacturing center and
was said to have more jewels and precious objects than the capital itself. Prince
Hsiao was not hesitant to put his resources to use, and he undertook an
extensive project to make Liang into one of the most attractive states in China.
He built an 'Eastern Park' which was over three hundred *li* square, enlarged
the capital of Sui-yang by seventy *li*, constructed palaces and other structures
including a thirty *li* elevated walkway from the main palace to P'ing Tower, a
pleasure palace in northeastern Liang. According to Ssu-ma Ch'ien: 'He had
received as a gift from the court flags and pennants of the Son of Heaven and,
when he left the palace, his entourage included a thousand carriages and ten
thousand riders. He went on hunting expeditions to the east and west in the
manner of the emperor and when he left the palace or returned, attendants
preceded him crying, "Clear the way! Attention!"'[72]

It is easy to understand how Prince Hsiao was able to attract the most
distinguished poets and scholars of the day to his court. It was during this
period that the princes made their last challenge to imperial authority. As in
the Warring States period, there was a renewed demand for men skilled in
disputation and persuasion, and like the Warring States rhetors, these men
travelled from state to state displaying their eloquence and offering advice to
the princes. Besides showing skill as persuaders, many of the scholars who
came to Liang were accomplished rhapsodists. These poets included Ssu-ma
Hsiang-ju, Tsou Yang (ca. 200–129 B.C.), Mei Ch'eng (?–141 B.C.), and

Chuang Chi (fl. ca. 154 B.C.). Coming to Liang gave the *fu* poet an opportunity he might not otherwise have had to develop his talent. The current emperor, Ching Ti (156–141 B.C.), had declared an aversion for *tz'u-fu*, as the rhapsody was often called, and poets were not welcome in Ch'ang-an.[73]

Mei Ch'eng is a typical example of the persuader-poet of the second century B.C. He was born in Huai-yin, which was once part of the ancient territory of Ch'u. He served briefly at the court of Liu P'i, Prince of Wu, but left for Liang after unsuccessfully trying to dissuade him from plotting rebellion. The memorials he wrote at this time are excellent specimens of early Han rhetoric.[74] His arrival in Liang was probably around 157 B.C.

The 'Treatise on Bibliography' credits him with nine rhapsodies. The texts of three pieces attributed to him survive as well as the title of a fourth.[75] The most famous of these poems, the 'Seven Stimuli' (*Ch'i fa*), is not titled a *fu*, but in terms of form and content clearly belongs to this genre.[76] The 'Seven Stimuli' represents a significant advance in the development of the rhapsody. Its most striking feature is its length, which exceeds that of Chia Yi's 'The Owl' by four or five times.

The rhapsody is constructed around a conversation between two persons: a prince of the state of Ch'u, who is suffering from an unspecified illness; the other is a guest from the state of Wu who has come to inquire of the prince's health. The guest begins with a long description of the prince's symptoms and identifies the apparent cause, over-indulgence. The guest declares that a medical cure is impossible and suggests that the only hope for recovery is to listen to 'essential words and marvelous doctrines' (*yao yen miao tao*). He then proceeds to describe for the prince a series of enticements: music, a delicious meal, a chariot ride, an excursion to a sightseeing area accompanied by beautiful women, a hunt, and a view of the tidal bore of the Ch'ü River in Kuang-ling. At the end of each of these descriptions the guest asks the prince if he feels well enough to get up from his sickbed and take part. Each time he responds negatively, although the description of the hunt almost succeeds in arousing him. It takes the seventh and last enticement, the promise to introduce him to the 'essential words and marvelous doctrines' of the sages and philosophers, to finally arouse the prince. Upon hearing this he leans on his stool, stands up, sweat pours from his body, and in a moment he is cured.

It is not difficult to trace the antecedents of the devices used in the 'Seven Stimuli'. The dialogue framework is directly derived from the Warring States persuasions. The idea of presenting a series of enticements to a sick king is found in the 'Summons' poems of the *Ch'u tz'u*.[77] Stylistically, the 'Seven Stimuli' is considerably different from anything written prior to this time (assuming that it antedates Ssu-ma Hsiang-ju's 'Master Void Rhapsody'). Mei Ch'eng relies heavily on ornament, and makes abundant use of cataloguing, repetition (particularly *expolitio*), the binomial descriptive, parallelism, and other devices of amplification.[78] The section on the tidal bore is especially full of what the Greeks called ecphrasis. There is this example of *expolitio* depicting the bore:

> *When one sees*
>
>> *What it leaps over,*
>> *What is plucks up,*
>> *What it tosses about,*
>> *What it collects together,*
>> *What it washes clean,*
>
>> *Though he be mentally equipped and verbally prepared,*
>> *He certainly cannot describe it completely.*

The poet even seems to characterize his own elaborate style when he tells of the poets who attend the excursion:

> *Thereupon, scholars of great learning and rhetorical skill*
> *Explain the origins of the mountains and rivers,*
> *Name all the plants and trees,*
> *Join things, link affairs,*
> *String words together, group categories.*

There then follows this catalogue of birds, trees, and plants:

> *The* hun-chang, *white heron,*
> *Peacock, pheasant,*
> *Yüan-ch'u, and red heron,*
> *Sport green crowns and purple neck feathers.*
> *The* Ch'ih *dragon and* Te-mu *bird*
> *Sing harmoniously in unison.*
> *The fish of brightness leap and jump,*
> *Spread their fins and shake their scales.*
> *Thick and profuse*
> *Grow the creeper grass and fragrant polygonum.*
> *There are tender mulberries and river willows*
> *With white leaves and purple stems.*
> *Miao pine and Yü-chang camphor*
> *Whose branches reach to the sky.*
> *Paulonia and coir palms*
> *Form a forest as far as the eye can see.*

Descriptions of this kind remind one of similar usages in medieval European literature.[79] Amplification was one of the important rhetorical devices of medieval literature, and the rhetorical handbooks fully discuss it. The best formulation is that of Geoffrey of Vinsauf (fl. 1210) in his *Poetria Nova*:

> *...multiplice forma*
> *Dissimeletur idem; varius sis et tamen idem.*[80]

One finds among the Han rhapsody writers a similar notion of amplification. Yang Hsiung, for example, claimed that 'a writer is required to speak by adducing examples, use ornate language to the extreme, grossly exaggerate, greatly amplify, and strive to make it such that another person cannot add to it.'[81] Difficult ornament became one of the identifying features of the rhapsody. This type of rhapsody I have chosen to call the *epideictic rhapsody*. Epideictic has traditionally referred to one of the most important branches of rhetoric. The word is derived from the Greek word meaning, 'to display', and in its widest sense refers to 'a style of prose in which ornateness is introduced in a conscious effort to please'.

An epideictic speech in its more technical sense was regarded among earlier rhetoricians as one whose sole or chief purpose was display, thus agreeing with the derivation of the word 'epideictic'. The hearer is to gain pleasure, at least, if not information. The style is to exclude topics of a practical nature where the thought of the auditor centers chiefly on the subject discussed or in the argument, or where his interests are to any extent affected by the conclusions reached or implied. Since the appeal is to the emotions more than the intellect, form is of greater importance than subject matter, and there is too little regard as to whether it is legitimate or not. Even truth may be disregarded in the interests of eloquence. 'A pomp and prodigality of words', well-balanced periods, a style half-poetic, half oratorical, are the qualities most desired.[82]

Because of the epideictic character of many rhapsodies, there has been confusion about the meaning and function of pieces like 'Seven Stimuli'. Burton Watson, for example, proposes that the sole function of the poem is as an exercise in epideictic rhetoric, 'a pretext for the poet to display his skill on a series of conventional themes'.[83] He considers the final moralistic section simply a perfunctory gesture inserted to observe 'didactic convention', and that its main purpose was to entertain and delight, not persuade.

To support his argument Professor Watson remarks that 'since the prince is already suffering from overindulgence, it seems odd that his visitor would attempt in this way to stimulate him to further excesses...'[84] Indeed, upon a cursory reading of Mei Ch'eng's poem, one might conclude that there is an inordinate emphasis on the pursuits the poet ostensibly wanted to discourage. However, if we examine the piece rhetorically, we can see that the portrayal of the sensual pleasures plays an important role in the scheme of persuasion.

The entire piece in a sense is a parable, a lesson for princes. The major theme is not that philosophy can cure illness, although this point is made, but that a young prince should spend more time in study and cease living a life of frivolity. Almost everything in the poem is designed to illustrate this point. First of all, we know that the prince is ill because of overindulgence, but he cannot be cured with 'medicines, acupuncture or cauterization'. Rather his illness must be '*shui ch'ü*' (persuaded away) with 'essential words and marvelous doctrines'. The cure prescribed is not a medical but a moral one, and the remedy is to refrain from wanton indulgence and to turn to more edifying activities. The use of the word *shui* (persuade) here is particularly significant, for it more directly links the guest's speech with the rhetorical tradition. *Shui* is the same word that appears in the expression *yu shui* (itinerant persuader), and also occurs numerous times in the *Intrigues* and other early Chinese rhetorical writings. Thus, the guest is a figure like the Warring States persuader, and the speech he makes is similar in form to the pre-Han persuasion.

The 'Seven Stimuli' also resembles the Warring States persuasion in its mode of argument, which is basically a modified version of the doubled persuasion. The poem contains two antithetic arguments: (1) the prince ought to give up his sensual pursuits if he is to be cured; (2) the prince ought to further indulge in idle pastimes. Unlike the dilemmas of the *Intrigues*, however, the persuader does not find both alternatives repugnant, and he clearly indicates a preference for the first alternative (give up sensual pursuits). Even though most of the speech is devoted to portraying the sensual pleasures, the manner in which they are portrayed serves to reinforce the persuader's main argument. For example, each of the enticements is presented in highly attractive terms; each is the ultimate in pleasure. Yet, all of his eloquence has little effect on the prince's condition, and he remains as sick as before, except for the slight improvement exhibited in the fifth and sixth stimuli. In the last stimulus it is not the sages nor their teachings, but the *suggestion* that the prince listen to them, that arouses him from the sickbed.[85] This subtle emphasis again hints at the necessity for a moral cure. The main point is clear: overindulgence cannot cure overindulgence, and the only way to complete recovery is for the prince to change his licentious habits.

Presentation of indirect criticism by means of this type of doubled persuasion is common in the Han rhapsody. Since the ruler-centered rhetoric of the time did not permit overt criticism of the ruler's behaviour, writers used a technique known as *feng*, a term that is often used to characterize the primary purpose of the rhapsody. *Feng* comes from the word meaning 'wind', and by Han times was used as a verb meaning 'to sway' or 'to influence'. From the sense of 'to influence' it came to refer to the rhetorical technique which is best translated as 'criticism by indirection'.[86] *Feng* also was combined with the word *chien* (admonition) in the expression *feng chien* (indirect admonition), which in at least one source was considered the most acceptable form of presenting criticism to the throne.[87]

In spite of the attempt to insert subtle moral reprimands in their poems, Han poets began to write more and more in the highly ornate style of the epideictic rhapsody. The poet most responsible for shaping the character of this type of rhapsody was Ssu-ma Hsiang-ju, the acknowledged poetic mentor of Yang Hsiung, and considered by some the greatest poet in the history of the genre. Ssu-ma Hsiang-ju was a prolific writer. According to the 'Treatise on Bibliography' he wrote a total of twenty-nine rhapsodies, but of these, only four of unquestioned authenticity survive. These include the 'Master Void Rhapsody' (*Tzu-hsü fu*), the 'Shang-lin Rhapsody' (*Shang-lin fu*), 'Rhapsody Lamenting the Second Emperor of Ch'in' (*Ai Ch'in Erh-shih fu*), and 'The Great Man Rhapsody' (*Ta-jen fu*).[88]

The most famous and influential of Ssu-ma Hsiang-ju's poems are his rhapsodies on hunts, the 'Master Void' and its companion piece 'Shang-lin'. Although these rhapsodies are technically two separate works, they properly form a single organic unit. 'Master Void' was written while Ssu-ma Hsiang-ju was serving at the court of Prince Hsiao of Liang, and is a description of the hunting parks of Ch'u and Ch'i. The poem came to the attention of Emperor Wu, who was greatly impressed with its elegant style. When he discovered that Ssu-ma Hsiang-ju was the author, he summoned him to the capital. Ssu-ma then offered to write a rhapsody on the Shang-lin Park, the great imperial hunting preserve located west of Ch'ang-an.[89]

The body of the two poems is structured around a debate between three imaginary envoys: Master Void (Tzu-hsü) from the state of Ch'u; Master Non-existent (Wu-yu hsien-sheng) from Ch'i, and Lord Not-real (Wu shih kung), who represents the emperor. All three gentlemen are attending a hunt given by the Prince of Ch'i. The 'Master Void' opens with Master Void describing in extenso the great Ch'u hunting preserve known as Yün-meng. He first presents a chorography of the park and enumerates in a series of catalogues the various products contained within its bounds: minerals, gems, flowers, herbs, trees, animals, and birds. He then follows with an account of a typical hunt, and the attendant festivities, which was so full of exaggeration and hyperbole the Prince was left speechless.

At this point, Master Non-existent interrupts, and chides Master Void for emphasizing the extravagance of the Ch'u hunts. What he should have stressed were the good customs of his kingdom, not the dissolute pleasures that take place in the Yün-meng Park. He then gives a brief hyperbolic description of Ch'i and all its marvels without going into the same detail as Master Void. The conclusion of the Ch'i envoy's speech marks the end of the 'Master Void Rhapsody'.

With almost no transition the 'Shang-lin Rhapsody' begins as Lord Not-real breaks in and criticizes both speakers, telling them that there is nothing in the world that can match the emperor's Shang-lin Park, which he then proceeds to describe. He begins by enumerating in an orderly sequence the main features of the park: the rivers, water animals and fowl, mountains, plants, land animals, palaces, stones and gems, trees, and the animials that dwell in them. After this detailed panoramic description follows an account of the great imperial hunt in which large numbers of animals are killed and captured.

After the hunt the procession moves to a large terrace where the emperor hosts a banquet at which there is dancing, music, and singing by captivating young girls. In the midst of this merriment, however, the emperor suddenly becomes lost in contemplation, and regrets the excessive extravagance of the hunt. He decides at this point to change his ways and give up such wasteful pursuits. He dismisses the revelers and declares that the park will now be open to the common people. From now on all of his attention will be focused on governmental activities, and learning from the classics. The emperor is thus completely superior to the princes of Ch'i and Ch'u, a fact which is immediately acknowledged by Master Void and Master Non-existent. Lord Not-real wins the debate.

The most obvious feature of the 'Shang-lin Rhapsody'[90] is the rhetorical structure. We have already seen that the convention of the debate is common in the early rhapsody, and that it was derived from the speeches of the Warring States persuaders. Each of the three imaginary gentlemen is the equivalent of an itinerant persuader who applies his rhetorical skill on his ruler's behalf.

There are several types of rhetoric operating in the poem. The first type, and the most obvious, is the direct rhetoric of the debate – the attempts by the gentlemen to overwhelm each other with powerful arguments and grandiloquence. The second kind of rhetoric is less obtrusive, less hortatory. This is the poet's attempt to persuade the emperor to abandon hunting as a pastime. This rhetoric is the oblique, indirect persuasion found in the 'Seven Stimuli'. The poet, instead of making a straight-forward appeal, puts his argument in the mind of the emperor himself, creating the impression that the emperor's self-reflection and decision to abandon hunting came to him independently. The poet does not remonstrate or harangue, but criticizes by presenting an imaginary portrait of the ideal Confucian emperor, which the current ruler ought to emulate.

The dominant rhetorical form, however, is the epideictic rhetoric that occupies most of the poem. The 'Shang-lin Rhapsody' is in effect a panegyrical poem eulogizing the three rulers and the realms in which they hold sway. Most of the imperial envoy's speech, for example, is devoted to a description of the Shang-lin Park, and relatively little space is given to a narrative of the hunt. The manner of this description is clearly designed to glorify and exalt the imperial majesty. Thus, hyperbole is one of the poet's favorite tropes. The opening *topographia* (situation of the place) is one example of this penchant for exaggeration:

> To the left of it is Ts'ang-wu,
> To the right of it is the Western Limits.
> The River Tan passes to the south,
> The Purple Pool runs to the north.[91]

This obviously is not an accurate geographical account of the park's dimensions. As Professor Hervouet has shown, none of these place names can be identified with any certainty, and even those that can be vaguely located do not necessarily rest in the direction attributed to them.[92] The impression the poet may wish to convey by such exaggeration and disregard for accuracy is that the park and its emperor occupy the center of the cosmos, and that everything radiates from the seat of imperial power.

Hyperbole is not the only descriptive device employed by Ssu-ma Hsiang-ju. Of equal importance is the enumerative catalogue, which we have already seen used to a limited extent in the 'Seven Stimuli'. Ssu-ma Hsiang-ju makes the catalogue a prominent feature of the rhapsody. He has lists of trees, animals, flowers, gems, stones, and other exotic objects, many of which are either legendary or quasi-imaginary, and are now impossible to identify. For example, there is this list of trees that resembles the tree catalogues of medieval European literature:

> Here grow citrons with their ripe fruit in summer,
> Tangerines, bitter oranges, and limes,
> Loquats, persimmons,
> Wild pears, tamarinds,
> Jujubes, arbutus,

Peaches and grapes,
Almonds, damsons,
Mountain plums and litchis...[93]

Verse catalogues of this kind, which are rhymed and follow a consistent rhythmic pattern (mostly four syllable lines) are particularly well-suited to a declamatory form like the rhapsody. Catalogues are relatively common in oral poetry, in which the ordered enumeration of names is used as a mnemotechnic means of 'transmitting a culture's necessary information'.[94] The names, which now seem to be simply dry, boring lists, at one time must have had a certain evocative effect. Even literate poets like Walt Whitman were aware of the power of particular details to convey cultural attitudes. He says in the poetic prose preface to the 1855 edition of *Leaves of Grass*:

The American poets are to enclose old and new for American is the race of races. Of them a bard is to be commensurate with a people...His spirit responds to his country's spirit...he incarnates its geography and natural life and rivers and lakes. Mississippi with annual freshets and changing chutes, Missouri and Columbia and Ohio and Saint Lawrence with the falls and beautiful masculine Hudson, do not embouchure where they spend themselves more than they embouchure into him ...When the long Atlantic coast stretches longer and the Pacific coast stretches longer he easily stretches them north or south. He spans between them also from east to west and reflects what is between them. On him rise solid growths that offset the growths of pine and cedar and hemlock and liveoak and locust and chestnut and cypress and hickory and limetree and cottonwood and tuliptree and cactus and wildvine and tamarind and persimmon...and tangles as tangled as any cane-break or swamp ...and forests coated with transparent ice and icicles hanging from the boughs and crackling in the wind...and sides and peaks of mountains...and pasturage sweet and free as savannah or upland or prairie...with flights and songs and screams that answer those of the wildpigeon and highfold and orchard-oriole and coote and surf-duck and redshouldered-cat-owl and water-pheasant and qua-bird and pied-sheldrake and blackbird and mockingbird and buzzard and condor and night-heron and eagle.[95]

Ssu-ma Hsiang-ju does essentially the same thing in his rhapsody: he enumerates names that conjure up associations of the magnificence and power of the Han empire. As Hervouet puts it 'Sseu-ma Siang-jou ne cherche qu'à décrire, à suggérer un paysage et l'abondance des noms, au moins autant qu'elle décrit dans son détail le spectacle offert devant les yeux, signifie seulement la profusion des beautés accumulées dans les parcs des rois et des empereurs.'[96] He was a poet intensely interested in language, and extended this interest into the field of actual linguistic investigations. He is the author of a dictionary, and it is significant to note that the manner in which his catalogues are constructed resembles somewhat the categorized word lists that served as dictionaries in the Han era. For this reason, scholars have suggested that the abstruse verbiage of Ssu-ma Hsiang-ju's rhapsodies may be related to his dictionary-making.

Indeed, the epideictic rhapsody is a type of lexical poetry or 'versified lexicography',[97] and in fact has been considered by some as the forerunner of the *lei-shu* or encyclopedia.[98] The association of lexicography and poetry is not as uncommon as one might think. Paul Demiéville points out that Rabelais, whose *Gargantua et Pantagruel* abounds in 'lexical enumerations', also dabbled in lexicography and glossography.[99] One could also add the example of the Greek poet Lykophron of Chalkis (3rd c. B.C.), who was an official in the Alexandrian Library and worked on a dictionary as just one of many philological pursuits. His *Alexandra* is one of the most abstruse poems of world literature – half of the words in it are exceedingly rare and more than a tenth are *hapax legomena*.[100]

The most abstruse words used by Ssu-ma Hsiang-ju are the binomial descriptives known as *impressifs*. As defined by Professor Demiéville, these words are disyllabic or polysyllabic expressions equivalent to what African linguists call *Lautbilder*, which are designated in Chinese as 'descriptives' (*mao*), 'c'est-à-dire des termes visant à rendre par leur contexture phonétique des *impressions* qui ne sont pas du tout nécessairement d'ordre auditif, ni même d'ordre sensorial'.[101] The sound-image is a common linguistic phenomenon, particularly in primitive languages. It is 'not confined to the imitation of noises but attempts to provide an auditory equivalent of appearances, odors, tactile sensations, tastes, and especially movements'.[102] They are words like English 'pell-mell', 'zig-zag', and 'helter-skelter' and often alliterate or rhyme. Here are a few examples from Ssu-ma Hsiang-ju: '*$*gli\hat{o}ng-dz'i\hat{o}ng$*' (lofty), *$*ngiəm-ngiəm$* (rugged), *$*xiung-d̦iung$* (rushing of water). Words of this kind are not original with Ssu-ma Hsiang-ju, and are found in both the *Book of Songs* and *Ch'u tz'u*, but as Hervouet correctly states, Ssu-ma Hsiang-ju is 'le plus grand créateur de ces expressions dans la littérature chinoise et aussi, proportionellement à la brièveté de son oeuvre, un des principaux utilisateurs'.[103] More than other rhapsody writers, including Mei Ch'eng, he tends to list them in a long series, which of course makes his poems extremely difficult to read.

The most difficult of Ssu-ma Hsiang-ju's rhapsodies from the standpoint of large numbers of *impressifs* is the 'Great Man Rhapsody'. This poem was written shortly after he presented the 'Shang-lin Rhapsody' to the

emperor. It describes the magical journey of the Great Man, acknowledged
to be Emperor Wu, into the cosmos of gods, spirits, and immortals. Both in
terms of content and language, the 'Great Man Rhapsody' closely resembles
the 'Distant Wandering' of the *Ch'u tz'u*. Like the celestial traveller of the
'Distant Wandering', the Great Man finds the sublunary world too small and
confining (his realm is only ten thousand *li* in size!), and therefore decides
to soar into the sky and go on a distant journey. Befitting his supernatural
status, the Great Man's carriage, which is decked out with banners made of
comets and rainbows, is pulled by a team of dragons. They are described in a
series of extemely rare *impressifs*, the sense of which cannot be approximated
in English. The words evoke, either explicitly or implicitly, images of 'a
caterpiller, a proud courser, a stubborn mount, a steep mountain, a frightened hare, beams of a roof, mosquitoes, sparks, lightning, fog...'[104] There
is nothing in earlier literature that matches this verbal portrait in sheer fantasy.

What follows is the account of the Great Man's journey in search
of immortals. He travels in all directions and has at his command the
entire pantheon of the astral regions. The climax of the trip is a visit to the
Mother Queen of the West (Hsi-wang-mu), who is portrayed in a somewhat
humorous manner:

> And now he sees the Mother Queen of the West,
> With her bright silvery hair and head ornaments she lives in a cave!
> Fortunately, she has a three-legged crow to wait on her.
> If one were to live as long as she without dying,
> Though it be for a myriad generations what joy could one have?[105]

Clearly, this less than complimentary portrait of the queen of the immortals is
intended as a reprimand to the emperor, who spent much of his time in
pursuit of elixirs of immortality and attempts to attract immortals. The
Mother Queen of the West was the center of a Han mystery cult that
promised immortality to its believers. Ssu-ma Hsiang-ju, by pointing out her
restricted, encumbered existence, is saying in a somewhat indirect fashion that
her type of immortality should not be emulated. I suspect that what the poet
really was objecting to was Emperor Wu's heavy reliance on Taoist magicians
and alchemists, many of whom were quacks and frauds, but who impressed the
emperor with their fantastic stories of immortals and spirits.

After his brief visit with the Mother Queen of the West, the Great Man turns
his carriage eastward until he reaches the Dark City Mountain (Yu-tu), where
he eats a meal. He dines on the food of the immortals: night dew, morning
mist, the fungus of immortality, and jasper flowers. His meal finished, the
Great Man soars again into the uppermost regions of the heavens. He

penetrates the fissure from which lightning flashes and crosses the domain of Feng-lung, the god of clouds and rain. From here he descends again to the earth, landing near the northern border of the empire. He now leaves his riders and charioteers behind as he stands alone in the realm of nothingness in which

> *In the sheer depths, below, the earth is invisible;*
> *In the vastness above, the sky cannot be seen.*
> *When one looks, his startled eyes see nothing;*
> *When one listens, his deafened ears hear nothing.*[106]

Except for the satirical portrait of the Mother Queen of the West most of the poem is highly laudatory of the supremely omnipotent emperor. This feature of the rhapsody has led Yang Hsiung to remark: 'In former times Emperor Wu was interested in immortals. Hsiang-ju presented the "Great Man Rhapsody" in order to criticize him by indirection. The emperor, on the contrary, had the intention of airily floating on the clouds. From this it is clear that the rhapsody only encourages and does not restrain.'[107] Yang Hsiung is certainly correct in noting the contradiction between the poet's desire to persuade and the fact that the fanciful eulogizing only reinforced the emperor's interest in immortals.

The reason for this apparent paradox is that Ssu-ma Hsiang-ju, in spite of his attempt to make the poem an ethical, suasory demonstration that would influence the emperor's behavior, let his interest in verbal decoration take precedence. 'La marque du poète', says Hervouet, 'ce n'est donc pas dans le contenu du poème qu'on la trouve…mais dans la forme. Car, dans le vocabulaire, dans la richesse des images qui décrivent les diverses étapes du voyage dans l'espace, apparaît le talent poétique caractéristique de Sseu-ma Siang-jou'.[108] For example, in this poem of about 750 characters there are 60 *impressifs*, and about thirty of these are 'original' to Ssu-ma Hsiang-ju (eight or nine appear to be *hapax legomena*).[109] With this poem Ssu-ma Hsiang-ju firmly established himself as the foremost representative of the school of rhapsody writers who were primarily concerned with the rhapsody as an aesthetic object, and who conceived the main purpose of the rhapsody as entertainment rather than pure instruction. There is rhetoric in his poems, but it is ornamental, epideictic rhetoric and not persuasive rhetoric that stands out. It was this feature of his poems that was the most influential on later rhapsodies.

The Rhapsody Used for Entertainment. During the Emperor Wu period the writing of rhapsodies was at its peak. I have mentioned only a few of the great number of rhapsody poets of this period. There was, for example, Mei

Ch'eng's son, Mei Kao (fl. 128 B.C.), who is credited with 120 rhapsodies. Mei served at court together with the famous court wit Tung-fang Shuo (ca. 161 B.C.–86 B.C.). They both composed rhapsodies under special orders from the emperor, including one poem celebrating the birth of the heir apparent.[110] Mei's main function was to accompany the emperor on excursions and tours of inspection and write poems on whatever subject the emperor might dictate. Particularly popular were rhapsodies on hunts and sacrifices.[111] The rhapsody was obviously becoming more and more a vehicle of entertainment, and with the emergence of epideictic rhapsodists like Ssu-ma Hsiang-ju, this tendency was reinforced.

With the accession of Emperor Hsüan in 74 B.C. the rhapsody seems to have been firmly established as a means of providing divertissement for the emperor and the court. The use of the rhapsody for entertainment of course conflicted with the fundamental function of the rhapsody as a suasory instrument, and raised a few eyebrows among the more sober Confucian scholars. Emperor Hsüan, like his predecessor, Emperor Wu, was also fond of taking poets along on his hunting expeditions. He usually asked them to compose extemporaneous rhapsodies for the enjoyment of the participants. Some of the emperor's advisers considered this an improper use of the genre, calling it an 'excessive and idle activity'. The emperor is reported to have made the following reply to this charge:

Are there not such games as dice and chess? To play them would certainly be better than doing nothing at all.[112] *The best of the rhapsodies have the same principle as the ancient poems; even the most mediocre are rhetorically ornate and designed to delight. They are like satin and crepe in a seamstress' work or the odes of Cheng and Wei in music. These currently are the things that please the ears and eyes. Rhapsodies, by comparison, still contain moral instruction about humaneness and propriety and much information about plants, animals, and trees. That is far better than the antics of court jesters or games like dice and chess.*[113]

This statement, while conceding that the primary purpose of the rhapsody was moral edification, did not hesitate to ascribe the genre with an aesthetic function. One suspects that the emperor really considered the epideictic rhapsody superior to the purely didactic rhapsody, which after all was frequently designed to criticize his own behavior! At any rate he clearly gave his endorsement to the notion that a poem could be enjoyed for its own sake, and this imperial approval must have carried considerable weight. The epideictic rhapsody tradition was reinforced and acquired a legitimacy it had had only informally and implicitly prior to this time.

How this new concept of the rhapsody manifested itself can be seen in the writings of the major poet of this period, Wang Pao (fl. 58 B.C.). Wang Pao, like Ssu-ma Hsiang-ju, came from the province of Shu, an area that produced so many great Han poets. He achieved recognition by a provincial official who asked him to compose several panegyrical poems which were to be set to music. These songs were submitted to the emperor, who was delighted with them. Eventually, Wang was summoned to the capital and found himself the recipient of the emperor's favor. He and another poet, Chang Tzu-ch'iao, always accompanied the emperor on his trips outside the palace, standing with brush in hand ready to write a rhapsody on any topic the emperor might suggest.[114]

It would appear that Wang Pao's poems were even credited with a medicinal as well as an entertainment function. One day the heir apparent was suffering from dizziness and loss of memory. Wang was summoned to the heir apparent's quarters to recite rhapsodies as a curative. He recited throughout the day and night, and returned only after the heir apparent had recovered.[115] Of the rhapsodies Wang Pao recited on this occasion, one the heir apparent particularly enjoyed was 'The Flute Rhapsody' (*Tung-hsiao fu*).[116] This piece is the first authentic example of a rhapsody on a musical instrument, a topic that was to be extremely popular in later times.[117] The poem begins with a description of the area where the bamboo for the flute grows. When the bamboo is picked, it is made into the *tung-hsiao*, a flute about thirty inches long with thirteen holes. Artists paint elegant patterns on it, and then the flute is given to a blindman, who, lacking any other means of expression, vents his feelings by playing the flute. He plays all types of music – sad, happy, martial sounds. The music is edifying, capable of influencing the most recalcitrant men. It even arouses the most hideous insects. The rhapsody ends with an epilogue which further describes the music.

'The Flute' is a good example of pure epideictic rhetoric. The poem is almost completely divorced from any suasory intent (except for the remarks about the edifying qualities of the music), and concentrates on ornate description. The language of the poem is extremely difficult and abounds with *impressifs* and other expressions that elude the linguistic acumen of Li Shan and other commentators of *The Literary Selections*. There are even notable landscape descriptions:

> The place where the bamboo for the flute grows
> Is a hillock south of the River Chiang.
> The bamboo stretches long and has few knots.
> On top the vegetation is dense and spreads in all directions.
> By just looking at the slope on which it stands,

One sees it is steep and declivitous.

[.   .   .   ]

One observes it spans a broad area;
The bamboo finds enough enjoyment in such a tranquil spot.

[.   .   .   ]

The soaring wind whistles through its branches,
Winding rivers and flowing streams pour down the mountain.
White caps swelling, beads of water splashing,
With a roar they flow into a deep chasm.[118]

Epideictic rhapsodies of this kind continued to be written into the reign of Emperor Ch'eng (32–7 B.C.) whose interest in amusements and pleasures exceeded that of both Emperor Wu and Emperor Hsüan. During his reign even scholars like Liu Hsiang (77–6 B.C.) were not averse to writing somewhat frivolous poems. Good examples of rhapsodies written for pure entertainment are Liu's 'Elegant Zither Rhapsody' (*Ya ch'in fu*)[119] and 'Encirclement Chess Rhapsody' (*Wei ch'i fu*).[120] Yang Hsiung, who was born in 53 B.C., was a young man when the epideictic rhapsody was at the peak of its popularity. Because of the geographical isolation of his home province of Shu, it is possible that Yang was unaware of the literary fashion of the capital. However, the conventions of the epideictic rhapsody had already been established by his compatriot, Ssu-ma Hsiang-ju, whose rhapsodies were familiar to almost any educated Chinese of this period. Yang Hsiung himself acknowledges his literary debt to Ssu-ma Hsiang-ju, and in his youth he wrote imitations of Ssu-ma's rhapsodies.[121] Yang Hsiung did not remain an imitator, nor did he continue to write in the pure epideictic manner. Yang, in fact, eventually rejected the *fu* as a proper medium of poetic expressions. Yang's handling of this genre, and his reaction to the epideictic tradition, is the subject of the remainder of this book.

3

The 'Sweet Springs' and 'Ho-tung' Rhapsodies

One state ceremony of Han times that was often the subject of poetic treatment was the imperial sacrifices. The rhapsody, with its tendency toward elaborate, hyperbolic description, was an ideal medium in which to celebrate these grandiose spectacles. Poets were usually invited to attend the ceremony, and were commissioned to write rhapsodies in honor of the occasion, which would then be submitted to the throne. Yang Hsiung wrote two poems on the sacrifices, the 'Sweet Springs Rhapsody' (*Kan-ch'üan fu*) and 'Ho-tung Rhapsody' (*Ho-tung fu*) to commemorate imperial sacrifices that were performed in 11 B.C.[1]

The 'Sweet Springs Rhapsody' is one of Yang Hsiung's longest and most famous poems. The occasion of its writing was the sacrifice to the supreme heavenly deity known as T'ai-yi or the Great Unity, held at the Sweet Springs Palace in Yün-yang Commandery, east of Ch'ang-an (northwest of modern Ch'un-hua, Shensi). The sacrifice to the Great Unity was originally established by Emperor Wu on the advice of an alchemist, who suggested that worshipping this god would bring the emperor his long-desired immortality. The Great Unity became so important in the Emperor Wu period that it replaced all other gods in importance, including the Five Emperors who were designated the Great Unity's assistants.[2] In 113 B.C. Emperor Wu ordered the construction of a special altar at Sweet Springs called the Great Altar (T'ai-chih) for conducting sacrifices to the Great Unity.[3] In addition, in order to accommodate the great numbers of people attending the sacrifices, elaborate halls, palaces, and viewing towers were built.[4] In the same year an altar for the Sovereign Earth (Hou-t'u), the chief earth spirit, was erected at Fen-yin, northeast of Ch'ang-an.[5]

The sacrifices to both of these deities continued throughout the dynasty until the accession of Emperor Ch'eng. In 32 B.C. Emperor Ch'eng's chief advisers, K'uang Heng and Chang T'an, recommended that the heavenly sacrifices be moved from Sweet Springs to the southern suburbs of the capital, and the earth sacrifices be transferred from Fen-yin to the northern suburbs. The recommendation was the subject of a debate at court, and eventually a vote was taken in which the partisans of K'uang and Chang won an overwhelming majority.[6]

K'uang Heng addressed a memorial to the throne stating in detail why the sacrificial sites should be changed. His argument consisted of three reasons: (1) in ancient times the sacrifices to Heaven were performed in the southern suburbs of the capital while those to Earth were held in the northern suburbs; (2) the journey to Yün-yang and Fen-yin was too dangerous for the emperor and his party; (3) the sacrifices were too expensive and imposed a heavy burden on the local inhabitants of the sacrificial sites.[7] K'uang also recommended changes in the ritual which would eliminate the ostentatious display that was particularly associated with the Sweet Springs sacrifices.[8]

With the transfer of the sacrifices, the controversy did not end. Shortly after the move had been made, a wind storm destroyed part of the Sweet Springs Palace complex, and uprooted over a hundred trees. The emperor, concerned that this was an evil omen, questioned his Confucian adviser, Liu Hsiang, about it. Liu addressed a long reply to the throne suggesting that the sacrifices be restored to their former places, citing all the favorable omens associated with these areas in the past.[9] The emperor did not act on Liu Hsiang's suggestion immediately, but in 16 B.C., because Emperor Ch'eng was without an heir, the Empress Dowager was requested to issue an edict ordering the sacrifices restored to Sweet Springs and Fen-yin.[10] The emperor then held a series of sacrifices in both of these areas hoping the spirits would bless him with a son. This was the purpose of the sacrifices Yang Hsiung attended in 11 B.C., and for which he wrote the 'Sweet Springs Rhapsody'.

Yang Hsiung's piece is not the only Han poem on the Sweet Springs sacrifices. Both Wang Pao and Liu Hsin wrote poems on the subject, but their compositions survive only in fragments.[11] In addition, Yang Hsiung's friend Huan T'an wrote a rhapsody which might be connected with the same sacrifice attended by Yang Hsiung.[12]

The text of the 'Sweet Springs Rhapsody' survives both in the 'Autobiography' and *The Literary Selections*.[13] The 'Autobiography' contains a short preface which also was included in *The Literary Selections* version of the poem. Since the preface comes from the 'Autobiography' it is likely that it was written by Yang Hsiung. This preface gives the details of the poem's composition:

During the reign of Emperor Ch'eng one of the emperor's retainers recommended my writings as resembling the style of Ssu-ma Hsiang-ju. The emperor was about to perform the suburban sacrifices at the Great Altar in Sweet Springs and to the

Sovereign Earth at Fen-yin, in order to seek an heir to succeed him. He summoned me to await orders in the Ch'eng-ming Hall.[14] *In the first month I accompanied the emperor to Sweet Springs. When they returned I presented the 'Sweet Springs Rhapsody' as an indirect criticism of the emperor.*[15]

The preface is followed by the main text of the poem, which consists of three parts: a prose introduction, repeating the circumstances of the poem's composition; the body of the piece, which is predominantly in verse; and a *luan* or epilogue.[16]

I

In this tenth generation of Han there is to be a suburban sacrifice to the Upper Dark. They set up the Great Altar, embrace the 'Divinely Good', and honor the 'Bright Titles'.[17] *The emperor matches tally with the Three August Ones, has recorded merits that equal those of the Five Emperors.*[18] *He is anxious for heirs to be granted in great numbers, to expand his heritage and develop his line. Thereupon, he orders a multitude of officials to calculate an auspicious day and select a propitious hour. The stars spread out and Heaven begins to move.*[19]

II

7. *He summons the Twinkler and the Great Yin,*
    Cowering before him, the Angular Arranger manages the troops.[20]
8. *He assigns K'an and Yü to the ramparts,*
    Beats K'uei-hsü and flogs Hsü-k'uang.[21]
9. *The eight spirits race off to clear the road,*[22]
    Dressed for battle, they stir up a clamor.
10. *Warriors like Ch'ih-yu wearing Kan-chiang swords and carrying jade axes*[23]
    Fly in disarray and run helter-skelter.
11. *Evenly grouped and massed, they stick tightly together;*
    Quick as the wind, swift as the clouds, rapidly they scatter.
12. *Arranged in groups and ordered in ranks, arrayed like rows of fishscales;*
    Ragged and uneven, they jump like fish and soar like birds.
13. *They are like gathering fog and converging mist;*
    They cast off a lustrous glow and form a pattern.

III

14. *Thereupon, the emperor*[24]
    Mounts a phoenix
    Shades himself with a flowery mushroom.
15. *He hitches up four green dragons,*
    And six white dragons.

16. *Twisting and slithering,*
    They stream out in long procession.
17. *Quickly darkness closes in,*
    Suddenly light opens out.
18. *They ascend the clear empyrean, cross the floating sunbeams,*
    How the falcon-flags and tortoise-snake-banners on tall staffs do flutter!
19. *Shooting-star yak-tail pennants flash like lightning,*
    Blend with kingfisher canopies and phoenix banners.
20. *They gather a myriad riders in the central camp;*
    Assemble a thousand jade chariots.
21. *With a continuous rumbling noise,*
    The light vanguard speeds like thunder, races the whirlwind.
22. *They ascend the lofty heights of a tall expanse;*
    Cross the clear purity of a sinuous, winding course.
23. *They climb mount Ch'uan-luan as far as the heavenly gate;*
    Gallop to Ch'ang-ho and enter the shivering cold.[25]

IV

24. *At this moment they have yet to reach Sweet Springs;*
    Then they gaze at the high-reaching Heaven Penetrating Tower.[26]
25. *The base, hidden in the shade, is chilly and cold;*
    The top is huge, jumbled and tangled together.
26. *Straight, tall, lofty it reaches Heaven,*
    Its height truly cannot be measured.
27. *The level plain, extending vast and long,*
    Is lined with peonies in forests and thickets.
28. *Collected here are coir palms and mint;*
    Profusely scattered about without limit.
29. *Lofty hills and mounds stand stately and tall;*
    Deep moats, steep and abrupt, form ravines.
30. *Here and there are touring palaces illuminating one another;*
    Interconnected and joined stretch Great Peak and Stone Gate.[27]

V

31. *Thereupon, a great building as illusive as clouds, as deceptive as waves,*
    Piled up precipitously forms a viewing tower.[28]
32. *When one lifts his head and looks up high,*
    His eyes become blurred and he sees nothing.
33. *Straight ahead the view is overflowing and vast,*
    Pointing to the limitless expanse of the east and west.

34. One is simply giddy and confused:
    The soul is perplexed and befuddled.

35. One leans on the railing and looks all around;
    Suddenly the vista is boundless, without limit:

36. Viridescent hues of green jade trees;[29]
    Ornate splendor of nephrite horses and rhinos.

37. Bronze men bold and intrepid hold the bell-stands;[30]
    They are inlaid with coarse, rough dragon scales,

38. Brandish bright, burning torches,
    Cast off a blazing, fiery flame.

39. They are fit for the Hanging Garden of the Lord's abode;[31]
    Symbols of the awesome spirit of the Great Unity.

40. The enormous tower stands out prominent and alone;
    It reaches the supreme heights of the Pole Star.

41. Constellations touch the upper eaves,
    The sun and moon pass through the main rafters.

42. Thunder drones in the caverns and recesses;
    Lightning flashes in the walls and fences.

43. Even ghosts and demons cannot reach the end;
    They go halfway and then tumble back down.

44. It passes through the 'falling sunlight' and crosses the 'flying bridge',
    Floats over the 'gnats' and brushes Heaven.[32]

VI

45. To the left is the Comet, on the right Hsüan-ming;[33]
    In front is the red watchtower, in the rear a receiving gate.

46. Its shadow reaches the Western Sea and the Dark City;[34]
    The bubbling sweet waters spurt forth to form a stream.

47. A dragon is coiled around the eastern bank;
    The white tiger fiercely guards the K'un-lun.[35]

48. He looks all about the Kao-kuang Palace,
    Wanders leisurely in the Western Purity Hall.[36]

49. The front hall stands tall and imposing,
    Mr Ho's jade glistens and glimmers.

50. Flying beams with floating columns soar above,
    Spirits still and quiet hold them up.

51. It is lofty, empty, and spacious,
    Resembling the great heights of the Purple Palace.

52. Buildings joined, interconnected, spreading out,
    Rest like rocky peaks ranged together.

53. He climbs a pavilion in the clouds, looks up and down:
     All is chaotic, obscure, formed in confusion.
54. It trails a streaming red lustre;
     Wafts a spiraling green vapor.
55. It is heir to the Jade Building and Jasper Palace.[37]
     It is as if one had climbed high and were looking into the distance;
     He is awe-struck as if on the edge of an abyss.

VII

56. A whirlwind releases its boiling fury, scatters cinnamon and pepper, gathers
     almond and willow.
57. A fragrance, pungent and strong, fills the air;
     It strikes the beam-pillars, reaches under the eaves.
58. Sounds reverberate and collide;
     The noise loudly passes from bell to bell.
59. The breeze pushes open the jade door, lifts the bronze knocker,
     Sets forth the aroma of orchid, melilotus, and cnidium.
60   Curtains rustle as they are brushed by the wind;
     It gradually becomes darker, the silence is deep.
61. Major and minor, clear and turbid, the stately notes all in harmony;[38]
     As if K'uei and Ya were playing their lutes.[39]
62. Upon hearing it Pan and Ch'ui would put down their axes and chisels;
     Wang Erh would throw away his compass and plumb-line.[40]
63. Even the immortals Cheng Ch'iao and Wo Chüan
     Would be confused, as if in a dream.[41]

VIII

Thereupon, affairs change and things transform; the eyes become alarmed and the
ears frightened. The Son of Heaven stands sedately in the midst of intricately carved
precious towers, pleasure lodges, jade inlaid end-beams, and jade petals. This is the
place to cleanse his mind and purify his soul, to gather his energy and concentrate
his attention, to influence Heaven and Earth, and receive blessings from the Three
Spirits.[42]

Then, he begins to search for a partner, to seek a mate, officials like Kao and Yi,[43]
men of first-rate talent and ability, who are embued with the kindness of the ' Sweet
pear tree',[44] and embrace the disposition of the ' March east'.[45] They gather
together in the Yang-ling Palace.

70. He weaves castor plants into mats,
     Breaks jasper branches to make perfume.

71. *He sips the flowing mist from the clear clouds,*
    Drinks dew from the petals of the Jo tree.[46]

72. *They congregate into the park where gods are worshipped;*
    Ascend the hall where earth-spirits are eulogized.

73. *They erect tall banners shimmering with light;*
    Display the magnificent colorful sunshade.

74. *The emperor grasps the Armillary Sphere*[47] *and looks below;*
    His eyes wander over the San-wei mountains.[48]

75. *The mass of chariots spread out onto the eastern slope;*
    Jade linchpins in perfect formation, they race downward.

76. *They float over the dragon pool and circle the Nine Divisions;*
    Peer under the earth and then return above.

77. *A breeze blows up to support the axles;*
    Bustling phoenixes guide the streamers.

78. *They cross the Weak Water as if it were a brook; Traverse Mount Pu-chou as*
    if it were a gentle slope.[49]

79. *Thinking of the Mother Queen of the West joyfully he wishes her long life;*
    He rejects the Jade Maiden, expels Fu-fei.[50]

80. *The Jade Maiden has no place to twinkle her clear eyes;*
    Fu-fei can no longer display her moth-eyebrows.

81. *Only now does he hold the essence and strength of the Way and Power;*
    Becomes an equal of the Divine Luminaries, and consults with them.

IX

82. *Thereupon,*
    He reverently makes a burnt offering, offers respectful prayers. He burns
    incense to August Heaven; he shakes and agitates the Great Unity.[51]

83. *They raise the Hung-yi banner;*
    Plant the Magic Pennant.[52]

84. *Flame and smoke burst into the sky;*
    Spread into the four directions.

85. *In the east it illumines the Green Sea;*
    In the west it dazzles the Flowing Sands.[53]

86. *In the north it brightens the Dark City;*
    In the south it warms up Cinnabar Cliff.[54]

87. *The black, curved libation ladle*
    Overflows with black-millet wine.

88. *The fragrance:*
    Spreads out in great density,
    Powerful and aromatic.

89. The flames activate the yellow dragon;
    The sparks arouse the giant unicorn.
90. He summons Shaman Hsien to call to the celestial gate,
    Open the heavenly court, invite all the spirits.
91. They gather in great numbers, descend to the pure altar;
    There are good omens in great numbers, piled up like mountains.

X

Thereupon, the affair ends with great success. They turn around their chariots and return. They pass the San-luan Tower and rest at the Pear Palace.[55]

93. The threshold to Heaven is agape, the boundary to earth is open;
    The eight wastes are in harmony, the myriad states are in accord.
94. They climb the Ch'ang-p'ing slope, drums are rumbling like thunder;[56]
    Heavenly sounds arise, bold warriors increase their fervor;
95. Clouds soar on high, rain pours in great profusion.
    Blessings are shared by all, they remain beautiful for a myriad generations.

XI

The Epilogue:

96. The lofty round mound
    Is so high it obscures the sky.
97. Up and down, from side to side,
    It encompasses a large circle.
98. The storied palaces stand in uneven rows,
    Joined together like rugged hills.
99. They are tall and deep,
    Of limitless expanse.
100. The affairs of Heaven
    Are mysterious and hard to fathom.
101. The sage ruler is dignified and solemn,
    A worthy counterpart of Heaven.
102. He comes to reverently sacrifice,
    The spirits trust him.
103. Leisurely, deliberately,
    The spirits come to rest.
104. With a blinding brilliance,
    They send down their blessing:
105. 'Son after son, grandson after grandson,
    Long and without limit!'

KHR

As one might expect in a rhapsody written under imperial auspices, the protagonist of the 'Sweet Springs Rhapsody' is the emperor. Emperor Ch'eng, who is not mentioned by name (he is referred to by metonymy in 1. 14 and appears under the designation 'Son of Heaven' in 1. 65), is portrayed as a super-magician on the order of the Great Man of Ssu-ma Hsiang-ju's 'Great Man Rhapsody' (*Ta-jen fu*). In 11. 7–8 the emperor, like the Great Man, is attributed with complete control over the gods and spirits of the terrestial and astral regions. Also like the Great Man, he has a magnificent cortège. He mounts a phoenix (*feng-huang*) which is shaded by a 'flowery mushroom' (*hua chih*), and he drives a team of twisting, slithering dragons. This description may not be as fantastic as it seems, for in Han times the imperial carriage was an imagined representation of the retinue of the celestial gods. The emperor's carriage was called a *feng-huang chü* (phoenix carriage)[57] and was shaped like a large *feng-huang* or decorated with small gold *feng–huang* figures. The *hua-chih* could refer to the *hua-kai* or 'Flowery Baldachin', which was part of the emperor's immortality-quest paraphernalia. Wang Mang had a 'Flowery Baldachin' eighty-one feet high pulled by six horses and three hundred men.[58] Dragons, of course, were common designations for magnificent horses.

This is a good example of the difficulty posed by such seemingly fantastic descriptions in the Han rhapsodies. Because the actual ceremony was a temporal replica of the supernatural, one never knows if the poet is speaking figuratively or literally. Thus, what may appear to be hyperbole and exaggeration may have had a basis in fact. What is significant, however, is that whether the poet is describing an actual scene or not, his language clearly brings his portrayal into the realm of the fantastic and imaginary. This feature is well-illustrated by the extensive use of *impressifs*. For example, 1. 22 actually contains no nouns, and what I have translated as nouns are really *impressifs*. The line literally reads: 'ascend: tall expansive/lofty-high,//cross: sinuous-winding/clear pure.'[59] In each part of this line there is an action verb followed by a succession of *impressifs* where one would normally expect a noun. Thus, instead of naming the thing being described, the poet gives only its attributes. The effect of this technique is to give the description a vague, impressionistic quality, with the emphasis on certain states, conditions, or attributes of the scene (e.g. the condition of 'highness') rather than concrete details (e.g. 'high hill').

The fanciful, impressionistic aspect of the descriptions clearly emerges as the poem progresses. Already by 1. 23 the emperor and his party have been transported into the celestial environment of the Ch'ang-ho Gate, the gateway to Heaven. Then, in 1. 31 when the Sweet Springs Palace first comes into view the scene has an almost terrorizing effect on the observer as for a moment his vision is blurred and 'he sees nothing'. Then, his view expands and he takes in the entire panorama which is 'overflowing and vast,/Pointing to the limitless expanse of the east and west' (1. 33). This is followed by another statement of fright and befuddlement, with a subsequent widening of the vision (11. 34–5). Thus, the poet moves between two extremes, a kind of clouded vision caused by his terror, and absolute clarity which beholds a broad vista.

This contrast of extremes is common in other rhapsodies as well,[60] and often takes the form of a juxtaposition of concrete detail with fantasy, hyperbole, and exaggeration. Thus, 11. 36–8 focus on the specific objects contained in the palace: jade trees, bronze statues, nephrite horses and rhinoceroses. Then, the poet turns his attention to a giant tower, whose heights are portrayed in the most extravagant language. It rises as high as the Pole Star, constellations brush its eaves, and the sun and moon pass through the rafters. It is so tall ghosts and demons cannot climb it, and its spire reaches into the uppermost limits of the sky.

As in Ssu-ma Hsiang-ju's rhapsodies, the supernatural imagery and hyperbole seem to be primarily designed to glorify the imperial majesty and are not intended to present a realistic description. In this case, it is difficult to conceive a mundane counterpart for the fanciful images. This, in fact, seems to be true for most of the 'Sweet Springs Rhapsody', where one really never gets a clear idea exactly what the palace looks like. Even when he is depicting a specific object, such as the bronze statues in front of the palace, the poet cannot resist his penchant for introducing supernatural associations (11. 37–8):

> *Bronze men bold and intrepid hold the bell-stands;*
> *They are inlaid with coarse, rough ragon scales,*
> *Brandish bright, burning torches,*
> *Cast off a blazing, fiery flame.*

After this relatively straightforward account, Yang ends up saying:

> *They are fit for the Hanging Garden of the Lord's abode;*
> *Symbols of the awesome spirit of the Great Unity.*

In spite of the great amount of fantasy in this poem, Yang Hsiung's primary purpose was not to display his verbal virtuosity but to write a poem of persuasion. This view is clearly stated in the preface, where he says he wrote the rhapsody to '*feng*' or 'criticize by indirection'. This point is reaffirmed in a short critique that follows the poem in the 'Autobiography', and which may also have been written by Yang Hsiung. After enumerating the palaces and towers built by Emperor Wu, the critique says:

The palace violated the regulations in which wood is polished but not carved, walls are plastered but not painted, such as the palace built by King Hsüan of Chou,[61] *the city moved by P'an-keng,*[62] *and the low palaces of the Hsia, the timbers, rafters and three steps of T'ang and Yü.*[63] *Yet, it had been built a long time ago and was nothing constructed by Emperor Ch'eng. If one wished to admonish, it was the wrong time, and if he wished to remain silent, he could not. Thus, I elaborated and exhalted it, comparing it to the Purple Palace, the residence of the Lord of Heaven. It is like saying: this is not made by human effort; one supposes only ghosts and spirits could do it.*

Furthermore, at this time, the Brilliant Companion Chao was in great favor. Everytime the emperor went up to Sweet Springs she accompanied him in the panther-tail section of the entourage. Thus, when I lavishly speak of the multitude of the horsemen and chariots, double and triple teams, means that this is not the way to 'influence Heaven and Earth' or 'receive blessings from the Three Spirits'.[64] *When I say further, 'He rejects the Jade Maiden and expels Fu-fei',*[65] *this is a slight warning to the emperor to be grave and reverent in conducting his affairs.*[66]

There are several places where Yang Hsiung has obviously allowed criticism to emerge. The first of these is at the end of the elaborate description of the palace environs. He concludes the section with the following remarks (1. 55):

> *It is heir to the Jade Building and Jasper Palace:*
> *It is as if one had climbed high and were looking into the distance;*
> *He is awe-struck as if on the edge of an abyss.*

The Jade Building (Hsüan-shih) was an excessively ornate palace built by the last of the Hsia rulers, King Chieh, and the Jasper Palace (Ch'iung-kung) was an equally ostentatious structure erected by the last of the Shang rulers, King Chou. One of the reasons commonly given for the downfall of these rulers was their obsession with luxury and frivolous living. Implied in the last two lines of this passage, particularly in the figure of standing on the edge of an abyss, is that Emperor Ch'eng should be sobered by the great danger present in his preoccupation with hedonistic activities.

A similar criticism is made toward the end of the rhapsody (11. 64–6):

Thereupon, affairs change and things transform; the eyes become alarmed and the ears frightened. The Son of Heaven stands sedately in the midst of intricately carved precious towers, pleasure lodges, jade inlaid end-beams, and jade petals. This is the place to cleanse his mind and purify his soul, to gather his energy and concentrate his attention, to influence Heaven and Earth, and receive blessings from the Three Spirits.

Again, the emperor attains a state of sobriety in the midst of the ostentatious environment of the palace. It seems clear that Yang Hsiung is attempting to demonstrate the incompatibility of the high solemnity of the sacrifice with the sumptuous setting in which it takes place. Thus, his laudatory remarks that this is the place 'to influence Heaven and Earth, and receive blessings from the Three Spirits' are unquestionably ironical. This is corroborated by the lines that follow, in which the emperor is portrayed as now pursuing more serious endeavors (11. 66–9):

Then, he begins to search for a partner, to seek a mate, officials like Kao and Yi, men of first-rate talent and ability, who are embued with the kindness of the 'Sweet pear tree', and embrace the disposition of the 'March east'. They gather together in the Yang-ling Palace.

Like the Great Man of the 'Great Man Rhapsody', the emperor then partakes of the ambrosia of the immortals (11. 70–1) which is then followed by a magical journey, in which the emperor and his party make a rapid circuit of the cosmos and even journey below the earth (11. 75–8). The details of the trip are less explicitly stated than in the 'Distant Wandering' and the 'Great Man Rhapsody'. The significant part of the journey, as in the voyage of the Great Man, is a meeting with the Mother Queen of the West (1. 79). Unlike Ssu-ma Hsiang-ju, Yang Hsiung does not ridicule her, but instead has the emperor reject her attendants, the Jade Maiden and Fu-fei. The Jade Maiden and Fu-fei are frequently mentioned in Han literature. Fu-fei was the goddess of the Lo River and is famous as the object of the poet's quest in the 'Li sao'. Ch'ü Yüan describes his encounter with her as follows (11. 114–17):

> *In a great flurry and frenzy we met and parted;*
> *Suddenly she became obstinate, difficult to move.*
> *In the evening she returned to abide in Ch'iung-shih;*
> *In the morning she washed her hair at Wei-p'an.*
> *She preserved her beauty with arrogance and pride;*
> *Daily pursuing pleasures and licentious gamboling.*
> *Though truly fair she lacks propriety;*
> *Come! Abandon her and search for another!*

From this portrait, Fu-fei seems to have a reputation for fickleness and illicit behavior.

Less is known about the Jade Maiden. She is a servant of the immortals in Huan T'an's 'Rhapsody on Viewing the Immortals', and in Chang Heng's 'Pondering the Great Mystery Rhapsody' (*Ssu-hsüan fu*) she is termed the goddess of Mount T'ai-hua, and as in the 'Sweet Springs Rhapsody', serves with Fu-fei as an attendant to the Mother Queen of the West.[67] Professor Pokora equates her with the 'Hairy Girl' of Taoist lore.[68]

Regardless of the correct identification of the Jade Maiden, it is clear that she and Fu-fei belong to the category of goddesses who were so diligently pursued by the shaman-suitors and frustrated scholar-officials, the latter being an allegorical representation of their quest for a sympathetic ruler. In Yang Hsiung's use of the motif there is no quest, and certainly no failure on the part of the suitor-emperor in making his tryst. Instead, it is the emperor himself who rejects the goddesses, and in this rejection Yang Hsiung has inserted a reprimand. The dismissal of these highly attractive female spirits is a symbolic representation of what should be the emperor's abandonment of frivolous behavior.

It is even possible a more specific reference is intended. As the 'Autobiography' notes, it was during this period that the Brilliant Companion Chao enjoyed the emperor's favor. She and her elder sister, Chao Fei-yen, had so captivated the emperor that almost all of his time was spent in the boudoir. He built for the Brilliant Companion a huge palace and squandered a great portion of the imperial treasury catering to her desires. Apparently he even allowed her to accompany the procession to Sweet Springs, something that would offend a ritual-conscious Confucian like Yang Hsiung.[69] It is thus tempting to read into the allusion to the two morally depraved, fickle goddesses a veiled criticism of the Brilliant Companion and her sister. It could be these beauties that Yang Hsiung wishes the emperor to dismiss. At the very least Yang Hsiung seems to be suggesting that the Brilliant Companion be forbidden from attending the sacrifices.

No matter how one interprets these lines, one cannot deny that some criticism is implicit in them. Note particularly that only after he has rejected the two goddesses can the emperor 'hold the essence and strength of the Way and Power', and become 'an equal of the Divine Luminaries' (1. 81). It is also only after he has purged himself to these evil influences that he can successfully perform the sacrifices to the Great Unity.

Yang Hsiung's opposition to the ostentation of the Sweet Springs sacrifices is significant in view of the controversy that had existed prior to this time. This would suggest that even after the emperor had revived the sacrifices, there were still political and/or doctrinal divisions among the Confucians. Liu Hsiang, who was as staunch a Confucian as Yang Hsiung, had strongly favored returning the sacrifices to their former location. Yang Hsiung seems to have taken a position close to that of K'uang Heng (K'uang had been dismissed from the government by this time), stressing particularly the extravagance and expense of the Sweet Springs Palace, and perhaps the long journey to the sacrificial site, on which even members of the harem were allowed to go.

Yang Hsiung's attempts at effecting criticism of the emperor in this poem, no matter how artfully conceived, are extremely feeble when measured against the poem as a whole. As persuasive rhetoric the rhapsody is rather ineffective, for the overwhelming emphasis of the piece is on epideictic rhetoric. With the exception of the 'Shu Capital Rhapsody' (*Shu tu fu*), the 'Sweet Springs Rhapsody' is Yang Hsiung's most ornate composition. The poem abounds in *impressifs*. For example, Yang uses the following binomial descriptives to portray the movement of the procession: *mung-ńiung* (helter-skelter), *ḷiôk-liang* (wild-chaotic), *tsung-tsung tswən-tswən* (gathering, collecting), *klôg-kât* (adhering, sticking together), *piwang-ńiang* (scattering), *dzəp-dəp* (confused, mixed), *dz'ar-dz'ar*(?) *ts'iəm-ts'ia* (uneven, ragged), *xiəp-xăk xmət-xwâk* (glossed as 'descriptive of opening and closing'). Many of the *impressifs* appear to be *hapax legomena*, if one can judge by their single occurrence in the *Dai kanwa jiten*. For example, out of a total of some 90 *impressifs* over 20 are found only in this poem. Many of them are rare characters, and one can only guess at their exact meaning.

Surprisingly, in spite of his great reputation as an imitator of Ssu-ma Hsiang-ju, there are relatively few borrowings from Ssu-ma's poems. There is really only one line that appears directly derived from the 'Great Man Rhapsody', the piece Yang Hsiung's rhapsody most closely resembles.[70] There are other lines that seem to be imitations of the 'Shang-lin Rhapsody' and the 'Li Sao', but generally the language shows great originality.[71] Yang is particularly fond of using strange metaphors which state a comparison only implicitly. For example, he describes the movement of the emperor's cortège as follows (1. 12): 'Ranked, ordered, with fishscales juxtaposed,/Uneven, ragged, fish jumping, birds soaring.' A similar implied comparison is used to portray the Sweet Springs Palace as seen 'from a distance (1. 31): 'Great structure, cloud illusion, wave deception.'

The rhapsody also contains what appear to be kennings, much like those found in Old Norse and Old Germanic poetry. Heaven is given the descriptive appellation 'upper dark', auspicious omens are called 'the divine and beautiful', and Heaven and Earth are referred to by the enigmatic terms *k'an* (*k'əm*) and *yü* (*zio*), which may mean 'the cover' and 'the container'. The Duke of Shao is referred to as 'Sweet Pear', which is the title of a poem in praise of him in the *Book of Songs*. Similarly, the Duke of Chou is called 'The March East', which is a phrase in a panegyrical ode about him, also in the *Songs*.

Yang Hsiung's concentration on linguistic embellishment and ornate description in the 'Sweet Springs Rhapsody' indicates that the epideictic rhetorical tradition was still strong at this time. As Yang makes clear in the preface to the poem, his intention was to write his piece as a persuasion, to reprimand the emperor for his excessive interest in ostentation. As we have seen, Yang Hsiung does attempt to chide the emperor with ambages and circuitous allusions to improper behavior. But, like the 'Great Man Rhapsody', the moral message is obscured by verbal ornament. Of course, Yang Hsiung was commissioned by the emperor to write this rhapsody, and it would have been impossible to insult his patron with strong criticism. The main significance of the piece is that Yang Hsiung made any attempt at all to persuade.

'HO-TUNG RHAPSODY'

The 'Ho-tung Rhapsody' was written the same year as the 'Sweet Springs Rhapsody' on the occasion of the sacrifices to the Sovereign Earth (Hou-t'u) in Ho-tung commandery.[72] The text of the poem is contained in the 'Autobiography',[73] and like the 'Sweet Springs Rhapsody' has a preface giving the details of composition:

In the third month sacrifices to the Sovereign Earth were to be held. The emperor then led his multitude of ministers across the Great River, and gathered at Fen-yin. After the sacrifices, he made an excursion along the Chieh mountains,[74] toured around An-yi,[75] saw Lung-men,[76] viewed Salt Pond,[77] climbed the Li Viewing-tower,[78] and ascended the Western Peak,[79] from which he viewed the eight wastes. He walked in the traces of the ruins of the Yin and Chou dynasties, and pondered carefully the influence left by T'ang and Yü.[80] I considered that it was better to return and make a net than to stand by a pool and admire the fish.[81] When I returned, I presented the 'Ho-tung Rhapsody' as an exhortation.[82]

The preface is followed by the standard prose introduction and main body of the poem in verse. There is no epilogue.

I

In this year in the last month of spring in order to perform sacrifices[83] to the Sovereign Earth and conduct ceremonies for the earth-spirits the emperor visits Fen-yin in the eastern suburbs. He uses this opportunity to have his exalted name engraved and hand down his great achievements, produce good omens and let descend kind blessings. He reverently follows the Divine Luminaries. Splendid! Magnificent! It cannot be described completely!

II

4. *Thereupon,*
    He orders his multitude of ministers:
    To prepare the ceremonial robes,
    Arrange the imperial carriage.
5. *Then,*
    He strokes the kingfisher phoenix carriage,[84]
    Yokes a six-horse front-shadow chariot.[85]
6. *They wave flowing red meteor pennants;*
    Draw tight the Heavenly Wolf's magnificent Bow;[86]
7. *Unfurl black banners gleaming in the sun;*
    Raise the left tu *streamer, unfold cloud banners,*[87]
8. *Crack lightning whips, harness thunder baggage-trains;*
    Sound great bells, erect the five flags.[88]
9. *Hsi-ho is in charge of the sun;*
    Yen Lun handles the carriages.[89]
10. *They race like the wind, move like a whirlwind, soar like spirits, speed like*
    demons.
11. *A thousand chariots in thunderous confusion;*
    A myriad riders, bold and strong,
12. *Laugh and shout with pride,*
    Making Heaven and Earth quake and quiver.
13. *They shake the hills, leap the peaks,*
    Burst over the Wei, jump the Ching.
14. *The Ch'in spirit sinks in terror;*
    His soul gives a start, he clings to the bank.[90]
15. *The River Spirit is startled;*
    He grasps Mount Hua, tramples Mount Shuai.[91]
16. *Then, they reach the Yin Palace:*
    They are majestic and solemn,
    Walking in a stately manner.

III

17. *When the holy earth-spirits lean our way,*
    The five positions follow their proper order.[92]
18. *The black and yellow forces of Heaven and Earth*
    Will greatly increase his descendants.
19. *Thereupon,*
    The emperor paces contentedly,

Wanders about at ease
Viewing the Chieh mountains.[93]

20. *He praises Duke Wen, laments for T'ui;*[94]
     He is impressed by the diligence of Great Yü at Lung-men:

21. *Yü diverted the great flood into the open waterways;*
     His distributed the Nine Rivers into the Eastern Sea.[95]

22. *The emperor:*
     Climbs the Li Viewing-tower and gazes into the distance,
     Roams about, making his plans.

23. *He enjoys the influence left from the past,*
     Delights in the place once plowed by Yü-shih.[96]

24. *He views the lofty heights of the Emperor T'ang;*
     Sees the great peace of the splendid Chou.[97]

25. *He paces back and forth unable to leave;*
     Frowns at Kai-hsia and P'eng-ch'eng.[98]

26. *Foul is the ragged and rough Nan-ch'ao;*
     Smooth are the level and even Pin and Ch'i.[99]

27. *He mounts a green dragon and crosses the River,*
     Ascends the high and towering slopes of the Western Peak.

28. *Thick clouds welcome his arrival;*
     Flowing moisture falls down to the earth.

29. *It is bleak, desolate, and dark;*
     Rain pours forth in great torrents.

30. *He shouts orders at the Wind Earl in the south and north;*
     Yells commands at the Rain Master in the east and west.[100]

31. *He stands alone, a trio with Heaven and Earth;*
     So grand an expanse he has no equal.

IV

32. *The emperor:*
     Follows the long road home;
     The great Han that envelops all of China –
     How could they match its accomplishments?[101]

33. *He establishes the proper signs of Ch'ien and K'un;*
     He will assemble them all with a dragon horde.[102]

34. *He harnesses Kou-mang and Ju-shou to the outside;*
     Hitches Hsüan-ming and Chu-jung to the inside.[103]

35. *He urges the crowd of spirits to show the way;*
     Promotes the Six Classics to broadcast praise.[104]

36. It surpasses the 'continuous brightness' of 'Oh, how August',
    Exceeds the concord of 'Pure Temple'.[105]
37. He overtakes the distant traces of the Five Emperors;
    Follows the high footsteps of the Three August Ones.
38. Now that he begins his journey on a level plain,
    Who would consider the road too far to follow?

Unlike the 'Sweet Springs Rhapsody', this poem is almost exclusively devoted to the emperor's excursion after the sacrifices. The emperor's retinue is described with the standard hyperbole: the phoenix carriage, powerful horses, meteor pennants, splendid bows. The procession is so large and impressive even spirits are frightened (11. 14–15). The sacrifice itself is disposed of in two lines (11. 17–18). Everything that follows is an account of the emperor's excursion.

The emperor sees the famous historical sites of the area. This was where Duke Wen lamented the death of his loyal minister Chieh Chih-t'ui and the Great Yü bored the hole in Mount Lung-men. The emperor is moved at the memory of these events. He climbs a pavilion and looks into the distance, and continues to contemplate the historical significance of the area. All the great rulers of the past were here: Shun, Yao, and King Wen. He compares the site with the southern battlefield of Kai-hsia, where Hsiang Yü and the Han founder, Liu Pang, contended for power, and finds it inferior to the Ho-tung area. He prefers the recollection that the historical seats of the Chou, Pin and Ch'i, are not too far from here.

The emperor then mounts a 'dragon' (either figuratively or literally, meaning a horse), crosses the Yellow River and ascends the Western Peak. Thick clouds come out to welcome him and allow their moisture to inundate the earth. He then shouts orders to the Wind Earl and the Rain Master, presumably to make them control the waters. He then stands alone with only Heaven and Earth his equal.

The final portion of the poem consists of a series of laudatory epithets for the emperor and the Han dynasty. The rhapsody concludes with no reprimand, and in fact the entire piece is highly panegyrical. Yang Hsiung himself describes the purpose of the poem as ch'üan, 'to exhort' or 'to encourage'. It seems clear that Yang Hsiung probably wished to encourage the emperor's interest in the sage kings of the past, and thus he constructs a model of ideal behavior which he recommends to the emperor. The proverb of the net and fish used in the preface most likely is a subtle hint to the emperor that he ought to return to the palace and apply the lessons he has learned here to his government.

The 'Ho-tung Rhapsody' is much shorter than the 'Sweet Springs Rhapsody' and is much less linguistically ornate. The poem has 25 binomial descriptives, most of which are extremely common. Only five appear to be *hapax legomena*. There are also several unusual uses of verbs. For example, in describing the processions movement over the hills and rivers, Yang says (1. 13):

> *They* winnow *the hills, leap the peaks,*
> Bubble *the Wei, jump the Ching.*

Similar language is used to depict the River Spirit's fright (1. 15):

> *He* claws *the Hua*, tramples *the Shuai.*

Examples of this kind are relatively few, and most of the poem's language is undistinguished. It is not one of Yang Hsiung's best compositions, and Hsiao T'ung had good reason to exclude it from *The Literary Selections* while including its companion piece 'The Sweet Springs Rhapsody'.

4

The 'Barricade Hunt' and 'Ch'ang-yang' Rhapsodies

Yang Hsiung is commonly characterized in both modern and traditional Chinese literary criticism as a servile imitator of Ssu-ma Hsiang-ju. Except for the fragmentary 'Rhapsody on the Shu Capital' (*Shu tu fu*), which is of dubious authenticity,[1] it is difficult to find many linguistic or even structural similarities between the poems of Yang Hsiung and Ssu-ma Hsiang-ju. For example, the 'Sweet Springs Rhapsody', which bears a superficial resemblance to the 'Great Man Rhapsody', is hardly a faithful imitation of its reputed prototype. The 'Ho-tung Rhapsody' does not resemble in any way the extant poems of Ssu-ma Hsiang-ju. The poem that probably influenced Yang more than any other was the 'Shang lin Rhapsody'. This influence can be seen in the 'Barricade Hunt Rhapsody' (*Chiao-lieh fu*), a poem written in the winter of 11 B.C.[2] This rhapsody deals with a subject made famous by Yang Hsiung's compatriot, an imperial hunt in the Shang-lin Park.

The similarities between the two pieces, however, are again only superficial. For example, unlike the 'Shang-lin Rhapsody', Yang Hsiung's poem deals with a specific hunt.[3] The 'Annals of Emperor Ch'eng' record for 11 B.C.: 'In the winter, the emperor travelled to the Ch'ang-yang Palace. Accompanying him were guests from the Hu tribe. He held a great "barricade hunt"'.[4] Yang Hsiung was allowed to attend the spectacle, which obviously was a type of military review intended to impress the non-Chinese visitors from Central Asia. After the hunt, he was commissioned to write a rhapsody describing the event.

The 'Barricade Hunt Rhapsody' is contained both in the 'Autobiography' and *The Literary Selections*, where it is listed under the title 'Plume Hunt Rhapsody' (*Yü lieh fu*).[5] Both of these texts contain a long preface, most likely by Yang Hsiung, explaining the circumstances of the poem's composition.

In the twelfth month there was a 'plume hunt',[6] which I attended. I believed that anciently under the Two Emperors and Three Kings[7] the palace lodges, towers, ponds, gardens, forests and preserves were just enough to provide for the suburban and temple sacrifices, to entertain the guests, and fill the imperial kitchen.[8] *They did not seize the people's fertile grain and mulberry lands. The women had surplus cloth and the men had surplus grain.*[9] *The state was wealthy, and both superior and inferior had enough. Thus, sweet dew fell in the court-yard and sweet springs flowed by the temple path.*[10] *The phoenix nested in the trees, the yellow dragon swam in the ponds, the unicorn came into the garden, and the Holy Bird perched in the forest.*[11]

Formerly, when Yü employed Yi the Forester, superior and inferior were in harmony and the grasses and trees flourished.[12] *Ch'eng T'ang enjoyed hunting but the resources of the empire were sufficient. King Wen's park was a hundred* li *but the people thought it too small; King Hsüan of Ch'i's park was forty* li *but the people considered it too large. The difference was that one was generous with the people and the other took from them.*[13]

Emperor Wu enlarged the Shang-lin Park southeast to Yi-ch'un, Ting-hu, Yü-hsiu, and K'un-wu,[14] *west along the Southern Mountains to Ch'ang-yang and Wu-tso.*[15] *In the north it encircled the Yellow Mountains and followed the bank of the Wei River eastward.*[16] *It had a circumference of several hundred* li.

They dug the K'un-ming Lake in imitation of the Tien-ho.[17] *They built the Chien-chang, Feng-ch'üeh, Shen-ming, and Sa-so.*[18] *The Chien Tower and T'ai-yi in imitation of the ocean were surrounded by the islands Fang-chang, Ying-chou, and P'eng-lai.*[19] *The excursions were extravagant, utterly marvelous, and extremely beautiful. Even though he cut somewhat from his three borders to provide for the common people, the places of limited access built for armored chariots, war-horses, machinery, and stores used in the 'plume hunt' were still elaborate and ostentatious. It violated the principle of the 'three-sided battue' of Yao, Shun, Ch'eng T'ang, and King Wen.*[20]

Furthermore, I was afraid that later generations would revive former interests, and that they would not decide on the middle course recommended for Ch'üan Tower.[21] *Thus, I used the pretext of the 'Barricade Hunt Rhapsody' to make an indirect criticism of the emperor.*[22]

The main text follows.

I

'Some people praise Fu-hsi and Shen-nung.[23] *Could they be deceived*[24] *by the increasing ostentation of later emperors and kings?'*

A critic says, 'No. Each decides what is appropriate to his own time. Why must their rationale coincide exactly? If it did coincide, how could there have been seventy-two different ceremonies for the feng *sacrifices on Mount T'ai?*[25]

Therefore, those who found an enterprise and hand on a tradition cannot perceive their errors. Whether as far back in time as the Five Emperors or as recent as the Three Kings, who can determine what is right and what is wrong?'

Consequently I have composed a eulogy which reads:

5. Elegant indeed the divine sage!
   He abides in the northern palace.
6. In wealth he is as rich as Earth;
   In honor he is as exalted as Heaven.
7. Duke Huan of Ch'i would never be worthy to support his wheel hubs;
   Duke Yen of Ch'u would never deserve to be his Chariot Companion.[26]
8. Constricted by the narrow confinement of the Three Kings,
   Uplifting himself on high, rising greatly,
9. He exceeds the Five Emperors in breadth;
   Surpasses the Three August Ones in scope.
10. He establishes the Way and Power as his teacher;
    Takes Kindness and Rightness for a friend.

II

11. Thereupon,
    In dark winter's final month
    With Heaven and Earth at the highest intensity,[27]
12. The myriad things germinate within,
    While they wither without.

The emperor is about to plan a hunt in the Holy Park. He opens the northern boundary, receives the control of the northwest wind, and from beginning to end is under the direction of Chuan-hsü and Hsüan-ming.[28]

15. Then, he orders the foresters to prepare the preserve:
    East to the environs of K'un-ming,
    West to the Ch'ang-ho Gate.[29]
16. They gather all the provisions;
    Troops line the road.
17. They chop the thick brambles,
    Mow the wild grass;
18. Declare out of bounds the Ch'ien and Wei,
    Lay out the area of Feng and Hao.
19. It sprawls and flows so far
    In and out go the sun and moon,
    Heaven and Earth intersect there.

20. *Then,*
    They barricade Mount San-tsung for the Marshall's Gate,
    Enclose a hundred li *for the palace portal.*[30]
21. *Outside, it stretches due south to the sea;*
    To the left it borders on Yü-yüan.[31]
22. *The field is vast and wide,*
    Marked off by lofty mountains.

When the compound is completely enclosed, they first place the provisions south of Po-yang Lodge,[32] east of the holy K'un-ming. Warriors like Pen and Yü,[33] hidden by shields, carrying plumes, leaning on Mo-yeh swords, spread out in the ten thousands.

25. *The rest carry nets that hang from the sky,*
    Stretch mesh all the way to the steppe;
26. *Wave vermillion sun-and-moon staffs,*
    Trail flying comet pennants.
27. *Blue clouds serve as tassels,*
    Red rainbows are the streamers.
28. *They extend as far as the K'un-lun wastes:*
    Spreading out like heavenly constellations,
    As grand as waves in rolling water.
29. *Marching, advancing, steadily onward*
    Front and rear, they block the road.
30. *Comets form the crenels;*
    The sun and moon act as lookouts.
31. *Fiery Mars decides life and death,*
    The Heavenly Bow takes charge of shooting.
32. *Swiftly, rapidly, in uneven groups,*
    Massed together, they fill the road.
33. *The banner cars, quick and powerful,*
    Stretched out, lined together,
34. *Rumbling and thundering,*
    Cover the hills, follow the slopes.
35. *In the utter darkness and extreme distance*
    They congregate on a high plateau.
36. *Plumed riders race to and fro,*
    Each with distinct markings, different tasks,
    In great numbers speeding back and forth.
37. *In an unbroken, continuous line,*
    At times bright, at times dim,
38. *They scatter into the green forest.*

III

39. Thereupon, the Son of Heaven at the break of day first comes out of the
northern palace.

40. They toll the huge bells,
Raise the nine dragon-flags.

41. Six white tigers
Pull the imperial carriage.

42. Ch'ih-yu marches beside the wheelhubs;
Duke Meng acts as the vanguard.[34]

43. They carry banners that touch Heaven,
Trail pennants that brush the stars.

44. Thunder out of the lightning fissures,
Spits its fire, applies its whip.

45. Speeding en masse as a river in flood,
Soaking and moistening a broad expanse,
They signal the eight corners to open their passes.

46. The Wind Earl and Cloud Master
Pant and puff.

47. They are arrayed like ranks of fishscales,
Gathered like rows of dragon wings.

48. With a bustling clamor
They enter West Park,
Approach Shen-kuang Palace.[35]

49. Heading toward P'ing-lo Lodge,
They pass through a bamboo forest,

50. Trample the melilotus gardens,
Tread over the orchid paths.

51. They raise a beacon, light a fire,
And the charioteers display their skill.

52. Galloping together, a thousand teams;
Nimble horsemen, ten thousand riders;

53. Like a file of roaring tigers,
They gather in all directions.

54. Sobbing like whirlwinds, droning like thunder,
Rumbling and booming,

55. The din and clatter
Shake Heaven and Earth.

56. When the flood of riders disperses,
The ground is desolate for mile after mile.

IV

57. Bold warriors, noble and heroic,
    Facing different directions, racing separate ways,

58. East and west, north and south,
    Gallop toward their pleasure, speed toward their desire.

59. They drag down grey boars,
    Crush rhinos and buffalo,
    Trample fleeing deer,

60. Cut giant badgers in two,
    Pummel black apes,

61. Soar into the air,
    Clamber up intertwined trees,

62. Walk over gnarled limbs,
    Play amidst the streams.

63. All is dusty and disordered:
    Valleys shake with whirlwinds,
    Forests are filled with dust clouds.

64. Then, strong hunters and fighters[36]
    Topple firs and cypress,
    Grasp the prickly pear.

65. They hunt in thickets,
    Run down birds with their chariots;

66. March over striped-head felines,
    Make belts of giant snakes;

67. Jab red panthers with hooks,
    Pull away elephants and rhinos.

68. They cross peaks and gullies,
    Traverse plains and slopes.

69. Chariots and riders gather like clouds,
    Ascending and descending in dense darkness.

70. The great Mount Hua is their banner,
    Hsiung-erh is their streamer.[37]

71. The trees fall, the mountains revolve,
    They seem to spill out beyond Heaven.

72. The riders amble along the great river bank,
    Wander at random throughout the universe.

V

73. Thereupon, the sky clears and the sun comes out.
74. P'eng Meng takes careful aim,
    Sir Yi draws his bow.[38]
75. The imperial carriage rolls and rumbles,
    Its light envelops Heaven and Earth.
76. Wang Shu tightens the reins,
    Slowly swerves into Shang-lan Lodge.[39]
77. They move the enclosures, switch formations,
    Gradually crowd the regiments together.
78. The divisions are tightly massed,
    Each keeps to his file and squad.
79. Like the Ramparts rotating in Heaven,
    Warriors strike like ghosts and lightning.
80. Whatever they meet is smashed;
    Whatever they approach is broken.
81. Birds cannot fly away in time;
    Beasts are unable to escape.
82. The army startles them, the troops terrify them,
    They scrape clean the field, sweep down the earth.
83. When the chariots with nets begin to soar about,
    Strong horsemen speed here and there.
84. They trample fleeing leopards,
    Lasso hyenas,
85. Pursue the Heavenly Treasure,
    Which comes from one direction.[40]
86. It resounds with a loud roar,
    Flashes a flowing light.
87. They search throughout the steppe and mountains,
    Bag both males and females.
88. Teeming, crawling, countless beasts,
    Shake their snouts within the nets.
89. The Three Armies in throngs
    Exhaust the fleeing, block the faltering.
90. Just see the swift birds beat their wings in vain!
    Rhinos and buffaloes butt their heads without effect!
91. Bears and sloths tug and pull at their ropes,
    Tigers and leopards tremble with fear.

92. *They can only strike horns and heads on the ground,*
     Stand shaking and quivering.

93. *Their soul and animus is lost;*
     They catch their necks in moving spokes.

94. *Even when archers shoot wildly they hit their mark;*
     Whether they step forward or back they trample or catch something.

95. *Their cuts are deep, the wheels wound,*
     The dead accumulate in mounds and heaps.

VI

96. *Thereupon, the beasts are decimated, shot to death;*
     All gather at a lodge of still repose, near a marvelous pond.

97. *It is fed from the Ch'i and Liang mountains,*
     Watered by the Chiang and Ho.

98. *In the east one can look as far as the eye can see;*
     In the west it extends without limit.

99. *Sui pearls and Ho jade*
     Dazzle on its banks.

100. *Jade stones serrated and rough,*
     Glisten with a blue twinkle.

101. *The Han nymph submerges in the water;* [41]
     Eerie creatures lurk in the darkness:
     They cannot be described completely.

102. *Black phoenixes, peacocks,*
     Kingfishers, cast off a radiance.

103. *Ospreys scream and screech,*
     Geese honk and cackle.

104. *Flocks of them play here,*
     Twittering and crying in unison.

105. *Duck, widgeon and flocking egrets*
     Soar and dive, wings drumming,
     A noise like thunder.

106. *Then, tatooed men demonstrate their skill;*
     They wrestle scaly reptiles in the water.

107. *They cross the solid ice,*
     Defy the awesome pool.

108. *They search the rocky shore and twisting banks,*
     Seeking out dragons and crocodiles.

109. They step over otters and muskrats,
      Grab turtles and lizards,
      Seize the magic tortoises.
110. They enter the Grotto;
      Come out at Ts'ang-wu.[42]
111. They mount huge sea monsters,
      Ride giant whales,
112. Float over Lake P'eng-li,
      See Yu Yü.[43]
113. They beat open the lapus-lazuli covering of the Night-light jewel,
      Cut open the pearl shell around the Moon-bright gem.
114. They flog Fu-fei of the River Lo,
      Offer food to Ch'ü Yüan, P'eng and Hsü.[44]

                              VII

115. Thereupon, great teachers, grand scholars,
      In high carriages and hats
      Colored jackets and skirts,
116. Men who study the Canon of T'ang,
      Who find rectification in the Odes and Hymns,[45]
117. Bow ceremoniously to the front,
      Emit a radiance and glow,
      Which scatters with magical speed.
118. Through them word of the imperial kindness tames the Northern Ti;
      The justice of our military policies influences the Southern Lin.[46]
119. Thus, kings of the felt and fur wearers,
      Chiefs of the Hu and Mo tribes,
120. Send precious objects in tribute,
      Raise their hands, declare themselves subjects.
121. The front of their line enters the compound door;
      The rear extends back to Mount Lu.[47]

    Officials and palace attendants, men like Yang Chu and Mo Ti,[48] declare
sighing: 'Lofty indeed the emperor's virtue! Although there is the eminence of
T'ang, Yü, the great Hsia, Ch'eng, and Chou, how could they surpass this? The
rulers of antiquity held audiences on the Eastern Peak, conducted shan sacrifices at
the foot of Mount Liang, but other than you who now can do likewise?'

VIII

But the emperor is modest and says no to the praise.

127. He now plans to hunt above for blessings from the three supernatural forces; [49]
      Below to let flow the nourishing waters of the sweet springs.

128. He opens the cave of the Yellow Dragon,
      Peers into the nest of the phoenix,

129. Approaches the park of the unicorn,
      Visits the forest of the divine peacock.

130. He considers Yün-meng an extravagance,
      Finds Meng-chu a waste,[50]

131. Condemns Chang-hua,
      Approves of Ling-t'ai.[51]

132. He rarely goes to his touring palaces and he halts sightseeing excursions.

133. He does not permit buildings to be ornamented,
      Nor does he allow wood to be carved.

134. He helps the people in their farming and sericulture;
      Urges them not to be idle.

135. Men and women are properly matched, none are married at improper times.

136. Concerned that the poor do not share in the widespread abundance,
      He opens the forbidden parks,
      Distributes the public stores.

137. He constructs parks of the Way and Power,
      Increases his foresters of Kindness and Charity,

138. Gallops and shoots in the garden of divine illumination,
      Examines and inspects the needs of his subjects.

139. He releases the pheasants and hares,
      Gathers the nets and snares.

140. The deer and grass are shared with the people:
      In this way he reaches his present greatness.

141. Thereupon, he purifies his vast and penetrating virtue,
      Develops further the standards of his glorious age.

142. He exerts himself more than the Three Kings,
      Strives harder than the Five Emperors.

143. Is this not the utmost in excellence?

144. Then, he honors men of reverence and harmony.

145. He establishes divisions between ruler and subject,
      Honors the deeds of worthies and sages.

146. He has no time for the beauty of his parks,
      Or the extravagance of hunting expeditions.

147. *Thus, he turns around his carriage, reverses the yoke,*
      Puts his back to O-fang Palace,[52]
      Returns to Wei-yang.[53]

The 'Barricade Hunt' provides an excellent example of the narrative skills
of the Han rhapsodist. One can see from my translation that the poem falls into
distinct divisions, which are clearly marked in the original by such words as *yü
shih* (thereupon), *jo fu* (as for), or *yü tzu hu* (and then). Except for the first
section, each division of the 'Barricade Hunt' advances the narration.

Section II sets the scene of the hunt. It is winter over which Chuan-hsü and
Hsüan-ming, gods of the north, winter, and destruction, have control. The
emperor orders foresters to prepare the Shang-lin Park for a hunt. They cut
down the brambles and wild grass, erect barriers and enclosures, and then
declare the area off limits to the local inhabitants. The hunters gather outside
the park carrying nets and banners. Chariots and riders speed over the road,
and arrive at the edge of the forest to await the beginning of the hunt.

Section III sets the beginning of the emperor's procession. As the Son of
Heaven emerges from the palace bells are tolled and flags are raised. His
retinue is splendid; stalwart warriors march beside him. They enter the park
in the early dawn and light huge bonfires to provide illumination for a chariot
race.

In Section IV the hunt proper begins. The hunters kill animals of all types
in sundry fashion. The slaughter and destruction is immense and awe-
some. Then, in Section Five, the sun comes out and the archers perform. The hunters surround the remaining animals who cower from fear
and fatigue. The climax of the hunt is the capture of the Heavenly Treasure
(T'ien-pao), a legendary supernatural creature with the features of a giant
rooster.

In Section VI, the animals being completely decimated, the group moves to
a pond where a water show is held. Tattooed men from the south wrestle
dragons, crocodiles, and other aquatic monsters, and make a long underwater
swim. This section concludes with a food offering to martyrs of the past who
committed suicide rather than compromise their principles: Ch'ü Yüan, P'eng
Hsien, and Wu Tzu-hsü.

Section VII, which is extremely brief, describes the appearance of the
scholars who attend the hunt. Because of their presence the barbarian
participants know of the splendor and glory of the Han empire. The section
ends with a brief eulogy for Emperor Ch'eng.

The final section begins with the emperor rejecting the inordinate praise
heaped upon him. He now condemns the hunt as extravagance and harmful to

the people. He resolves to return to the proper endeavors of government, and opens the park to share its products with the common people.

It is clear from this outline that the narrative order of the poem follows the sequence of the hunt. The piece begins with the preparation of the hunting ground, progresses through the gathering of the troops, the emergence of the emperor's cortège, the capture and killing of the animals, the water spectacle, the appearance of the scholars, ending with the emperor's conversion.

The narration of the 'Shang-lin Rhapsody', on the other hand, displays an entirely different orientation. The poem begins with a long enumeration of the mountains, rivers, lakes, animals, birds, minerals, stones, trees, flowers, and herbs which the park contains. This enumeration continues for many lines before the reader is actually aware that the subject of the rhapsody is a hunt. The section dealing with the hunt itself is relatively brief (about forty lines). Thus, there really is no narrative structure, only a series of enumerative catalogues.

In the discussion of the 'Shang-lin Rhapsody' we saw that the most distinguishing feature of the piece was the fantastic and imaginative description. This element was also present to a high degree in the 'Sweet Springs Rhapsody'. The 'Barricade Hunt', compared with the 'Shang-lin Rhapsody' and 'Sweet Springs Rhapsody', is relatively free of many flights of the fancy. While Ssu-ma Hsiang-ju devoted much space to a panoramic description of the park, Yang's poem has virtually no description of the setting in which the hunt takes place. Almost the entire piece is devoted to portraying the movement of the hunting procession around the park with little notice of the surroundings. The center of the poet's attention is the emperor and his entourage. Where the park is described, it is pictured in the most hackneyed hyperbole (11. 19, 21–2):

> It sprawls and flows so far
> In and out go the sun and moon,
> Heaven and Earth intersect there.
> [.   .   ]
> Outside, it stretches due south to the sea;
> To the left it borders on Yü-yüan.
> The field is vast and wide,
> Marked off by lofty mountains.

There is nothing, for example, resembling Ssu-ma Hsiang-ju's description of the rivers:

> North, south, east and west
> They gallop and race,
> Emerging from the gap in Pepper Hill,

> Running along the banks of the river islets,
> Passing through the middle of a cassia forest,
> Crossing a broad, expansive plain.
> They speed along en masse,
> Tumble down the hill slopes,
> And butt into giant boulders,
> Smash against the river banks.
> They leap and whirl,
> Spout and swell,
> Clash and collide,
> Flow sideways, run backwards,
> Jump and splash,
> Making a loud and angry din.[54]

The 'Barricade Hunt', furthermore, lacks the descriptive catalogues used so frequently by his predecessor. The only thing resembling a catalogue is the brief description of the pond where the water show took place (11. 99–105), but even this is not a catalogue in the sense that Ssu-ma Hsiang-ju's lists are catalogues. One sees that it is interspersed with verbs of motion that lend it a dynamic, kinetic quality. In fact, much of the 'Barricade Hunt' consists of kinetic descriptions that convey the manner in which things move, such as the description of chariots gathering for the hunt in 11. 33–8. Being concerned with movement, Yang uses many verbs of motion. In the section relating the capture of animals, the verbs are particularly rich. There are five different words meaning 'to trample': b'wât, kiwat, liər, d'ôg, and niáp; three meaning 'to pull away': t'â, pâk, and k'ien; and various other words describing how the beasts were caught: tsiak, 'to cut in two'; lien, 'to run over'; and ku, 'to seize with a hook'.[55]

Although the 'Barricade Hunt' has less in the way of fanciful descriptions than the 'Shang-lin Rhapsody' or 'Sweet Springs Rhapsody', this does not mean that this poem is completely devoid of fantasy. In fact, there is one extremely puzzling passage that stands out because it is not typical of the rest of the piece. It occurs in the final part of the water spectacle (11. 110–14):

> They enter the Grotto;
> Come out at Ts'ang-wu.
> They mount huge sea monsters,
> Ride giant whales,
> Float over Lake P'eng-li,
> See Yu Yü.

Somehow the procession has been transported from Shang-lin Park, in the north, to south China. The Grotto (Tung-hsüeh) is another name for the Cavern of Yü (Yü hsüeh), located in the Kuei-chi mountain range. Ts'ang-wu is the legendary burial place of the Emperor Shun (Yu Yü). P'eng-li is the ancient name for P'o-yang Lake in northern Kiangsi province.

Why has the poet suddenly shifted the scene of his water spectacle from north China to a region in the south? Several possibilities suggest themselves. First of all, the poet may be using that device common in the rhapsody, hyperbole. He thus exaggerates the strength of the performers, comparing the distance of their swim to the distance between the Grotto and Ts'ang-wu. Yet, there is more than mere hyperbole here, for in the world of this poem, if not in the hunt itself, the performers do go south. They emerge near Shun's grave and spy him out (literally 'eye' him) as they float over P'o-yang Lake. Then, they leave the scene of the hunt altogether as the description becomes even more fantastic (11. 113–14):

> They beat open the lapus-lazuli covering of the Night-light jewel,
> Cut open the pearl shell around the Moon-bright gem.
> They flog Fu-fei of the River Lo,
> Offer food to Ch'ü Yüan, P'eng, and Hsü.

There is here an entire string of mythological associations. The three martyrs, Ch'ü Yüan, P'eng Hsien, and Wu Tzu-hsü, had failed to dissuade their kings from persuing a disastrous policy and committed suicide. They were all later worshipped as water spirits.[56] Fu-fei, the legendary daughter of the Emperor Fu-hsi, was the dissolute and fickle goddess of the Lo River already discussed in the chapter on the 'Sweet Springs Rhapsody'. Thus, if one conjures a picture of huge tattooed men, mounted on sea serpents and whales, snapping whips in pursuit of a female demon, while others prepare a food sacrifice to the three martyrs, he finds a scene that is completely ultra-mundane and imaginary. The very presence of spirits suggests the supernatural.

This is not a simple magical flight that one finds in the 'Distant Wandering' or the 'Great Man Rhapsody', which depict the celestial journey into the realm of gods and spirits mainly as an escape from the confinement of the human world. It is possible to interpret this extra-worldly journey symbolically. As in the 'Sweet Springs Rhapsody', Fu-fei would represent lechery and depravity, or more specifically, the extravagance of spectacles such as the current hunt. Her beating seems to represent a rejection of hedonistic pastimes. The three martyrs were scholar-officials who died in an attempt to save their rulers from perdition. They represent in the context of the entire poem either a return to the activity of good government, or at least a warning of the consequences of extravagance and dissipation. They are fed, so to speak, on the flesh of the debauched, pleasure-loving river goddess.[57] This idea is reinforced by the opening lines of Section VII, which describe the entrance of the scholars, whose goodness, not frivolous and wasteful hunts, was the real strength of the empire. It is also consistent with the 'conversion' of the emperor, some ten lines later, where the emperor indeed rejects hunting as a pastime.

In Yang Hsiung's use of fanciful and supernatural imagery he seems to differ somewhat from Ssu-ma Hsiang-ju. Ssu-ma generally inserted fantastic description into his poem primarily for its own sake or for the purpose of embuing the object he was portraying with supernatural significance. Yang Hsiung also does this, as in the description of the Heavenly Treasure in ll. 85–8, but Yang also uses the magical and supernatural for rhetorical purposes. It is one method of conveying indirect criticism. In this rhapsody, one observes that rhetoric is less unobtrusive than in the 'Sweet Springs Rhapsody'. This is readily apparent in the prose introduction of Section I, which is in a conventional rhetorical form. An anonymous questioner first poses a proposition that Fu-hsi and Shen-nung are praised for frugality primarily because they appeared parsimonious compared with later rulers (such as King Hsüan of Ch'i and Emperor Wu mentioned in the preface) who indulged in ostentatious display. These later rulers were in violation of the classical Confucian precept which condemned these activities. The critic (*lun-che*) rejects this argument, claiming that different periods had different conditions and needs. For this reason, history has known many different types of display, of which the seventy-two sacrifices on Mount T'ai are an example. Since times and practices vary, there can be no standard by which to judge all rulers. Implied here is the idea that the present age is a glorious one, and its splendors should be celebrated. The hunt is one means of demonstrating the glory and prosperity of the time, and hence, a legitimate enterprise.

The form of this introduction thus is somewhat similar to the debate structure of the rhapsodies of Ssu-ma Hsiang-ju and Mei Ch'eng. In the 'Barricade Hunt' Yang has inserted a small debate minus the *dramatis personae*. It is an excellent example of the old Chinese rhetorical device known as the doubled persuasion, which we have seen involves presenting two arguments or alternatives to a proposed action with the intention of showing one superior to the other.

At first glance, it would appear that the second argument has successfully countered the first proposition, and that the poet seems to be justifying elaborate spectacles as the proper duty of a virtuous ruler. Yet, we know from reading the entire piece that the contrary view continues to be expressed. How, then, do we account for this ambivalence on the part of the poet? One obvious explanation is that since he was writing this rhapsody under imperial auspices he could not insult the emperor with direct reprimand. As we have already seen, the ruler-centered rhetoric of ancient China required that the persuader's criticism be delivered in an oblique and circuitous manner.

One finds in the 'Barricade Hunt' an abundance of indirect reprimands. The rhymed eulogy that follows the introduction (11. 5–10) is one example. On one level this eulogy is simply hackneyed hyperbole. However, it is, in addition, said in a somewhat ironical vein. We know, for example, that Emperor Ch'eng is engaging in an activity of which Yang Hsiung does not approve. We can assume that either this eulogy is an insincere statement or that it harbors satire. It is tempting to read into the allusion to Duke Huan of Ch'i and Duke Yen (= Chuang) of Ch'u, both of whom built huge hunting parks that were a great hardship of the people of their states, a veiled criticism of the emperor's indulgence in idle pastimes. This also could be similar to the fanciful eulogizing used by Ssu-ma Hsiang-ju in the 'Great Man Rhapsody', in which he hoped to dissuade Emperor Wu from his baneful interest in immortals by excessive praise.

The most sustained persuasive rhetoric of the rhapsody comes in the conclusion, which contains the emperor's conversion. Here Yang borrows almost directly from Ssu-ma Hsiang-ju's 'Shang-lin Rhapsody', which describes the emperor's rejection of the hunt in almost identical terms. The emperor obtains all of the favorable omens such as the yellow dragon, phoenix (*feng-huang*), unicorn (*ch'i-lin*), and divine peacock. He condemns the lavish parks of Yün-meng and Meng-chu as extravagances, and vows to rid his establishment of ornament, and to make the park available for the benefit of the peasants of the area. Instead of engaging in revelry he now turns his attention to the activity of government.

All throughout this section one should notice that the poet does not criticize the emperor directly. Instead, he puts the argument into the mind of the emperor himself, making it appear that the self-reflection and conversion came to him independently and spontaneously. We have seen that this technique was used both by Ssu-ma Hsiang-ju and Mei Ch'eng. The main purpose of presenting this portrait of an idealized ruler is to set up a contrast with the emperor who engaged in the hedonistic and extravagant hunt. When Yang records the hunt, the emphasis is on the great destruction and sadistic behavior of the participants, as in 11. 89–95 where the animals are completely annihilated. Implicit in descriptions of this kind is a criticism of the excesses of the hunt. According to the ancient ritual of the hunt, the hunters were required to use a three-sided battue, allowing the beaters on three sides only, letting the game in front escape. The impression given here is that everything was decimated, that nothing escaped.

In this context, then, Yang Hsiung's comparisons of the emperor to the sage kings of the past are clearly intended to be ironic. Even if irony were not intended, this is certainly the effect. The nature of the irony may be illustrated in the scholar's eulogy in 11. 122–5, which the emperor refuses to accept.

Officials and palace attendants, men like Yang Chu and Mo Ti declare sighing:
' Lofty indeed the emperor's virtue! Although there is the eminence of T'ang, Yü, the
great Hsia, Ch'eng, and Chou, how could they surpass this? The rulers of
antiquity held audiences on the Eastern Peak, conducted shan sacrifices at the foot
of Mount Liang, but other than you who can do likewise?'

But the emperor is modest and says no to the praise.
He now plans to hunt above for blessings from the three supernatural forces;
Below to let flow the nourishing waters of the sweet springs.

The emperor's rejection of the eulogy betrays the ironic character of the hyperbole. Implied in it is the idea that a sage ruler who spends all his time hunting does not qualify as a sage king, and certainly is unworthy to perform the *feng* and *shan* sacrifices. There may even be some significance in the allusion to Yang Chu and Mo Ti. These two thinkers, whose names are often associated, represented antithetic philosophical positions in ancient China. Yang Chu was the egoist-hedonist who Meng-tzu claimed refused to give even a single hair to save the world.[58] Although it is possible the hedonism ascribed to him in the *Lieh tzu* is a later creation,[59] probably by the time of Yang Hsiung it was considered an essential part of his school. Mo Ti's philosophical position is well known, and stressed among other things frugality and simplicity, and condemned any ostentatious display. It may not be reading too much into this poem to claim that Yang Hsiung did not choose these names at random, but intended them to symbolize the two arguments around which the rhapsody is centered – the dichotomy between prodigality and parsimony, and the choice the emperor must make between them. Even though the emperor rejects both philosophers and follows what the Confucians would call a middle course, the position adopted in the conclusion is extremely close to the Mohist one.

Whether or not these names have the special significance I have attributed to them, the evidence is clear that this poem was not simply a virtuoso exercise in *epideixis*, but that it was intended to convey a moral message by means of an extremely subtle but not altogether unobtrusive rhetoric. To be sure, this piece does contain ornament – Yang uses over fifty binomial descriptives – but it is subordinate to his primary interest, persuasion. Whether or not he succeeded in convincing Emperor Ch'eng is irrelevant, for the important thing is that Yang made a conscious attempt to revive the rhetorical purpose of the rhapsody. It is not surprising to find that his next poem, the 'Ch'ang-yang Rhapsody', is almost pure persuasive rhetoric.

'CH'ANG-YANG RHAPSODY'

The 'Ch'ang-yang Rhapsody' (*Ch'ang-yang fu*) is a sequel to the 'Barricade Hunt' and probably deals with the same hunt Yang Hsiung so skillfully portrayed in the earlier piece.[60] It is contained both in the 'Autobiography' and *The Literary Selections*,[61] and like the 'Barricade Hunt' has a preface outlining the details of the poem's composition:

The next year[62] *the emperor, wishing to impress the Hu tribes with the great number of animals in the hunting preserve, in the autumn commanded the Yu Fu-feng*[63] *to dispatch people into the Southern Mountains. West from Pao and Hsieh,*[64] *east to Hung-nung,*[65] *and south to Han-chung*[66] *they spread nets and snares, caught bears, porcupines, tigers, panthers, long-snouted apes, macaques, foxes, rabbits, and deer which they loaded in portable cages and transported to the Bear Shooting Lodge at the Ch'ang-yang Palace.*[67] *They made circular pens out of the nets and released animals into them. They let the barbarians fight them with their bare hands and take away their own catch. The emperor personally came to observe the hunt. At this time, the farmers were unable to harvest their crops. I accompanied the emperor to the Bear Shooting Lodge. Upon our return I presented the 'Ch'ang-yang Rhapsody'. Since I wrote this composition with brush and ink I used Brush Forest as host and Master Ink as guest for the purpose of expressing indirect criticism.*[68]

The text reads:

The guest, Master Ink, asked the host, Brush Forest, ' I have heard that a sage ruler sustains his people by imbuing them with kindness and bestowing them with grace. He does not act for his own sake. This year we hunt at Ch'ang-yang.

3. *They first command the Yu Fu-feng*
    With great Mount Hua on the left and Pao-Hsieh on the right,
4. *To pound the Tz'u-yeh mountains into tethering posts,*
    To coil the Southern Mountains into nets.
5. *They place a thousand chariots in the forest meadow,*
    Arrange a myriad riders on the mountain slopes;
6. *Lead the troops to gather the pens,*
    Grant booty to the Jung, a catch to the Hu.

7. They grab bears,
    Drag out porcupines,
8. Wood pressed together, bamboo poles intertwined
    Serve to form the barricade.

This is the most marvelous spectacle in the empire. Even so, it is rather hard on the farmers. For over a month they have toiled extremely hard, and now their work is in vain. I am afraid an impartial observer, viewing the hunt from the outside would simply consider it a pleasure excursion, or looking at it from the inside would think it had nothing to do with providing dried meat for the sacrifices.[69] How is it conducted for the benefit of the people? Moreover, a ruler should instill his spirit with mysterious silence and make tranquility his virtue. Now he revels in going out far away in order to manifest his magnificent charisma. By repeated movement the charioteers and armored troops have become exhausted. This is not an important activity with which a ruler should engage himself. In spite of my youthful folly I have doubts about it.'

The host, Brush Forest, said, ' Bah, why do you say this? It seems to me that from what you have said you only know one part of the reason and have yet to perceive the other aspects. You have seen the superficial points but have failed to recognize the deeper ones. I have become exhausted from talking and cannot explain this in detail to you. I beg your indulgence to briefly describe the general theme and let you observe the fine points for yourself.'

The guest said, ' Please do.'

The host said, ' In ancient times the powerful state of Ch'in acted like a giant boar to its officers and oppressed the people like a Ya-yü.[70] The likes of the Chisel Fangs[71] gnashed their teeth and contended against each other. Powerful heroes were as thick as bubbling congee and arose like a confused cloud mass. For this reason the people knew no peace.

Thereupon, the Lord on High looked kindly on Kao-tsu. Kao-tsu received the mandate.

27. Followed the Dipper and Pole Star,
     Rotating round the Heavenly Barrier.[72]
28. He traversed the Great Sea,
     Shook the K'un-lun Mountains,
29. Picked up his sword and shouted.
30. He pointed to a city and seized it,
     Defeated its generals and lowered its flags.
31. The battle of a single day
     Cannot be described completely.

32. While toiling this greatly
     He had no leisure to comb his dishevelled hair,
     Though hungry he had no time to eat,
33. His helmet teemed with lice,
     His armor was soaked with sweat,
34. Thus, for the sake of the people he begged for a mandate from August
     Heaven.
35. Then, he released them from oppression,
     Saved them from deprivation;
36. He made plans for one hundred thousand years,
     Sought to expand the imperial heritage.
37. Within seven years the empire was at peace.

When the sage Emperor Wen ascended the throne, he followed tradition and custom, and concentrated his attention on perfect peace. He was restrained and frugal in conduct. His gray pongee clothes, though worn, he never changed; his leather boots, though with holes, he always wore. He did not live in large buildings nor did he decorate his wooden vessels. And then, in the rear palace he condemned the use of tortoise shells and removed all the pearls.

43. He rejected kingfisher decorations,
     Removed carved ornaments,
44. Detested elaborate beauty, would not go near it;
     Cast aside fragrant perfumes, did not allow them around.
45. He suppressed voluptuous music played by strings and reeds,
     Disliked hearing the enticing music of Cheng and Wei.
46. Therefore
     The Jade Balance was correct and the Great Stair was level.[73]
47. After this
     The Hsün-yü began to threaten,
     The Eastern Yi rebelled at will.
48. The Ch'iang-jung glared in anger,
     The Min-yüeh were in turmoil.[74]
49. On this account the people far away were insecure,
     And the central states become involved in their distress.
50. Thereupon
     The Sage Emperor Wu flew into a rage,
     And marshalled his troops.
51. He then commanded the Swift Cavalry General and Wei Ch'ing[75]
     Who in a great flurry and frenzy
     Gathered like clouds and struck like lightning.

52. They rose like whirlwinds and flowed like waves;
    Faster than snapping triggers, swifter than bees,
53. They sped like shooting stars,
    Attacked with the noise of thunder,
54. Smashed the enemy chariots,
    Tore down their tents,
55. The Gobi was strewn with their skulls;
    The Yü-wu River was filled with their marrow.[76]

Then, they hunted in their royal court: they drove away their camels, burned their cheese, split up the khan's territory, and portioned out the dependent states. They levelled the valleys, plucked the salt-grass, chipped boulders from the hills, trampled corpses, chariots crushed their attendants, fetters bound the old and feeble. Those scarred and marked by sharp lances, deeply wounded by bronze arrow-heads numbered one hundred thousand.

62. All kowtowed with their chins erect,[77]
    Grovelled along the ground, cowering like ants.
63. For over twenty years
    They did not dare to take even a quick breath.
64. The Heavenly troops covered the four directions:
    The Dark City was the first to be attacked.[78]
65. When they turned their lances in the opposite direction,
    The Southern Yüeh destroyed each other.
66. Waving their insignia, they marched west,
    The Ch'iang and Po galloped east to submit.

Thus, in the realm of far away regions, distant custom, remote neighbourhoods, cut-off villages, where men had yet to be transformed by imperial kindness, or pacified by his splendid virtue, all raised their feet, lifted their hands, and begged to present their treasures, making the world tranquil. Never again would there be the disasters at the border walls or troubles of war.

71. Now
    The court is embued with pure humaneness,
    Follows the Way and manifests rightness.
72. It embraces the forest of learning,
    Sage influence spreads like the clouds.
73. Blossoms and flowers[79] sink and float in profusion,
    Inundate the eight sections of the empire.
74. Everywhere covered by Heaven,
    All are soaked and drenched by them.

75. *If there were a gentlemen who did not praise the kingly Way,*
    Even a woodcutter would laugh at him.
76. *It is my opinion that glory is inevitably followed by decline,*
    Prosperity is succeeded by deterioration.
77. *Therefore, in peace we cannot neglect peril,*
    Nor in security can we ignore danger.

In the past after a bountiful harvest the emperor dispatched the troops, marshalled the chariots, and urged on the army. They activated the hosts at Wu-tso and exercised the horses at Ch'ang-yang. They chose the strong to fight the powerful brutes and test the stalwart against swift beasts.

81. *Then en masse*
    They climbed the Southern Mountains,
    Gazed afar at Wu-yi,[80]
82. *In the west subdued the Moon Grotto,*
    In the east terrified the Sun Region.
83. *Yet, they feared later ages would be deluded by a one-time event, considering it a regular endeavor of state,*
84. *They would hunt without restraint or moderation*
    Leading to degeneration that could not be withstood.
85. *Thus*
    They did not halt their chariots,
    And before the sun could shift the banners' shadow,
86. *The entourage, vague and indistinct,*
    Dissolved its ranks and returned home.
87. *This is also a way*
    To emulate the deeds of the Great Ancestor,
    To follow the principles of Wen and Wu,
88. *Restore the hunts of the Three Kings,*
    And revive the forester office of the Five Emperors.
89. *This allows*
    The farmers to continue harrowing,
    The weavers to remain with their looms,
90. *Marriage to be conducted at the proper time,*
    Not a single man or woman will miss the season.
91. *The emperor dispenses tranquility and joy,*
    Practices simplicity and ease,
92. *Shows concern for labor and toil,*
    Gives respite to the corvée,

93. *Visits the hundred-year olds,*
     Inquires about the orphaned and weak.
94. *He leads them together,*
     Shares their suffering and joy.
     Then
95. *They display music of bells and drums,*
96. *Sound the harmony of hand drum and chime,*
     Erect the bell-stand that roars like a tiger,
97. *Tap and strike the singing sphere,*
     Bend with the dance of the eight ranks.
98. *For wine they drink 'true excellence'*
     For meat they eat 'happiness'.[81]
99. *Hearing reverent care in the ancestral temple,*
     The spirits give a manifold blessing.
100. *The songs are in accord with the* Hymns;
     The music is in harmony with the Odes.
     Diligence like this earns a reward from the spirits. Now he waits for a good
       sign
102. *In order to make a* shan *sacrifice at the base of Mount Liang,*
     And increase the height of Mount T'ai,[82]
103. *Extend a great brilliance to the future,*
     And match the blessings received by rulers in the past.

  How is it we are only engaging in excessive spectacles, only galloping through rice fields, gallivanting in the pear and chestnut forests, trampling down the grazing lands, boasting to the common people, collecting a splendid crop of monkeys, and catching a great number of deer?
  The blind cannot see a foot in front of their face but Li Lou could spy into a cranny a thousand li *away. You only begrudge that the Hu tribes are catching our animals. You do not know that we also have caught their rulers.'*[83]
  Before the host had finished speaking the Ink Guest fell down on the mat and repeatedly lowered his head saying, 'Grand indeed is your lesson. Certainly not one as humble as I could match it. How you have exposed my folly! I see vast and clear!'

  In spite of its title, the 'Ch'ang-yang Rhapsody' is not a description of a hunt. Instead it is a debate between two imaginary figures called Master Ink Guest and Brush Forest Host. The poem begins with Master Ink characterizing a sage ruler as one who 'sustains his people by imbuing them with kindness and bestowing them with grace' (1. 2). He then mentions that the emperor has ordered the officials to prepare the area of Yu Fu-feng for a hunt.

The area is prepared, and the animals are led into the pens and barricades for the Hu participants to capture.

Master Ink concedes that this is a grand spectacle, but comments that it is also rather hard on the peasants. 'For over a month they have toiled extremely hard and now their work is in vain' (1. 11). The reference obviously is to the hunters' trampling of the farmers' rice and grain crops, and the destruction of the natural game and vegetation of the forests (as opposed to the artificially transported plants and animals of the game preserve). In the 'Barricade Hunt' Yang Hsiung alludes to this great destruction:

> *Then, strong hunters and fighters*
> *Topple firs and cypress*
> *Grasp the prickly pear.*
> *They hunt in thickets,*
> *Run down birds with their chariots;*
> *March over striped-head felines,*
> *Make belts of giant snakes;*
> *Jab red panthers with hooks,*
> *Pull away elephants and rhinos.*
> *[.   .   ]*
> *The trees fall, the mountains revolve*
> *[.   .   ]*
> *Whatever they meet is smashed;*
> *Whatever they approach is broken.*[84]

The guest remarks that 'an impartial observer, viewing the hunt from the outside would simply consider it a pleasure excursion, or looking at it from the inside would think that it had nothing to do with providing dried meat for the sacrifices. How is it conducted for the benefit of the people?' (11. 12–13).

Indeed, the people who lived in or near the imperial park suffered great hardship because of the hunters' disregard for their property. Tung-fang Shuo complained of this in a memorial addressed to Emperor Wu at the time he was considering enlarging the Shang-lin Park:

From the mountains of the area come jade, gold, silver, lead, iron, camphor, rosewood, wild mulberry, and exotic objects, so many they cannot be counted. These provide material for the craftsman and supply the needs of the people. There is also millet, rice, pears, chestnuts, mulberry, hemp, large bamboo, and dwarf bamboo. The land is suitable for ginger and taro, the waters produce many frogs and fish. The poor obtain enough to supply their families' wants and have no concern about hunger or cold. Thus, the area between the rivers Feng and Hao is called ' land fat' and is worth one gold-piece a mou. *If there now be a law to make this area into a park and cut off the profit from the ponds and marshes, and take away the people's fertile lands, you first deprive the state of its resources and second take away the occupations of agriculture and sericulture. We give up success, bring about failure, and lessen the supply of the five grains. This is the first objection.*

To fill a forest with brambles and thorns and raise deer, expand a park of foxes and rabbits, enlarge a wasteland of tigers and wolves, ruin the mounds and graves of the people, raze the houses and cottages of the people, causes the young and feeble to think of the land they have lost with nostalgia and the aged and old to cry with sadness. This is the second objection.

...Thus, to endeavor to enlarge a park without concern for agriculture is not the means to strengthen the country and enrich the people.[85]

The position of the guest seems to be similar to that maintained by Tung-fang Shuo a half-century earlier. Brush Forest replies to the criticism of the hunt that the guest's knowledge of the reasons for the hunt is superficial. He offers to outline the rationale for holding such expensive and elaborate spectacles. When the guest assents, Brush Forest launches into an extensive discussion of Han history, and China's relationship with the people of the border areas. He begins by telling of the oppression of the Ch'in dynasty, and the revolt by Liu Pang (Kao-tsu) which established the Han. He singles out Emperor Wen, who was distinguished for his frugality and distaste for ostentation. Shortly after Wen's reign, the tribes on all of China's borders posed a serious threat to the empire's security. Emperor Wu reacted by appointing the generals Huo Ch'ü-ping and Wei Ch'ing to lead expeditions against the Hsiung-nu. They succeeded in utterly routing the enemy, and as a result of these campaigns all the tribes subsequently submitted to the Han.

Brush Forest then characterizes the great peace and prosperity of the present age. The court encourages learning and the Confucian virtues. The host then mentions the hunt being held at the Ch'ang-yang Palace and the fears of some that 'later ages will be deluded by a one-time event,/considering it a regular endeavor of state' (1. 83). He then explains how the hunt actually benefits the common people (11. 89–90):

> *This allows the farmers to continue plowing*
> *And the weavers to stay on their looms.*
> *Marriages are conducted at the proper time,*
> *Men and women are wed at the proper age.*

Because of the great care and consideration for the people, the spirits grant blessings to the emperor. He will be able to make a *feng* and *shan* sacrifice, the supreme evidence of a virtuous ruler. The host concludes by accusing the guest of only begrudging the catch to the Hu tribes while failing to realize that this is one way of obtaining the Hu tribes' allegiance.

The guest immediately falls down on the mat and lowers his head as a sign of respect, and acknowledges the greater merits of the host's argument. Superficially, it appears then that the opinion of the host in defense of the hunt is also the poet's opinion. However, anyone familiar with the Han rhapsody will not be misled by this common rhetorical device. As Burton Watson has correctly suggested, 'one feels very strongly that Yang Hsiung's own views are expressed in the words of the scholar-critic, and that the so-called rebuttal of them, for all its eloquence, is no more than a rather grudgingly offered sop to the imperial conscience'.[86] We have already seen in the 'Barricade Hunt' a reduced application of the doubled persuasion in which a persuader argues for and against something in order to make one argument seem more appealing than another. We have also seen that the argument that seems to win the debate is not necessarily the poet's own opinion. In the 'Ch'ang-yang Rhapsody' Yang Hsiung has made effective use of irony which clearly betrays his objection to the hunt. The host, in his account of the great blessings the spirits have bestowed on the emperor, remarks:

How is it we are only engaging in excessive spectacles, only galloping through rice fields, gallivanting in the pear and chestnut forests, trampling down the grazing lands, boasting to the common people, collecting a splendid crop of monkeys, and catching a great number of deer? (11. 104–7)

If Yang Hsiung wished to support the host's argument, he would hardly have elaborated on the specific destruction caused by the hunt. This statement is one of the best examples of irony I have seen in early Chinese literature. Furthermore, the perfunctory manner in which the host relates the hunt to its alleged purpose of gaining the barbarians' allegiance seems to indicate that the host's speech is indeed a 'sop to the imperial conscience'.

The style of the rhapsody is a good reflection of its purely suasory intent. There are almost no binomial descriptives, and much of the piece is unrhymed. In one section there are rather unusual words, which appear to be transcriptions of the Hsiung-nu language. The greater part of the diction, particularly when compared with Yang's other poems, is extremely simple and consists of common words. The poem in many ways resembles a Warring States persuasion.

5

The Rhapsody Criticized and Reformed

Yang Hsiung in his later years turned away from literature and focused his attention on philosophy. This interest, however, did not preclude him from developing ideas on literature, and the rhapsody in particular. One must remember that in Han times literature was considered an inherent part of learning in general. The modern word for literature, *wen-hsüeh* or 'refined learning', in fact designated not *belles lettres* but learning, scholarship, erudition, and education.[1] The study of *wen-hsüeh* primarily involved a knowledge of the classics and the ritual (*li*), and secondarily the ability to compose, both orally and in writing. During the Emperor Wu period *wen-hsüeh* was virtually institutionalized when a 'devotion to *wen-hsüeh*' (*hao wen-hsüeh*) became one of the chief requirements for obtaining governmental appointment.[2]

There were words in Han times that referred to what one might call *belles lettres* or literature in the modern sense. The most common of these is probably *tz'u*, which simply means 'words', whether written or spoken. *Tz'u*, used alone, or in the compound *wen-tz'u* (refined words), came to be a general designation for the artistic, ornamental, and imaginative use of language – *belles lettres*. Thus, the anthology of Ch'u poetry collected in Han times is called *Ch'u tz'u*, which really means 'Literature of Ch'u'.[3] The rhapsody itself was frequently called *tz'u-fu*, probably because of the verbal effusion that characterized many of the pieces in this genre.

Central to early Chinese literary theory were also the concepts of *wen* and *chih*, which are rough equivalents to the Western notions of 'form' and 'content'. The term *wen* is an extremely complex concept and involves a number of elements. Arthur Waley has made one of the best explanations of its many senses:

The original meaning of the word wên *is criss-cross lines, markings, pattern. It also means a written character, an ideogram…* Wên, *again, means what is decorated as opposed to what is plain, ornament as opposed to structure, and hence things that vary and beautify human life, as opposed to life's concrete needs. In particular,* wên *denotes the arts of peace (music, dancing, literature) as opposed to those of war…It is clear that* wên *means something very like our own word culture and served many of the same purposes.*[4]

Chih refers to some of the opposites of *wen:* substance, essence, simplicity, disposition, matter, and content.

Confucius was the first to posit a theory of *wen* and *chih.* He says in the *Lun yü:*

> *When natural substance* (chih) *prevails over ornamentation* (wen), *you get the boorishness of the rustic. When ornamentation prevails over natural substance, you get the pendantry of the scribe. Only when ornament and substance are duly blended do you get the true gentleman.*[5]

Confucius appears to give equal weight to both *wen* and *chih* so that neither form nor content should be overemphasized. He insists that a balance be maintained between them.

Yang Hsiung was the first philosopher after Confucius to develop a detailed and coherent theory of *wen* and *chih,* particularly as aesthetic concepts. In *The Great Dark,* for example, there is a tetragram that represents the concept of *wen* and outlines the cyclical development of *wen* and *chih* as cosmic forces. It might be useful to present a complete translation of this tetragram in order to illustrate the exact nature of Yang's view:

Tetragram 47: Wen
The yin *gathers substance; the* yang *disperses form.*
When form and substance are properly manifested, the myriad things are in splendid array.

This opening statement proposes the proper relationship that should exist between substance/content and pattern/form. Content is governed by the *yin* principle, while form is controlled by the *yang.* When *yin* and *yang,* and in turn, form and content, are properly balanced, everything in nature is in harmony.

1. [Dawn. Birth of consciousness.]
An embroidered gown is covered with plain silk. Jade pure.
  Judgment: An embroidered gown is covered with plain silk. Form lies within.

The first stage of the tetragram represents an embryonic period of consciousness. Here the embroidered gown, which has been covered with plain, unadorned silk, represents the undifferentiated pattern or form that has not yet emerged fully into consciousness. External form lies latent, overshadowed by non-ornamented substance. The embryonic attachment of form to content indicates the dominant role of the latter. Its purity is that of jade in its crude, uncarved, unpolished state.

2. [Night. Conscious reflection.]
Form emerges as resplendent; content is obstructed.
   Judgment: Form emerges as resplendent; content is obstructed. Both are unable to remain in pure harmony.

As form emerges into consciousness, it breaks away from substance (content) and exhibits a splendor that upsets the balance between them. Content then cannot find a means for expression.

3. [Dawn. Formulation of definite ideas.]
Grand form (ta wen) *becomes more and more pure and simple. Truth only seems in insufficient supply.*
   Judgment: Grand form becomes more and more pure and simple. Substance is in excess.

The grand form or grand pattern is the normative pattern of the Sage. It is the true form, and is characterized by simplicity as opposed to ornamentation that only obstructs the conveyance of ideas (content). Although truth seems to be lacking because of increased simplicity, this is only superficially so. Truth need not and must not rely on ostentatious display, which only obscures it.

4. [Night. Extension of ideas into conduct.]
Polished and adorned: the pattern of tiger and leopard. It is not received by Heaven. Obstruction.
   Judgment: Obstruction with respect to elegance and adornment. How do they deserve praise?

Here Yang evokes the images of the tiger and leopard from Hexagram 49 of the *Book of Changes* where the tiger is the symbol of the Great Man (*ta-jen*) and the leopard, the Gentleman. In *The Great Dark* the tiger and leopard are singled out for the elegance of their appearance. The former has his stripes, and the latter his spots. However, this outward elegance is only a facade and a disguise hiding their internal essence (that of evil, dangerous animals). By concentration on external pattern, substance is obstructed.

5. [Dawn. Manifestation in achievement.]
Bright and elegant: form that is esteemed is manifested clearly. One deserves his carts and robes.
   Judgment: Elegant above; the pattern of Heaven is bright.

In the fifth position of the tetragram all is in harmony. It is the apex of good fortune, and form is no longer obscured but reflects that of Heaven which is supreme brightness and clarity.

6. [Night. Greatest achievement.]
Vast form [or: the pattern of geese] lacks standards. Restraint is thrown off in the river.
  Judgment: Vast form lacks standards. It behaves as it likes.

Here normative influences are lacking. The individual loses control over form and it simply runs away with itself, as when the formation of geese dissolves when the flock lands in a river.

7. [Dawn. Decline and loss.]
The pheasant is unfed [= untamed] while the chicken eats his fill.
  Judgment: the pheasant is unfed. He is difficult to domesticate.

The highly adorned pheasant abides in the wilds but must forage for food. The plainly adorned chicken, however, since he has been tamed, eats to satiation. Thus, adornment or pattern without a normative influence is symptomatic of impending disaster.

8. [Night. Disintegration and collapse.]
Carving of intricate objects: caring for grain and weaving of cloth is neglected. At this time, pattern is disordered.
  Judgment: The carving of intricate patterns: simply a waste of time.

When time is spent on non-essential things such as creating highly ornate patterns at the expense of the essentials (caring for grain and weaving cloth), disorder ensues. At this stage all normative influences have disappeared.

9. [Dawn. Destruction and annihilation.]
Pattern that is elaborate to the extreme: substitute sacrificial robes for it.
  Judgment: The substitution for pattern that is elaborate to the extreme: the substitution ought to be with substance.

Here Yang Hsiung inserts an optimistic interpretation to the stage of the tetragram most symbolic of destruction. Form reverts to content, to which it was subject in the first stage. The sacrificial robes, although highly ornamented, convey the proper function to which certain elaborate patterns may be put. They are not the mere carving of intricate objects, but play an important part in the ritual.

Yang Hsiung's position on the *wen* and *chih* question is clearly stated here, although it is presented in a somewhat cryptic and unsystematic fashion. He believes, first of all, that form is subordinate to content, even though they ideally should be in harmony. Form should be a natural embodiment of the substance, not an artificial creation. Yang also indicates that elaborate and intricate patterns in language and conduct only lead to obfuscation. Thus, the pattern or form must serve an appropriate function. It must be normative and adhere to certain restrictions. The cultivation of form for the sake of form cannot be tolerated. The same theme is elaborated more fully in the *Model Sayings:*

Someone asked, ' Suppose there were a person who said his name was K'ung and his style was Chung-ni, that he entered Confucius' door, mounted his hall, and leaned over his table. Could one consider him Confucius?'

Yang Hsiung answered, ' His outer form is that of Confucius, but his essence is not.'

' I venture to ask you what you mean by essence.' Yang Hsiung said, ' Suppose there were an animal whose essence was that of a sheep but wore a tiger's skin. If it saw grass it would rejoice. However, if it saw a wolf, it would tremble. This is because it would forget that it wore a tiger's skin. A sage is a type of tiger: he is distinguished by the brilliance of his adornment. A gentleman is a type of leopard; he is distinguished by the elegance of his adornment. A sophist is a type of fox; he is distinguished by the bushiness of his adornment.'[6]

Yang Hsiung's concept of the normative pattern as applied to literature is explained in a short essay appended to *The Great Dark:*

What is to be esteemed in a writer is his compliance with and embodiment of nature (tzu-jan)*...The writer concentrates on the situation and ignores the language* (tz'u)*. He allows the permutations to increase but does not allow form* (wen) *to be in excess. If his language is not restrained, his theories will be unclear. If it is not concise, the application of his ideas will not be broad...Thus, it is by means of form that content can be seen, and it is by means of language that circumstances can be viewed. By observing the application of language, what the heart desires can be seen.*[7]

Yang Hsiung says a number of things here that relate to his general theory of literature. First of all, he borrows from Taoism the concept of spontaneity and natural simplicity that cannot be added to or subtracted from. Artificially fabricated adornment leads to feeble and disordered writing. By concentration on things as they are (*tzu-jan*) the fundamental principles of the universe can be expressed. Thus, language is a potent instrument, a vehicle of the emotions and the mind.

Yang Hsiung's concept of language is strikingly modern in the awareness of the symbolic power of language to express ultimate reality. However, to him language is a dangerous force that can be misused. When one concentrates too heavily on the decorative and descriptive aspects of words at the expense of natural simplicity, it becomes a useless tool. Such language is not a product of the mind (*hsin*) or emotions, and hence does not convey essential truths.

In the *Model Sayings* Yang Hsiung develops further the theory of language as the vehicle of expressing the ultimate reality which itself springs from the mind.

When words are unable to express the mind and writing is unable to convey words this makes for great difficulty. Only a sage can attain the proper content in words or the proper style in writing. Both content and style possess clarity as if illumined by the sun and washed by the Chiang and Ho. The writing is so vast nothing can resist it. Colors and language seem to run back and forth.

For expressing the desires that come from the deepest part of the mind and conveying vexations, nothing is better than words. To restore the events of the past, clarify the distant, publicize marvels from antiquity, and transmit wonders from a thousand miles distant, nothing is better than writing.

Thus, words are the sound of the mind; and writing is the image of the mind. When sound and image take form, it is evident whether one is a gentleman or an ordinary man. Sound and image are the means by which the gentleman and the ordinary man express their feelings.[8]

Here words are again made the product of the mind. Writing (*shu*) is a particular manifestation of words, which in the hands of the proper person, the sage, possesses unmatched clarity and scope. Language, it seems, stems from the deepest layers of the mind, expressing all the frustrations and emotions that it contains. When language expresses the mind in writing, feelings can be transmitted over long distances of time and space. Words and writing, which are representations of the mind, are an important means of distinguishing men from each other. Implied in this statement is the notion that the writing of the gentleman (*chün-tzu*) is a more faithful reflection of the feelings than that of the ordinary man, who tends to obfuscate reality with his excessively ornate verbiage.

This view influenced Yang Hsiung's opinion of the rhapsody. For example, in the *Model Sayings*, when asked if a gentleman esteems only ornate language, he replies:

The gentleman adheres to the description of the situation. When his description of the situation is emphasized at the expense of ornate language one has a dry discourse. When the language is emphasized at the expense of the description of the situation, one has a rhapsody. When the description of the situation and the verbiage are in balance one has a classic.[9]

Thus, the rhapsody is a type of writing in which the style and verbal display are pre-eminent, and tend to distort the accurate portrayal of a situation (*shih*).

The statement is only a partial representation of Yang Hsiung's view of the rhapsody. His most extensive comments on the genre come in a series of remarks made in the second chapter of the *Model Sayings*.

Someone asked, 'When you, sir, were young did you not enjoy writing rhapsodies?' Yang said, 'Yes, as a child I indulged in worm-carving and seal-character cutting.'[10] *He hesitated and said, 'But a grown man does not go in for such things.' Someone asked, 'But can't a rhapsody be used to criticize by indirection?' Yang said, 'To criticize by indirection? If it criticizes by indirection, it should stop there. If it does not stop there, I am afraid it cannot avoid encouraging the behavior it criticizes.'*

Someone said, 'But does it not have the intricate beauty of misty gauze?' Yang said, 'It is only a moth in a seamstress' work.'[11]

Obviously, at the time Yang wrote this, he had long abandoned the writing of rhapsodies, which he considered a puerile endeavor. His remarks reflect two views of poetry: one, that a poem is a moral and ethical instrument used primarily for persuasion; and the other, that it is an aesthetic object concerned with the artistic manipulation of language for its own sake. Although Yang rejects both views with respect to the rhapsody, he clearly is partial to the former view.

One should note that Yang does not dismiss the idea that the legitimate function of the rhapsody, or any poetry for that matter, is suasory. His objection is that the effusive verbal display that characterizes the genre made it impossible for the moral message to be conveyed. This point is elaborated by Yang in a following passage:

Someone asked, 'Were not the rhapsodies of Ching Ts'o, T'ang Le, Sung Yü, and Mei Ch'eng of any value?' Yang said, 'They were necessarily unrestrained.' 'What do you mean by "unrestrained?"' Yang said, 'The rhapsodies of the Song writers (shih jen chih fu) *are beautiful but maintain standards. The rhapsodies of the writers who concentrate on ornate language* (tz'u jen chih fu) *are beautiful but unrestrained. If the Confucian school had used the rhapsody, Chia Yi would have mounted the hall and Ssu-ma Hsiang-ju would have entered the inner compartments. But they did not use the rhapsody, so what of it?'*[12]

These statements are essentially an extension of Yang Hsiung's theory of form and content. He attacks, first of all, the unrestrained language of the rhapsodists who immediately followed Ch'ü Yüan. He speaks favorably of the *shih jen chih fu*, which is a somewhat ambiguous designation. Some believe it refers to one of the three modes of expression supposedly used in the Songs, namely 'direct narration'.[13] The concept, however, is more general than this, and actually is a representation of Yang Hsiung's poetic ideal, which is embodied in the canonical collection of poems titled *Shih*. According to Yang Hsiung, the classics are the chief repositories of all truth and ethical principles. The poems in this collection are considered the sincere expression of the feelings and the mind, and are a key to the ultimate reality and natural substance of things. Theoretically they are unfettered by elaborate and ornate linguistic structures, which only obscure the moral message they contain. These poems, while primarily designed for emotive expression, are essentially suasory and rhetorical, and are meant to teach and instruct.

The *tz'u jen* (literally, the 'language men') are the epideictic rhapsodists, who, as the term indicates, are obsessed with ornate language. In their writings the moral message is obscured. Even though many of these poems are intended to persuade, the effusive verbiage renders the poet's rhetoric ineffective. Thus, rhapsodies of this kind have little practical value. They are like Ssu-ma Hsiang-ju's rhapsodies, which Yang Hsiung characterizes in a later *Model Sayings* chapter as 'beautiful writing but of little use'.[14]

Yang Hsiung, as one of the leading writers of rhapsodies in the Han dynasty, was in a good position to recognize the conflict that existed between the two types of rhetoric that operated in the rhapsody, the persuasive and the ornamental. One was designed to teach and instruct while the other was intended to delight and entertain. Yang believed that the proper function of the rhapsody, along with the poems of the *Shih*, was to influence human behavior. He could not justify the excessive use of verbal embellishment that characterized the epideictic tradition of his time. Even though he made an extremely skillful use of rhetoric in the 'Barricade Hunt' and 'Ch'ang-yang Rhapsody', Yang finally concluded that the genre was an ineffective ethical instrument.

It should be noted, however, that Yang Hsiung's condemnation of excessive ornament does not mean that he completely disavowed the use of refined poetic language. In 'Dissolving Objection' (*Chieh nan*), the piece he wrote in response to a critic's remark that the language of *The Great Dark* was too abstruse for the ordinary man to understand, Yang expresses the view that great ideas are necessarily clothed in difficult and refined language, and are not meant for the eyes and ears of the masses. Burton Watson labels this an 'exclusive and obscurantist view of literature'.[15] This characterization is hardly appropriate in view of Yang's other statements about the obfuscation caused by elaborate adornment in writing, but it is certainly true that Yang Hsiung maintained an elitist notion of literary beauty (note his remarks about the sage being best able to write beautiful literature). What Yang Hsiung was really saying is that the ideas and the language used to express them are inseparable, and that the ideas as well as the language are difficult for someone with less intelligence than the sage to understand.

POEMS OF FRUSTRATION

Yang Hsiung did not cease writing poetry when he formally rejected the rhapsody as an effective suasory instrument. He in fact wrote two rhymed compositions shortly after he made his famous denunciation of the genre. These are the 'Dissolving Ridicule' (*Chieh ch'ao*) and 'Dissolving Objection'. The latter piece has been discussed above, and need not be further elaborated on here.

The 'Dissolving Ridicule' is contained in the 'Autobiography' and *The Literary Selections*.[16] Its immediate literary antecedent is Tung-fang Shuo's 'Response to a Guest's Objection' (*Ta k'o nan*).[17] Like the earlier piece, the poem is a dialogue between an unnamed guest, who criticizes Yang's low position and impractical devotion to scholarship, and Yang himself, who offers a long defense of his position. Yang's argument is identical to that of Tung-fang Shuo: the man of integrity does not live in an age that will accept his ideas.

'Dissolving Ridicule'

A guest said, ' I have heard that a scholar of the past generations served as model and principle for other men. If he had never been born that would be the end of the matter, but since he was born in the world, he was obliged to honor his lord above and glorify his parents below.

4. *He split a tablet with his lord,*
   Accepted rank from his lord,
5. *Embraced a tally from his lord,*
   Partook of a salary from his lord.
6. *Bound up in blue, trailing purple,*
   He vermillioned his wheel hubs.[18]

Now you are fortunate enough to encounter a bright and glorious age, to dwell in a censure-free court, and to associate with a multitude of worthies. You have long passed through the Golden Gate[19] *and ascended the Jade Hall,*[20] *but you have never devised a single scheme or produced a single plan.*

10. *Nor do you*
    Persuade the ruler above,
    Debate with the ministers below,
11. *Or with eyes blazing like stars,*
    A tongue like flashing lightning,
12. *Argue now vertically, now horizontally,*[21]
    So that no critic can rebut you.
13. *All you do is silently write your five thousand character* Great Dark;
14. *Its leaves and branches spread all over,*
    Which alone makes an explanation of some one hundred thousand
        words.
15. *Where it is deep it penetrates the Yellow Springs,*
    Where it is high it reaches the blue sky.
16. *Where it is large it encompasses the primal force;*
    Where it is minute it enters the finest crevice.
17. *However,*
    You hold the position of Gentleman in Attendance,
    Have been selected merely as Servitor at the Yellow Gate.

It is my opinion that your "dark" (hsüan) is still "white".[22] *Otherwise, why have you failed so miserably in your career?'*

Yang-tzu laughed and answered, ' *You only want to vermillion my wheel hubs. You do not seem to know that just one slip will redden my entire clan'.*[23]

22. *In the past*
    Chou's net of control was loosened,
    A herd of deer raced away in flight.[24]
23. *They separated into twelve parts,*
    Joined into sixes and sevens.[25]
24. *Split into fours, paired into fives,*
    Combined became the Warring States.
25. *The scholar had no permanent ruler,*
    The state had no reliable officials.
26. *Those who obtained scholars became wealthy,*
    Those who lost them became poor.
27. *Scholars flapped their wings, shook their quills,*
    Alighted wherever they pleased.
28. *Therefore,*
    Sometimes a scholar hid himself in a sack,
    Or fled by drilling a hole in a wall.[26]

29. For this reason
    Tsou Yen, because of his stiff-necked arrogance, was employed by the
        world.[27]

30. Even though Meng K'o suffered hardships, he became the teacher of a
        powerful lord.[28]

31. Now, the great Han
    With the Eastern Sea on the left,
    Ch'ü-sou on the right,[29]

32. P'an-yü to the front,
    Chiao-t'u to the rear,[30]

33. Has one governor for the southeast,
    One overseer for the northwest.[31]

34. The entire country is bound together with ropes,
    And is controlled with the executioner's axes,

35. They disseminate the Rites and Music,
    Extend moral influence with Poetry and History.

36. They spend years and months
    Building schoolhouses.

37. The scholars of the empire,
    Moving like thunder, gathering like clouds,

38. Arrayed like fishscales,
    All hasten into the eight regions.

39. All fancy themselves a Chi or Hsieh;
    Each considers himself a Kao-yao.[32]

40. Sophists wearing hair-nets and cap-strings all compare themselves with A-heng.
    A five-foot boy is ashamed to be compared to Yen Ying or Yi-wu.[33]

41. Those who hold high position lie abandoned in ditches and moats.

42. At dawn one holds power and is a minister;
    At dusk he loses power and becomes a commoner.

43. The court is like the bank of a river or lake[34]
    Or an island in a large gulf.

44. When a flock of geese alight there they don't constitute a great increase;
    When several of them fly away that does not make a great loss.[35]

45. In the past
    When the Three Humane Ones left Yin, it was reduced to ruins;
    When the Two Elders returned to Chou, it began to prosper.[36]

46. When Tzu-hsü died, Wu was destroyed;
    When Chung and Li survived, Yüeh became hegemon.[37]

47. When 'Five Sheepskins' entered Ch'in, Duke Mu was delighted;
    But when Yüeh Yi left Yen, King Hui was afraid.[38]

5

48. *Fan Chü had broken ribs and teeth but was able to threaten the Marquis of Jang;*
   Ts'ai Tse's deformed jaws made T'ang Chü laugh.[39]
49. *Therefore, in a time of emergency*
   Without ministers like Hsiao, Ts'ao, Tzu-fang,
   P'ing, Po, Fan and Huo there is no security.[40]
50. *In a time of no emergency*
   Students of paragraphs and phrases sit together and take care of things
   And there is no cause for worry.[41]

Therefore, when the world is beset with chaos, the sage and wise gallop around but they cannot adequately meet the situation. When the world is well-ordered, ordinary men can handle the government with their heads on a pillow and there is ability to spare.

53. *Among scholars of the past:*
   One was freed from fetters and became a minister;
   One took off his coarse clothing and became a king's adviser.[42]
54. *One leaned on Yi Gate and laughed;*
   One crossed the river depths and fished.[43]
55. *One persuaded seventy times but was never successful;*
   Another spoke once to a king and was made marquis.[44]
56. *One made a ruler of a powerful state bend into his humble alley;*
   Another moved a ruler to sweep the road ahead for him.[45]
57. *Thus, scholars stretched their tongues and moved their brushes.*
58. *They filled up gaps and stepped into openings without being supressed.*
59. *In the present*
   District magistrates do not summon scholars,
   Commandery governors do not invite teachers,
60. *High chancellors do not receive guests,*
   Generals and ministers do not condescend to look on a scholar.
61. *Those who speak the unusual are considered suspicious;*
   Those who do something different are punished.
62. *Thus*
   Those who wish to speak roll up their tongues and echo the consensus;
   Those who want to act walk with hesitation and follow others' footsteps.

Suppose distinguished scholars of the past lived today. If their memorials were not 'Class A', their conduct were not 'filial and pure', if they were not recommended as 'square and upright', all they could do is present memorials and periodically speak criticism. The best of them would be able to attain Candidate for Appointment;[46] *the worst of them would be heard and then dismissed. How could they obtain the blue and purple?*

67. Furthermore, I have heard that
    When a fire is at its hottest point it begins to die down;
    When thunder drones its loudest it begins to die out.
68. If we examine thunder, examine fire
    They will appear to be full and strong,
69. But the sky gathers the sound of thunder
    And the earth absorbs the heat of fire.
70. Similarly, a family at the apex of fame
    Will be spied out by the spirits.
71. Those who grab for power die;
    Those who remain silent survive.
72. Those who reach the highest positions endanger their family;
    Those who maintain themselves intact remain secure.
73. Therefore
    To understand the Dark, understand the silent
    Is to preserve the principle of the Way.
74. To be pure, to be tranquil
    Is to travel in the court of Spirit
75. To be quiet, to be still
    Is to preserve the abode of Power.
76. Times differ, circumstances change,
    But the Way of man never alters.
77. If we could change times with those of the past,
    We do not know which of us would be successful.
78. Now you
    Take the owl and laugh at the phoenix,
    Grasp the measuring-worm and mock the tortoise and dragon.
79. Are you not ill with error?
80. You laugh because my 'dark' is still 'white'.
81. I laugh at you because you are so ill with error.
82. How sad you have never met Yü Fu and Pien Ch'üeh.'⁴⁷

The guest said, 'If this is so, without a "dark" there is no way to achieve fame, is there? But what need did men like Fan and Ts'ai have for a "dark"'.

Yang-tzu said, 'Fan Chü was a refugee from Wei. He had his ribs broken and his bones crushed but escaped the shackles. He pulled in his shoulders, had someone stamp on his back, and he crawled into a bag. He excited a powerful lord and induced him to exile the lord of Ching-yang, to expel the Marquis of Jang, and let Fan take his place. He could do this because the opportunity was right.

' *Ts'ai Tse was a commoner from east of the mountains. He had a deformed jaw and broken nose, tears and spittle poured down his face. In the west he bowed to the minister of the powerful Ch'in, seized him by the throat, choked him with his eloquence, slapped him on the back and took his position.*[48] *He could do this because the time was right.*

' *When the empire was pacified and warfare had ceased, the capital was established at Lo-yang. Lou Ching abandoned his man-drawn cart, flashed his three-inch tongue, devised a plan that could not be uprooted, and proposed that the capital be moved to Ch'ang-an.*[49] *He could do this because the situation was right.*

' *The Five Emperors handed down the laws and the Three Kings transmitted the rites. These were not changed for a hundred generations. Shu-sun T''ung arose in a time of warfare, took off his armor, cast away his lance, and then composed a code of court ritual.*[50] *He could do this because he understood the needs of the time.*

' *The* Code of Fu[51] *was ineffective and the Ch'in laws were too harsh. When the sage Han established the regulations Hsiao Ho drew up the code. He could do this because the conditions were right.*

' *Therefore, if the code of Hsiao Ho had been drawn up in the time of T''ang and Yü, it would have been considered untimely. If the court ritual of Shu-sun T''ung had been composed in the Hsia and Yin periods, it would have been viewed with suspicion. If Lou Ching's plan had been devised in the time of King Ch'eng of Chou,*[52] *it would have been considered ridiculous. If the speeches of Fan and Ts'ai had been made to Chin, Chang, Hsü or the Shih,*[53] *they would have been considered silly.*

105. *The regulations of Hsiao that Ts'ao followed,*
  · *The plans devised by the Marquis of Liu,*
  The unusual policies formulated by Ch'en P'ing[54]

106. *Earned merit piled as high as a tall mountain,*
  Achieved fame that resounded like the noise of a collapsing hill.

107. *Even though these men possessed great wisdom,*
  They also met the proper time.

108. *Therefore*
  He who does what can be done at the proper time will be successful;
  He who does what cannot be done at the improper time will fail miserably.

109. *Master Lin achieved success at Chang Tower;*
  The four grey-heads plucked glory at South Mountain.[55]

111. *Kung-sun began his career at Gold Horse;*
  The Swift Cavalry General started out at Ch'i-lien.[56]

112. *Ssu-ma Hsiang-ju stole his wealth from the Cho clan;*
    Tung-fang Shuo cut off some sacrificial meat for his wife.[57]
113. *I certainly cannot be classed with these men.*
    Thus, silently and alone I guard my Great Dark.'

Although the 'Dissolving Ridicule' does not have the word *fu* in its title, it closely resembles à rhapsody of frustration. Yang Hsiung, because he had rejected the rhapsody, would not label his poem a *fu*, but this did not preclude him from writing a poem using many of the rhapsodic conventions. Thus, he makes extensive use of the historical example, almost to excess. In 11. 53–6 he has an enumeration of scholars who attained different degrees of success in various situations. In 11. 45–8 there is a list of scholars whose action or inaction influenced the decline or prosperity of their ruler's states. Yang also makes abundant use of the *topos* of time's fate. In 11. 84–100 he cites a series of examples of men who were successful because the time was right for their ideas to be accepted by the ruler. Finally, a rhapsody of frustration would not be complete without at least one example of the *topos* of the world upside down. Referring to the guest who criticizes him, he says (1. 78):

> Now you
> Take the owl and laugh at the phoenix,
> Grasp the measuring-worm and mock the tortoise and dragon.

The language of the 'Dissolving Ridicule' is less ornate than Yang Hsiung's other rhapsodies, and this poem is a much more effective rhetorical demonstration. Yang even inserts humor and sarcasm that are almost totally absent from his other rhapsodies. At one point he says to the guest (11. 79–82):

> Are you not ill with error?
> You laugh because my 'dark' is still 'white'.
> I laugh at you because you are so ill with error.
> How sad you have never met Yü Fu and Pien Ch'üeh.

(The reference here is to the critic's remark at the beginning of the poem that Yang Hsiung's 'dark' (*hsüan*) was still 'white' (*pai*), meaning that *The Great Dark* had not brought him any success or recognition. Yü Fu and Pien Ch'üeh are famous doctors of antiquity.)

The 'Dissolving Ridicule' represents a more forthright, personal expression than any of Yang's previous poems, and closely conforms to his concept of the 'rhapsody of the *Song* writers'. Yang still uses a rhyme-prose structure for ethical demonstration, and in fact it is remarkable how much of the piece is in rhyme. He also continues to use many of the conventions of the rhapsody, particularly those common to the rhapsody of frustration. Thus, although Yang eschewed the name of the genre, he did not abandon its form.

Among the works attributed to Yang Hsiung is one rhapsody which, if genuine, is a perfect example of what Yang Hsiung probably meant by the 'rhapsody of the *Song* poets'. This piece is the 'Expelling Poverty Rhapsody' (*Chu p'in fu*). The earliest text of this poem is contained in the *Compendium of Arts and Letters*.[58] It also survives in the *Garden of Ancient Literature*, which makes it somewhat suspect.[59] However, there is no evidence to indicate that Yang Hsiung is not the author, although it is strange that a rhapsody of this quality was excluded from the *History of the Former Han* and *The Literary Selections*.

'Expelling Poverty Rhapsody'

1. *I, Yang-tzu dwell in hiding,*
   Apart from the world, living alone.

2. *On the left my neighbors are the lofty mountains,*
   On the right I adjoin the vast wilderness.

3. *Over my next-door walls are beggars,*
   Always poor and destitute.

4. *Though deficient in ritual and propriety*
   They gather together in groups.

5. *Depressed and in despair*
   I called to Poverty and said:

6. *'When you lived amongst the Six Extremities,*[60]
   They cast you far into the wastes.

7. *You enjoyed working as a laborer;*
   Your punishments were heavy.

8. *Not only as a youth or lad*
   Did you merrily play in the sand.

9. *Now you are not merely my near neighbor,*
   But your house touches mine.

10. *Favor is lighter than fur or feather,*
    Propriety is thinner than wispy gossamer.

11. *I advance but not through virtue,*
    I retreat but receive no rebuke.

12. *Long have you been a lingering guest.*
    What is your intent?

13. *Others all wear patterned embroidery,*
    I wear unfinished coarse cloth.

14. *Others all eat rice and millet,*
    Only I eat brambles.
15. *In poverty I lack treasures and toys;*
    What can provide me pleasure?
16. *The clans with their banquets*
    Engage in revelry without end.
17. *I walk afoot with book basket on my back,*
    With only a single change of clothes to go out in.
18. *I work at a hundred labors,*
    My feet and hands are callused.
19. *I sometimes weed, sometimes hoe.*[61]
    My body is wet, my skin exposed.
20. *Cut off from my friends and companions,*
    My promotion in office is slow.
21. *Where does the blame lie?*
    It can only be your fault!
22. *I left you and fled far away*
    To the peaks of the K'un-lun mountains.
23. *But you followed me,*
    You flew and reached the sky.[62]
24. *I left you, and climbed a mountain,*
    I hid in cliffs and caves.
25. *But you followed me,*
    And climbed that high slope.[63]
26. *I left you, and entered the sea,*
    Tossed was my cypress boat.[64]
27. *But you followed me,*
    Now sinking, now floating.[65]
28. *I act, you move.*
    I am still, you rest.
29. *Couldn't you haunt someone else?*
    What do you seek from me?
30. *Now be gone!*
    Remain here no longer!'
31. *Poverty said, ' Very well, master,*
32. *I have been expelled.*
    Though the more I speak the sillier I sound
33. *I have been harboring something in my heart*
    And I would like to express it completely.

34. *Formerly my ancestor and yours*
    Displayed his bright virtue.

35. *He was able to assist Emperor Yao,*
    Warned him to make canons and rules.

36. *The earthen stairs and thatch roof*
    Were not carved, not decorated.

37. *Then, at the end of the era*
    Rulers gave free rein to dark folly.

38. *Gluttonous rapacious hordes*
    Through foul means greedily sought wealth.

39. *They belittled my ancestor;*
    They were arrogant and haughty.

40. *Their jade towers, jasper terraces*
    Buildings and houses were lofty and tall.

41. *They poured wine to make a pond;*
    Piled meat to make Mount Yao.[66]

42. *Then the swan flew away;*
    He would not set foot in their court.

43. *Three times a day I examine myself;*
    I find I am without blame.

44. *Since I have dwelled in your house,*
    There have been mountains of blessings.

45. *You have forgotten my great virtues;*
    You remember only petty grudges.

46. *You withstand cold, bear heat*
    Gradually I have gotten you used to them.

47. *Cold and heat are unwavering,*
    They are as long-lived as immortals.

48. *Chieh and Chih you do not heed,*[67]
    The greedy do not concern you.

49. *Others all lock themselves in,*
    You alone live in the open.

50. *Others all tremble with fear,*
    You along have no apprehensions.'

51. *When Poverty's speech was finished*
    His expression was stern, his eyes enlarged.

52. *He lifted his robe and rose,*
    Descended the stairs, left the hall.

53. *'I will leave you*
    And go to Mount Shou-yang.

54. *The two sons of Ku-chu*
    Will walk along with me.'[68]
55. *I then left my mat*
    Apologized for being so unforthright.
56. *'I beg not to make a second mistake.*
    Hearing rightness I yield.
57. *I will dwell with you always*
    I will never tire of your presence.'
58. *Poverty then did not leave,*
    He accompanies me always.

The most significant quality of 'Expelling Poverty' is that unlike other rhapsodies it is written entirely in the tetrasyllabic meter of the *Book of Songs*. In addition, the piece makes extensive use of *Songs* formulae (in 11. 19, 23, 25, 26, 27). It almost appears that the poet were attempting to write a rhapsody in the form of a classical *Song*. The diction is remarkably simple for a rhapsody, and in no way does it obscure the poem's message. Nevertheless, 'Expelling Poverty' still displays the essential qualities of a rhapsody. It is structured around a dialogue-debate, which conforms to the fundamental rhetorical character of the genre. The poem is an argument between the poet's persona (Yang tzu) and the allegorical figure of poverty. Unlike the debates of most rhapsodies, however, there is no hidden criticism or disguised persuasion. The argument is direct and personal, and there is no ambiguity at the conclusion. Although we cannot be certain if Yang Hsiung wrote this piece, and if he did write it, there is no way of dating it, my guess would be that it could come from a later period of his poetic production, and after he had ostensibly abandoned the writing of rhapsodies. It is possible that when Yang Hsiung condemned the rhapsody, and resolved never to write one again, he was referring only to the epideictic rhapsody. Thus, he could have written this poem as an attempt to compose a rhapsody more consistent with his poetic ideals.

In theory, and perhaps even in practice, Yang Hsiung sought a reform of the rhapsody. Yang's early compositions like the 'Sweet Springs Rhapsody' and 'Barricade Hunt Rhapsody' were attempts to write poems of criticism in the guise of epideictic rhapsodies, and evidently he considered them failures. Thus, already in the 'Ch'ang Yang Rhapsody' we see Yang using a structure and technique that is reminiscent of Warring States persuasions, although the argument is still disguised and not directly stated. Then, as his interests turn to philosophy, Yang rejects the epideictic rhapsody in favor of a more direct, less verbally ornate style, which does not obscure the moral message. The 'Dissolving Ridicule', with its profusion of historical *exempla* and other old rhetorical techniques, is not only more direct, but is the first of Yang's rhapsodies to make a personal expression. 'Expelling Poverty', even if it is not by Yang Hsiung (and I believe it is), is a noble attempt at putting Yang's new poetic principles into practice: directness, plain diction, personal statement, and didacticism.

6

Epilogue

There is no question that Yang Hsiung was considered the leading poet of his day, and that his rhapsodies continued to be admired in later ages. Huan T'an recalls with delight his first introduction to Yang's writings during his youth.[1] In the Later Han dynasty Yang Hsiung was generally ranked as an equal of Ssu-ma Hsiang-ju.[2] The great Six Dynasties critic, Liu Hsieh, praises Yang Hsiung as one of the greatest writers up to that time: '[Yang Hsiung] may be considered the most profound both in the language he employs and the themes he treats. His ability to couch his brilliant thought in firm language is due to his ideas, which are both sagacious and profound; to his relentless search for wondrous and beautiful expressions; and to his untiring effort to think things through.'[3] In T'ang times the poet Tu Fu (712–770) singled out Yang Hsiung as the model he hoped to emulate in writing his rhapsodies.[4] One could find example after example of favorable remarks of this kind.

In the Republican period, however, the assessment of Yang Hsiung's poetic contribution was somewhat different. Cheng Chen-to (1898–1958), perhaps the leading literary historian of the post-1920 era, spoke of Yang Hsiung in extremely derogatory terms:

He was a typical Han writer and took imitation as his speciality. Since he had no independent thought, and even less strong emotion, all he had was the labor of chasing down beautiful words and applying the strange phrases used by all Han writers...Yang Hsiung's rhapsodies such as 'Sweet Springs', 'Plume Hunt', 'Ch'ang-yang', etc. also are patterned after Ssu-ma Hsiang-ju's rhapsodies. Except for his piles of beautiful words and strange characters, and his firm and brilliant style, he has absolutely nothing.[5]

Ch'en Shou-yi makes a similar assessment, lamenting that Yang's writing was 'far removed from the life and feelings of the common people'.[6]

What accounts for the almost universal distaste for Yang Hsiung's poems in modern Chinese criticism? Part of the reason perhaps lies in the great antipathy of post-May Fourth Movement scholars for anything written in the classical language. In the case of Yang Hsiung, however, there are other reasons that account for such wide-spread condemnation. First of all, he had the reputation of serving a usurper, which still earned him much opprobrium, particularly during a time of rising patriotism. Secondly, as a general rule modern students of Chinese literature have a great aversion to the rhapsody. Cheng Chen-to was particularly caustic in his attack on the genre:

They [= rhapsodies] lack any profound spirit, are without any true poetic beauty; they are merely multicolored, empty, lacquered cupboards. They have no great creativity; their authors are not great poets. Ever since Chia Yi and Mei Ch'eng, Han rhapsody writers closely followed Ch'ü Yüan and Sung Yü. But they did not capture the true poetic imagination of Ch'ü and Sung – only their dregs. We can say that the period of the two Han dynasties was a time when poetic imagination dissipated and poets were few.[7]

Essentially what Cheng and many of his contemporaries were objecting to was the artificiality and preciosity that characterized the rhapsody of the epideictic tradition. When one thinks of the Han rhapsody, the first poem that comes to mind is probably the 'Shang-lin Rhapsody'. Because of the florid, ornamental style used by Ssu-ma Hsiang-ju, somehow all rhapsodies came to be identified with the verbal effusion of this poem. Statements such as the following are common: 'The word *fu* means "display", and is applied to compositions of a descriptive nature on given themes, in contrast to more spontaneous lyrical pieces.'[8] '[The *fu* is] essentially descriptive in nature.'[9] As we have already seen, however, the scope of the rhapsody extends beyond purely formal, descriptive, virtuoso pieces, and includes poems that are intensely emotional, lyrical expressions of despair and complaints against a hostile world.

The most pervasive ingredient to be found in the Han rhapsody is unquestionably rhetoric. Ideally, the rhapsody was meant to serve a rhetorical function, particularly those poems written at court. Not all rhapsodies conform to the generic ideal, however, and it was the increasing use of the rhapsody for non-suasory, purely aesthetic purposes that led Yang Hsiung late in life to reject the genre. Even though many rhapsodies are not purely rhetorical, it is significant that almost all observe, no matter how perfunctorily, rhetorical conventions. It is thus useful in evaluating a rhapsody to note the extent to which rhetoric operates, and what effect, if any, it has.

The diversity in the corpus of Yang Hsiung's own rhapsodies is a good illustration of the non-uniformity of the genre. His poems range from the highly descriptive, epideictic pieces such as 'Sweet Springs', in which the primary emphasis seems to be on verbal decoration, to more personal expressions, written in plain language, such as 'Expelling Poverty'. The epideictic pieces, which would also include 'Ho-tung', and 'Barricade Hunt', contain at least a modicum of persuasion rhetoric. The ostensible emphasis in these rhapsodies is on portraying a place or event, but they also contain a moral message, which is usually conveyed in an indirect manner. Usually the rhapsody expresses a reprimand or criticism, but occasionally, as in 'Ho-tung', it praises something the poet wishes to encourage. The purely rhetorical rhapsodies are those poems that are concerned exclusively with moral suasion, and make ethical demonstration rather than verbal display the central focus of the poem. Yang Hsiung's major pieces of this type are 'Ch'ang-yang', and 'Dissolving Ridicule'. Actually, all of Yang's poems are in varying degrees rhetorical. For example, of the epideictic poems, some rhapsodies make more effective use of rhetoric than others. Thus, 'Barricade Hunt' adapts fanciful description to convey reprimands, while 'Sweet Springs' and 'Ho-tung' tend to concentrate on elaborate and hyperbolic description for its own sake.

In fact, in spite of Yang Hsiung's primary interest in rhetorical demonstration, it is perhaps the descriptive features of his rhapsodies that are most appealing to the Western reader. Arthur Waley once described the *fu* descriptions as a kind of 'word magic' that achieves its effect by 'a purely sensuous intoxication of rhythm and language'.[10] This aspect of the rhapsody is virtually impossible to translate into a Western language. The language of a rhapsody appears to a modern Chinese reader much like the language of the alliterative *Pearl* poems with their extensive repetition of synonyms and unfamiliar words. The description of the hunting scenes in *Sir Gawain and the Green Knight* (11. 1421–40) is extremely redolent of similar descriptions in Yang Hsiung's 'Barricade Hunt'.

One must remember that the rhapsody was still chanted in court during the time Yang was writing his poems, and that it is entirely possible that his rhapsodies were chiefly intended for oral recitation. It is impossible to know the exact manner in which these poems were recited, but even reading these poems with Mandarin pronunciation gives some idea of the 'intoxication of rhythm and language' that Waley mentions. The sounds of the numerous alliterative and rhyming binomes, for example, must have had a certain evocative effect as the rhapsode intoned them before the emperor and his court guests.

Yang Hsiung's artistry is best displayed, however, in his rhetorical skill, particularly in his use of the techniques of indirect criticism. One can imagine that if Yang Hsiung had written a rhetorical manual on the rhapsody, it would have included a long section on the devices of indirect criticism. It is thus primarily in his use of persuasion rhetoric that Yang Hsiung may lay claim to originality. The charge that he was a slavish imitator of Ssu-ma Hsiang-ju is not entirely justified, especially if one compares the use of rhetoric in 'Barricade Hunt' and 'Shang-lin'. Admittedly, Yang shows a great debt to the conventions developed by his predecessor, but at the same time it appears that Yang had a clearer idea of what effect he was trying to achieve. Ssu-ma Hsiang-ju intended 'Shang-lin' as a reprimand to Emperor Wu, but devoted almost all of the piece to an elaborate description of the park. The effect, then, is to make the final rhetorical section appear perfunctory and insincere, when it really is not. Yang Hsiung, on the other hand, never loses sight of his fundamental purpose. The reader has no doubt at the end of the poem that Yang Hsiung disapproves of the hunt. Yang was so concerned about making his persuasion convincing that he eventually concluded that the rhapsody was an ineffectual means of conveying criticism. His candor is admirable, but Yang Hsiung's disparagement of his own writing should not prohibit us from appreciating his genius.

Appendix I: The Dates of Yang Hsiung's Imperial Rhapsodies

Shortly after his arrival in Ch'ang-an, Yang Hsiung was commissioned to write four rhapsodies for the emperor: 'Sweet Springs Rhapsody', 'Ho-tung Rhapsody', 'Barricade Hunt Rhapsody', and 'Ch'ang-yang Rhapsody'. The dating of these poems has been a question that has bothered many scholars who have studied Yang Hsiung.[1] The reason for the befuddlement is that the information contained in the early sources is highly confusing. First of all, there is a question about the date of Yang's arrival in the capital. Pan Ku gives an account of this event in his 'Appraisal' appended to the 'Autobiography': 'In the beginning, when Hsiung was over forty years of age, he traveled from Shu to the capital. The Grand Marshal and General of Chariots and Cavalry Wang Yin was impressed with the elegance of his writings and summoned him to be an official at court.'[2] Based on this account, Yang would have had to arrive in Ch'ang-an sometime after 14 B.C. (Yang's fortieth birth-year). However, Wang Yin died in 15 B.C., when Yang was only thirty-nine.[3] This inconsistency has led some scholars to believe that instead of Wang Yin, the text should read Wang Ken, who was made Grand Marshall and General of Agile Cavalry in 13 B.C.[4] Others have suggested that the character 'four' in the expression 'over forty years of age' should read 'three', since the old form of the character for four could be easily confused with the character for three.[5] Tung Tso-pin, who accepts this emendation, places Yang's arrival in the capital in 22 B.C., or when Yang was thirty-two.[6] Another possible interpretation is that the number forty could be an approximate number or perhaps an error on Pan Ku's part.[7]

The question is further complicated, however, by contradictory information concerning the dates of the four rhapsodies. In the introductions Yang Hsiung wrote to these rhapsodies, all of which are contained in the 'Autobiography', Yang detailed the circumstances of the writing of the poems, but he did not specify the exact year in which they were written or presented to the throne. In order to clarify matters, I shall produce the relevant passages from the 'Autobiography'.

' Sweet Springs Rhapsody':
During the reign of Emperor Ch'eng one of the emperor's retainers recommended my writings as resembling the style of Ssu-ma Hsiang-ju. The emperor was about to perform the suburban sacrifices at the Great Altar in Sweet Springs and to the Sovereign Earth at Fen-yin, in order to seek an heir to succeed him. He summoned me to await orders in the Ch'eng-ming Hall. In the first month I accompanied the emperor to Sweet Springs. When they returned I presented the 'Sweet Springs Rhapsody' as an indirect criticism of the emperor.[8]

' Ho-tung Rhapsody':
In the third month sacrifices to the Sovereign Earth were to be held. The emperor then led all his subjects across the Great River, and gathered at Fen-yin...When I returned, I presented the 'Ho-tung Rhapsody' as an exhortation.[9]

' Barricade Hunt Rhapsody':
In the twelfth month there was a 'plume hunt', which I attended...I used the pretext of the 'Barricade Hunt Rhapsody' to make an indirect criticism of the emperor.[10]

' Ch'ang-yang Rhapsody':
The next year, the emperor, wishing to impress the Hu tribes with the great number of animals in the hunting preserve, in the autumn commanded the Yu Fu-feng to dispatch people into the Southern Mountains...I accompanied the emperor to the Bear Shooting Lodge. Upon our return I presented the 'Ch'ang-yang Rhapsody'.[11]

According to these accounts, all of these pieces were written within the space of two years. 'Sweet Springs', 'Ho-tung' and 'Barricade Hunt' were written in the same year, and 'Ch'ang-yang' was written a year later. A different account of these dates, however, is contained in surviving fragments of Liu Hsin's *Seven Summaries* (*Ch'i lüeh*):

' Sweet Springs Rhapsody', presented to the throne by Gentleman Candidate for Appointment Hsiung in the first month of the third year of Yung-shih (14 B.C.).[12]
' Plume Hunt Rhapsody', presented to the throne in the twelfth month of the third year of Yung-shih (13 B.C.).[13]
' Ch'ang-yang Rhapsody', presented to the throne in the first year of Sui-ho (8 B.C.).[14]

No *Seven Summaries* remarks on 'Ho-tung Rhapsody' survive.

To complicate this problem, Pan Ku's 'Appraisal' records that one year after Yang was recommended to the emperor by Wang Yin he presented the 'Plume Hunt Rhapsody' (= 'Barricade Hunt').[15] If Yang were over forty years of age, say about forty-three, this would make the year of presentation 11 B.C.

There have been a number of attempts to rationalize the inconsistencies of these accounts. The main method has been to determine the dates of all the relevant sacrifices at Sweet Springs and Fen-yin, and to discover which date fits the circumstances of Yang Hsiung's rhapsodies. In 32 B.C. the imperial sacrifices were moved from the suburbs (Sweet Springs, Fen-yin, and Yung) to the capital.[16] However, because Emperor Ch'eng was without an heir, the sacrifices were restored to the suburbs almost two decades later. The *Annals of Emperor Ch'eng* gives the date for this revival as the tenth month of Yung-shih 3 (November, 14 B.C.),[17] but a memorial dated A.D. 5 says the sacrifices were restored in the third month of Yung-shih 1 (May, 16 B.C.).[18] If Yung-shih 3 is the correct date, Liu Hsin's date for 'Sweet Springs Rhapsody' is impossible since Liu says the poem was presented in the first month of that year (March, 14 B.C.). This date for the revival of the sacrifices is generally considered incorrect, however, mainly because Pan Ku records a suburban sacrifice at Yung for the tenth month of 15 B.C., which would mean that the sacrifices had already been restored.[19] Thus, the date 16 B.C. is most probably the correct one.

The *Annals of Emperor Ch'eng* records four sacrifices at Sweet Springs and Ho-tung for the period with which we are concerned: 13, 11, 9, and 7 B.C.[20] We can rule out the years 9 and 7 B.C. as probably being too late (Yang would have been at least forty-five). Timoteus Pokora believes that 13 B.C. is the most plausible date.[21] A more likely date, however, is 11 B.C., for it is the only year in which a hunt is recorded in the same year as the suburban sacrifices.[22] Remembering that the 'Autobiography' places 'Barricade Hunt' in the same year as 'Sweet Springs' and 'Ho-tung', it would seem that this date fits the circumstances better than any other date.

However, there still remains the problem of the date of 'Ch'ang-yang Rhapsody', According to the 'Autobiography', this poem was written a year after 'Barricade Hunt'. Liu Hsin dates it much later: 8 B.C. Ch'ien Ta-hsin (1728–1804), agreeing that 'Barricade Hunt' was written in 11 B.C., says that the 'Autobiography' is correct and dates 'Ch'ang-yang' in 10 B.C. even though no hunt is mentioned for this year in the annals.[23] Shen Ch'in-han (1775–1832) argues, on the other hand, that the 'Barricade Hunt' and 'Ch'ang-yang', describe the same hunt, the hunt mentioned in the annals for the year 11 B.C. His argument is based on the fact that the hunt recorded in the annals was specifically held to impress the barbarians, and he notes that the 'Ch'ang-yang Rhapsody' deals exclusively with a barbarian hunt. Thus, Shen believes that the 'Autobiography' account has confused the year the rhapsody was presented to the throne (most likely 10 B.C.) with the year the hunt took place.[24] Either of these interpretations is acceptable. The important point is that both scholars agree that the poem was written around 11 B.C.

Having determined with a degree of certainty the date of Yang Hsiung's first rhapsodies written at the capital it is possible to arrive at a more satisfactory date for Yang's arrival in Ch'ang-an. Yang's letter to Liu Hsin helps somewhat in solving this riddle:

When I was first able to write I composed the 'Inscription on the District Lodge', the 'Eulogy to Wang Erh', the 'Inscription on the Staircase and Inner Gate', and the 'Inscription on the Four Corners of Ch'eng-tu'. There was a man from Shu named Yang Chuang who was a Gentleman at Court. He chanted these writings to Emperor Ch'eng. Emperor Ch'eng liked them and considered that they resembled the style of Ssu-ma Hsiang-ju. Because of this I was able to leave Shu and have an audience at court.[25]

This account corresponds with the briefer statement in the 'Autobiography'. It seems clear that Yang's first introduction at court was not by Wang Yin, but by Yang Chuang. Thus, Yang Hsiung was most probably younger than forty when he first came to the capital. The 'Appraisal' account of Yang's age is inaccurate in several places. First of all, Yang could not have been 'over forty' when he met Wang Yin, for as was mentioned above, Wang died in 15 B.C. when Yang was thirty-nine. Secondly, if Yang wrote his rhapsodies in 11 B.C. obviously he could not have been recommended to the emperor one year before by a man who had been dead for three years! The age of 'over forty' does agree, however, with the age Yang would have been at the time he wrote his rhapsodies in 11 B.C. (forty-three). It is possible that Pan Ku somehow confused Yang Hsiung's age at his arrival in the capital with his age when he wrote his first poems for the emperor. Yang could have been recommended by Wang Yin at an earlier date, perhaps shortly after Yang arrived from Shu at the request of Yang Chuang. This recommendation could have taken place anytime between 22 B.C. and 15 B.C.

Appendix II: Rhapsodies of Doubtful Authenticity

In addition to the poems discussed in the main text, Yang Hsiung is credited with three other rhapsodies all of which are somewhat suspect. The first of these, 'Examining the Spirit Rhapsody' (*He ling fu*), survives only in fragments in Li Shan's commentary to *The Literary Selections*.[1] Not enough of it survives to allow an adequate evaluation. The second piece is 'The Great Dark Rhapsody' (*T'ai-hsüan fu*). It is a typical frustration rhapsody, which makes use of historical example and the *itineraria*. It is preserved only in the *Garden of Ancient Literature*, which immediately casts suspicion on it.[2] The most serious objection to the poem's attribution is that Yang Hsiung himself claimed that when he wrote *The Great Dark*, he wrote no more rhapsodies. Thus, it seems strange that he would write a rhapsody with this title. The poem actually seems to have been inspired partly from the 'Dissolving Ridicule' and has several lines that closely resemble lines in this piece.[3] The style of the piece is rather crude and hardly worthy of Yang Hsiung. Mainly for this combination of reasons I consider it a prosopopeia or perhaps even an outright forgery.

The third poem that seems of dubious authenticity is the 'Shu Capital Rhapsody' (*Shu tu fu*), a long composition describing the city of Ch'eng-tu. Although the present text is long, it is incomplete, and survives in several versions. The longest text is in the *Garden of Ancient Literature*.[4] A short excerpt is also found in the *Compendium of Arts and Letters*,[5] and it is quoted frequently in Li Shan's commentary to *The Literary Selections*.[6] The earliest testimony to Yang's authorship is much earlier: it is cited in Liu K'uei's (fl. A.D. 291–299) commentary to the 'Three Capitals Rhapsody' (*San tu fu*) by Tso Ssu (fl. A.D. 265–305).[7]

There is not much internal evidence to prove or disprove Yang Hsiung's authorship. It is possible that Tso Ssu made use of Yang Hsiung's rhapsody in writing his own rhapsody on the Shu capital, for there are a number of phrases in Tso's piece that appear to echo Yang's rhapsody.[8] Similarities in language do not prove too much, however, since it is virtually impossible to determine which work is quoting from which. It is also conceivable that the piece ascribed to Yang Hsiung is based on the Tso Ssu rhapsody.

I am inclined in this case to respect the traditional attribution to Yang Hsiung. The style of the poem is crude and suggests the hand of a novice. Since this would have been one of Yang's first attempts at writing a rhapsody, one might expect the piece to exhibit amateurish qualities. I also consider the early third century attribution by Liu K'uei a reliable testimony to Yang Hsiung's authorship.

Appendix III: Chronology

53 B.C. Born in Ch'eng-tu.

24 B.C. Writes 'Contra *Sao*'.

ca. 20 B.C. Travels to Ch'ang-an. Designated Candidate for Appointment.

11 B.C. Writes 'Sweet Springs Rhapsody', 'Ho-tung Rhapsody', 'Barricade Hunt Rhapsody', 'Ch'ang-yang Rhapsody'.

ca. 10 B.C. Appointed Attendant Gentleman and Servitor at the Yellow Gate.

ca. 7 B.C. Writes 'Admonition on Wine'.

ca. 2 B.C. Composes *The Great Dark*. Writes 'Dissolving Ridicule' and 'Dissolving Objection'.

A.D. 5 Compiles *The Annotations Compendium*.

ca. A.D. 7 Compiles *Regional Words*.

A.D. 10 Falsely implicated in anti-Wang Mang plot, leaps from T'ien-lu Gallery. Designated Palace Grandee Without Specified Appointment. *Model Sayings* completed (?).

A.D. 13 Writes 'Dirge for the Empress'.

ca. A.D. 14 Presents 'Criticizing Ch'in, Praising Hsin'.

A.D. 18 Dies.

Notes to the text

PREFACE

1. Reprinted in *Die chinesische Anthologie: Übersetzungen aus dem Wen hsüan*, ed. Ilse Martin Fang, 2 vols. (Cambridge, Mass., 1958).
2. *Intrigues: Studies of the Chan-kuo Ts'e* (Ann Arbor, 1964).
3. *Un Poète de cour sous les Han: Sseu-ma Siang-jou* (Paris, 1964).
4. *Fu no seiritsu to tenkai* (The Formation and Development of 'Fu' in Chinese Literature) (Matsuyama, 1963).
5. *The Key of Remembrance: A Study of Chaucer's Poetics* (New Haven and London, 1963).
6. *Webster's New World Dictionary of the American Language* (Cleveland and New York, 1958), pp. 1128.

CHAPTER 1

1. See below for further discussion and references.
2. See below for further discussion and references.
3. This work was known as *The Annotations Compendium* (*Hsün tsuan*) or by the longer title *Annotations Compendium to the Ts'ang Chieh* (*Ts'ang Chieh hsün tsuan*). The *Ts'ang Chieh* was a special dictionary compiled in the Ch'in dynasty by the famous minister Li Ssu (ca. 280–208 B.C.). The dictionary contained the correct orthography for characters in Small Seal forms. It was revised repeatedly during the Former Han, and several conferences were convened to update the work and to add phonological glosses. Yang's work, in eighty-nine sections, was the product of a conference summoned by Wang Mang in A.D. 5. See *Han shu* 30.1721, Peking, Chung-hua shu-chü 1962 ed., hereafter cited as HS; Hsü Shen's 'Postface to the *Shuo-wen chieh-tzu*' (*Shuo-wen chieh-tzu hsü*), *Ch'üan Hou Han wen* [Complete Later Han Prose], 49.3b (in Yen K'o-chün, ed., *Ch'üan shang-ku San-tai Ch'in Han San-kuo Liu-ch'ao wen* [Complete Prose of high antiquity, the Three Eras, Ch'in, Han, Three Kingdoms, and Six Dynasties], Taipei, Shih-chieh shu-chü 1963 ed; hereafter cited as CW), trans. by K. L. Thern, *Postface of the Shuo-wen chieh-tzu* (Madison, Wisconsin, 1966), pp. 13–14. The fragments of the work have been collected by Ma Kuo-han, *Yü-han shan-fang chi yi-shu* [Fragments collected in the Jade Case Mountain Studio], ts'e 74, 66.6a–7a (Ch'ang-sha, Lang-huan kuan 1883 ed.).
4. Some scholars have doubted the attribution of the *Regional Words* to Yang Hsiung. The best discussion of the question is by Paul L-M Serruys, 'Prolegomena to the Study of the Chinese Dialects of Han Time According to *Fang Yen*', Diss. University of California, Berkeley 1956. See also Serruys' *The Chinese Dialects of Han Time According to Fang Yen* (Berkeley and Los Angeles, 1959).
5. For a good collection of Yang's prose works see *Ch'üan Han wen* [Complete Han Prose], 51–54 (hereafter cited as CHW) in CW.
6. Ssu-ma Hsiang-ju is credited with a statement about the rhapsody in *Hsi-ching tsa-chi* [Western Capital Miscellany], SPTK, 2.4a, but it is probably not authentic.
7. Chu Hsi (1130–1200) was especially critical of Yang. For a brief account of the attacks on Yang Hsiung see Alfred Forke, *Geschichte der mittelalterlichen chinesischen Philosophie* (Hamburg, 1934), pp. 78–83.
8. See Yves Hervouet, *Sseu-ma Siang-jou*, pp. 14–17, 69–134; W. Jablonski, 'Wen Wong', *Rocznik Orientalistyczny*, 21 (1957), 135–40.
9. See Appendix II.
10. The text is found in HS 87A.3516–21. See my study and translation in 'Two Studies on the Han *Fu*', *Parerga* 1 (1968), 18–28.
11. These include a work called 'Sao Expanded' (*Kuang sao*) and 'Rebutting Grief and Sorrow' (*P'an lao-ch'ou*) mentioned in HS 87A.3516.

12. The exact date of Yang's arrival in the capital is not known precisely. See Appendix I.
13. Ssu-ma Hsiang-ju was appointed Gentleman (*lang*) after presenting the emperor with a rhapsody on the imperial hunt; see HS 57A.2575. Emperor Hsüan had Wang Pao, while he was still a 'candidate for appointment', write poems for hunts and excursions. Later, he was selected as Grandee Remonstrant (*chien ta-fu*); see HS 64B.2829.
14. This information is recorded in the 'Appraisal' (*tsan*) to Yang Hsiung's *Han shu* biography (HS 87B.3583), which because of certain anachronisms and inaccuracies must be used with caution.
15. Both the 'Sweet Springs Rhapsody' and 'Ho-tung Rhapsody' are translated and discussed in Chapter 3.
16. These two poems are translated and discussed in Chapter 4.
17. The 'Appraisal' says: 'Over a year later Yang presented the "Plume Rhapsody" [= "Barricade Hunt Rhapsody"]. He was promoted to Gentleman and Servitor at the Yellow Gate' (HS 87B.3583). Yang himself in a poem titled 'Dissolving Ridicule' mentions that he held the two posts of Attendant Gentleman and Servitor at the Yellow Gate (HS 87B.3566). The position of Servitor at the Yellow Gate apparently was called in Han bureaucratic parlance an 'added office' (*chia kuan*), meaning a position held concurrently with another post; see HS 19A.739. It should be noted that the Yellow Gate was the entrance to the emperor's living quarters in the palace. Officials assigned to the Yellow Gate had close access to the emperor, for they supervised the presentation of memorials and visits to him. In addition, there is evidence that the Yellow Gate was the residence of the palace entertainers such as singers, musicians, and jesters. Since the rhapsody often was used as a form of entertainment, particularly toward the end of the Former Han, the Yellow Gate would be an appropriate assignment for a skilled poet. On the Yellow Gate see Timoteus Pokora, 'The Life of Huan T'an', AO 31 (1963), 550 and Jean-Pierre Diény, *Aux Origines de la poésie classique en Chine: étude sur la poésie lyrique à l'époque des Han*, pp. 94–100 (on the Yellow Gate entertainers).
18. Cf. *Shih chi* 117.3063, Peking, Chung-hua shu-chü 1959 ed. (hereafter cited as SC): 'When Ssu-ma Hsiang-ju presented the "Eulogy to the Great Man" the Son of Heaven was so delighted he felt like airily floating over the clouds, and he seemed to have a longing to roam about heaven and earth.'
19. Ch'un-yü K'un was an adviser of King Hui of Liang (370–ca. 319 B.C.) famous for his witticisms. See SC 126.3197–9, Hellmut Wilhelm, 'Notes on Chou Fiction', *Transition and Permanence; Chinese History and Culture* (Hong Kong, 1972), pp. 252–8; David R. Knechtges, 'Wit, Humor, and Satire in Early Chinese Literature (to A.D. 220)', MS 29 (1970–1), 83–5. Jester Meng (Yu Meng) is a famous wit from Ch'u (see SC 126.3200–2).
20. HS 87B.3575.
21. See Chapter V.
22. This piece is 'Admonition on Wine' (*Chiu chen*). It is contained in HS 92.3712–3. For a translation and discussion see Knechtges, 'Wit, Humor, and Satire', pp. 93–4.
23. I am referring to 'Expelling Poverty Rhapsody' translated and discussed in Chapter 5.
24. These works are Chin Chü-hsiang, *Han tai tz'u-fu chih fa-ta* [The Development of the Han Rhapsody] (Shanghai, 1931) and T'ao Ch'iu-ying, *Han fu chih shih te yen-chiu* [A study of the history of the Han Rhapsody] (Shanghai, 1939). Hsü Fu-kuan's recent article 'Hsi Han wen-hsüeh lun lüeh' [Summary discussion of Western Han literature], *Hsin-ya shu-yüan hsüeh-shu nien-k'an*, 13 (1971), 99–121 offers many original ideas on the rhapsody.
25. *Fushi taiyô* [Outline history of the rhapsody] (Tokyo, 1936); Chinese trans. by Yin Shih-ch'ü (1942), rpt. Taipei, 1966.
26. *Fu no seiritsu to tenkai.*
27. Waley's *The Temple and Other Poems* (New York, 1923) consists mainly of rhapsodies.
28. These translations have been collected and reprinted in *Die chinesische Anthologie: Übersetzungen aus dem Wen-hsüan*, 2 vols. (Cambridge, Mass., 1958).
29. *Chinese Rhyme-Prose: Poems in the Fu Form from the Han and Six Dynasties Periods* (New York and London, 1971).
30. *Topics in Chinese Literature* (Cambridge, Mass., 1953), pp. 26–9.
31. See *Sseu-ma Siang-jou*, pp. 135–85.
32. See his *Early Chinese Literature* (New York and London, 1962), pp. 254–85 and *Chinese Rhyme-Prose*, pp. 1–18.
33. 'The Scholar's Frustration: Notes on a Type of "Fu"', *Chinese Thought and Institutions*, ed. J. K. Fairbank (Chicago, 1957), pp. 310–19, 398–403.
34. *Ibid.*, p. 314.
35. See 'Yang Shyong, the *Fuh*, and Hann Rhetoric', Diss. University of Washington 1968; 'Narration,

Description, and Rhetoric in Yang Shyong's *Yeu-lieh fuh:* An Essay in Form and Function in the Hann *Fuh'*, *Transition and Permanence: Chinese History and Culture* (Hong Kong, 1972), pp. 359–77.

36. Ch'en Pen-li, *T'ai-hsüan ch'an-mi* [Explaining the secrets of *The Great Dark*], 1a–13b (*Chü hsüeh hsüan ts'ung-shu* ed.); T'ang Ping-chen, 'Yang Tzu-yün nien-p'u' [Chronological biography of Yang Hsiung], *Lun hsüeh* (April, 1937), pp. 76–91; (May, 1937), pp. 25–44; (June, 1937), pp. 59–83; and Tung Tso-pin, 'Fang yen hsüeh-chia Yang Hsiung nien-p'u' [Chronological biography of the dialectologist Yang Hsiung], *Chung-shan ta-hsüeh yü-yen li-shih yen-chiu so chou-k'an*, 8 (June, 1929), 82–8.

37. 'The Philosopher Yang Hsiung', JNCBRAS, 66 (1930), 108–10; 'Der Philosoph Yang Hiung', *Sinica*, 7 (1932), 169–78; *Geschichte der mittelalterlichen chinesischen Philosophie*, pp. 74–99.

38. 'Yang Hiung und Wang Mang', *Sinica-Sonderausgabe* 1 (1937), 14–34.

39. 'Zur Verteidigung des chinesischen Philosophen Yang Hsiung', MS 1 (1935–6), 186–91.

40. 'Yang Hsiung's Fa-yên (Worte strenger Ermahnung): Ein philosophischer Traktat aus dem Beginn der christlichen Zeitrechnung', *Sinologische Beiträge*, 4 (1939), 1–74.

41. In *Chu-tzu p'ing-yi* [Critiques of the philosophers], chaps. 34–5.

42. Originally published under the title *Fa yen shu cheng* [Annotation and investigation of *Model Sayings*], this work was revised and printed under the title *Fa yen yi shu* [Annotations of the meaning of *Model Sayings*] in 1933. The edition I use is the reprint by Yi-wen yin-shu kuan, Taipei, n.d.

43. *Fa-yen yi-shu* 10.1a.

44. See *Fa-yen yi-shu* 11.13b and 18.16b–17a.

45. For a detailed explanation of the system of correlations see Suzuki Yoshijirô, *Taigen eki no kenkyû* [Studies of *The Great Dark*] (Tokyo, 1964), pp. 41–83.

46. In addition to Suzuki, secondary studies include: Mitarashi Masaru, 'Yo Yû to Taigen' [Yang Hsiung and *The Great Dark*], *Shinagaku kenkyû*, 18 (1957), 22–32 and Hellmut Wilhelm, 'Das Zusammenwirken von Himmel, Erde, und Mensch', *Eranos Jahrbuch* (Zürich, 1963), pp. 317–50.

47. Some scholars have doubted the authenticity of the 'Appraisal'. It is not in the form of Pan Ku's other 'Appraisals' and it contains several errors. For example, it says that Yang was recommended to be Staff Clerk (*men-hsia shih*) by Wang Yin. The position of Staff Clerk did not exist during the Former Han, and Wang Yin was already dead when he would have recommended Yang to this post.

48. See 'Yang Shyong', pp. 26–30 for a discussion of the autobiography. The autobiography portion of the chapter includes everything before the 'Appraisal'. I refer to this part as 'Autobiography'. There are two complete translations of the entire *Han shu* biography: 'Yang Shyong', pp. 393–497 and F. M. Doeringer, 'Yang Hsiung and His Formulation of a Classicism', Diss. Columbia University 1971, pp. 232–306.

49. HS 30.1755.

50. Hereafter cited as WH. The edition used is the SPTK.

51. On the Li Shan commentary see 'Yang Shyong', pp. 21–3.

52. Hereafter cited as PTSC. The edition used is the reprint by Wen-hai ch'u-pan she (Taipei, 1966). For more information see 'Yang Shyong', pp. 13–14.

53. Hereafter cited as YWLC. The edition used is the reprint by Chung-hua shu-chü (Peking, 1965). See 'Yang Shyong', pp. 15–16 for more information.

54. Hereafter cited as CHC. The edition used is the reprint by Chung-hua shu-chü (Peking, 1962). For more information see 'Yang Shyong', pp. 16–17.

55. See 'Yang Shyong', pp. 17–19.

56. See 'Yang Shyong', pp. 19–21. There are two different editions: one edited by Han Yüan-chi (1118–post 1179) in nine *chüan* published in 1179, and now contained in *Tai-nan ko ts'ung-shu* (hereafter cited as KWY-A); another edition in twenty-one *chüan* published in 1232 by Chang Ch'iao (fl. 1230) with a commentary, and contained in SPTK (hereafter cited as KWY-B). The nine *chüan* edition is the preferred text in most cases.

57. See CHW.

58. I use the Hsin-hsing shu-chü edition (Taipei, 1963).

59. The best edition is the rare 1706 Yang-chou shih-chü edition.

CHAPTER 2

1. The 'Tribute of Yü' (*Yü kung*) in the *Book of Documents* contains frequent examples of *fu* in this sense: cf. *Shang shu* 3.1b, 3.2a, 3.3a, etc. The *fu* was probably a military tax; see Yang Lien-sheng, *Studies in Chinese Institutional History* (Cambridge, Mass., 1961), pp. 104–7.

2. See *Shuo-wen chieh-tzu ku-lin* [Collected glosses on *Shuo-wen chieh-tzu*] 6B.2770b and Bernhard Karlgren, 'Grammata Serica Recensa', BMFEA 29 (1957), 47, no. 104 (hereafter cited as GSR).

3. See Bernhard Karlgren, 'Loan Characters in Pre-Han Texts'. BMFEA 35 (1963), 84, no. 306 and 'Glosses on the Book of Documents', BMFEA 20 (1948), 130, no. 1328.

4. See GSR, p. 47, no. 104.

5. Nakashima Chiaki has studied this quotation in detail. See his *Fu no seiritsu to tenkai* [The formation and development of the 'Fu' in Chinese literature] (Matsuyama, 1963), pp. 59–74 and his 'Saden inyô shi no imi' [The meaning of quoting songs in the *Tso chuan*], *Shinagaku kenkyû* 10 (1953), 43–56. See also Yang Hsiang-shih, 'Tso chuan fu shih k'ao' [An examination of *fu shih* in *Tso chuan*], *K'ung Meng hsüeh-pao* 13 (April 9, 1967), 89–124; rpt. Taipei: Chung-hua ts'ung-shu pien shen wei-yüan hui, 1972.

6. Several of these poems are now in the *Book of Songs*. See *Tso chuan*, Wen 6 (*Shih* 131); Min 2 (*Shih* 79); Min 2 (*Shih* 54); and Yin 3 (*Shih* 57). The *Tso chuan* also contains two extemporized poems not included in the *Book of Songs*; see Yin 1 and Hsi 5.

7. Cf. *Lun yü* 16.13.

8. This commentary does not survive. Part of the passage is quoted in Mao Heng's commentary to *Shih* 50 (*Mao shih* 3.5b) where the ability to recite is given as one skill a great officer should possess.

9. HS 30.1755–6.

10. It should be observed that the English term 'chant' is only an approximation of the Chinese word *sung*. The distinction I make between singing and chanting is essentially the same as the one made by Chao Yuen-ren: 'Singing a song differs from chanting in that the singer is expected to sing the same tune on repetition. The fixed tune may have been deliberately composed by a composer or simply have grown from tradition into one or possibly several alternate versions; in any case the singer has less liberty with the tune than in chanting.' See 'Tone, Intonation, Singsong, Chanting, Recitative, Tonal Composition and Atonal Composition in Chinese', *For Roman Jakobsen* (The Hague, 1956), p. 57. See also Chu Tzu-ch'ing, *Shih yen chih pien* [Study of 'Poetry Gives Voice to Feelings'] (Taipei, 1964), p. 19 where *sung* is defined as 'rhythmical unaccompanied singing'.

11. *Shina bungaku kenkyû* [*Studies in Chinese literature*] (Kyoto, 1925), pp. 321–50. There were blind reciters at court who were charged with chanting poems of criticism; see *Kuo yü* [Conversations of the states] 1.4b–5a and *Shih chi* 4.142 (Mh, I, 272–3); Jean-Pierre Diény, *Aux Origines de la poésie classique en Chine* (Leiden, 1968), pp. 5–6. The *Rites of Chou* (*Chou li*) purports to describe the recitation techniques of the blind reciters, who learned them from the Grand Music Master (*T'ai shih*). There were six methods of recitation (*liu shih*), and one of them was called *fu* (see *Chou li* 6.13a). However, this description is highly idealized and may not even ante-date the Han dynasty (but see Bernhard Karlgren, 'The Early History of the Chou li and Tso Chuan Texts', BMFEA, 3 [1931], 2–8). There is also the problem of the later confusion of the six recitation techniques with the six poetic principles (*liu yi*) enunciated in the 'Mao shih Preface', which is generally acknowledged to be the work of Wei Hung of the first century A.D. Nakashima Chiaki (*Fu no seiritsu to tenkai*, pp. 38–41) has convincingly shown that the notion of *fu* contained in the 'Preface', which is the name of a poetic trope meaning something like 'direct narration', is a relatively late development, probably of the Later Han, and thus should not be considered in determining the pre-Han sense of *fu*. Actually, I think *fu* as the name of a poetic trope did not evolve until the *fu* was well established as the name of a poetic genre, and the idea of 'direct narration' was derived from the narrative quality of the *fu*.

12. Cf. Diény, p. 64, who translated this same passage differently. *Teng kao* also occurs in *Han shih wai chuan* [External Commentary to the Han *shih*], 7/25 (Hightower, p. 248) where it clearly alludes to a mountain. See also *Shuo yüan* [The story garden] 15.8a–9b. On the entire problem of *teng kao neng fu* see *Fu no seiritsu to tenkai*, pp. 79–94.

13. See Chang Ping-lin, *Kuo-ku lun-heng* [Discourses on Chinese Philology], *Chang shih ts'ung-shu* ed., p. 105, and Hellmut Wilhelm, 'The Scholar's Frustration: Notes on a Type of "Fu"', *Chinese Thought and Institutions*, ed. John K. Fairbank (Chicago, 1957), p. 399, n. 9. Nakashima disagrees with Chang's interpretation (*Fu no seiritsu to tenkai*, pp. 82–3).

14. There is some question about the authenticity of the *fu* attributed to Hsün tzu; see p. 18. The *fu* ascribed to the pseudo-Sung Yü are most likely Han or later.

15. The earliest classification to label Ch'ü Yüan's works *fu* is the *Han shu* 'Summary on Songs and Rhapsodies'; see HS 30.7, 1747.

16. The earliest record of Ch'ü Yüan's life is in SC 84 (trans. *Records*, I, 499–508; David Hawkes, *Ch'u Tz'u* [London and New York, 1959], pp. 11–15).

17. There are several bibliographies that give a good indication of the great amount of research on this

subject. See J. R. Hightower, 'Ch'ü Yüan Studies', *Silver Jubilee Volume of the Zinbun-Kagaku Kenkyushyo, Kyoto University* (Kyoto, 1954), pp. 192–223; Jao Tsung-yi, *Ch'u tz'u shu-lu* [Bibliography of the *Ch'u tz'u*] (Hong Kong, 1956); and Chiang Liang-fu, *Ch'u tz'u shu-mu wu chung* [Five *Ch'u tz'u* bibliographies] (Peking, 1961).

18. There was a work known as *Ch'u tz'u* that circulated prior to Wang Yi (see SC 122.3143, HS 64A.2791, 64B.2821). Wang Yi claimed that Liu Hsiang arranged the *Ch'u tz'u* into sixteen *chüan*. No text of the *Ch'u tz'u* is mentioned in the 'Treatise on Bibliography', which has led some scholars to doubt this statement. One possible reason the 'Treatise' does not list the *Ch'u tz'u* is that unlike later bibliographies, the 'Treatise' had no *chi pu* or section for literary collections. The works of Ch'ü Yüan and others, which make up most of the *Ch'u tz'u*, were listed individually in the 'Summary on Songs and Rhapsodies', and need not have been catalogued again as *Ch'u tz'u*.

19. See Arthur Waley, *The Nine Songs: a Study of Shamanism in Ancient China* (London, 1955), and David Hawkes, *Ch'u tz'u* (London, 1959), pp. 35–44. Chen Shih-hsiang has recently tried to salvage the 'Nine Songs' as a single poem; see 'On Structural Analysis of the Ch'u Tz'u Nine Songs', *Tamkang Review* 2 (April 1971), 3–14.

20. Arthur Waley, *The Nine Songs*, p. 13.

21. Not all of the 'Nine Songs' consists of encounters between male and female deities. Some of the spirits may have been male, for whom there presumably were female shamans.

22. See his *Naissance de l'élégie chinoise* (Paris, 1967), pp. 154–73; 196–211.

23. See Hawkes, *Ch'u Tz'u*, p. 21.

24. Attempts have been made to read the 'Li Sao' as a love allegory, but as David Hawkes has remarked, 'in order to obtain a consistent interpretation as love-allegory, it would be necessary to suppose that the original poem had been subjected to interpolation on so large a scale as to constitute its total rewriting' (p. 213). On the 'Li Sao' allegory see the excellent study by C. H. Wang, 'Sartorial Emblems and the Quest: A Comparative Study of the *Li Sao* and the *Faerie Queene*', *Tamkang Review* 2.2, 3.1 (October 1971–April 1972), 309–28.

25. See 'The Quest of the Goddess', AM 13 (1967), 71–94.

26. Cf. David Hawkes, *Ch'u Tz'u*, pp. 6–7: 'I think there can be little doubt that Sao-style verse was evolved from the Song style and that it was designed for recitation of long narrative poems. Whether or not it was chanted to some sort of tune, it must have been nearer to speech than song...' Nakashima Chiaki, in examining the structure of the *sao* line, finds that it consists of two caesuras, a major caesura (at the *hsi*) and a minor caesura (at the key word). He believes the particles, while containing some meaning, are primarily used for rhythmic effect. See *Fu no seiritsu to tankai*, pp. 117–64, 208–11. On the prosody of the 'Li Sao' see A. C. Graham, 'The Prosody of the *Sao* Poems in the *Ch'u Tz'u*', AM 10 (1963), 119–61.

27. Note that Ssu-ma Ch'ien says in his 'Letter to Jen An' (*Pao Jen An shu*) that Ch'ü Yüan 'recited [*fu*] the "Li Sao!"' (HS 62.2735; the SC version reads 'Ch'ü Yüan composed [*chu*] the "Li Sao"' [SC 130.3300]).

28. 'Quest of the Goddess', p 82. See also Hellmut Wilhelm, 'The Scholar's Frustration'.

29. A term coined by Ernst Curtius for example of *adynata* (stringing together impossibilities) in medieval Latin literature. See *European Literature and the Latin Middle Ages*, trans. Willard R. Trask (New York and Evanston, 1953), p. 95.

30. See 'Quest of the Goddess'.

31. *Ch'u tz'u pu chu* [Supplementary commentary to *Ch'u tz'u*] 5.268–88, Hong Kong, Chung-hua shu-chü 1963 ed., trans. Hawkes, *Ch'u Tz'u*, pp. 81–7.

32. 'Quest of the Goddess', p. 87.

33. For a more thorough discussion of this work see my article 'The *Fu* Chapter of *Hsün-tzu*', in *Wen-lin* II, ed. Chow Tse-tsung (Madison, Wisconsin, 197?).

34. *Hsün tzu*, SPTK, 18.9b–15a. The entire chapter has been translated by Hermann Köster, *Hsün-tzu* (Kaldenkirchen, 1967) and in my article listed above, where other translations are noted.

35. 'The Scholar's Frustration', pp. 316–17.

36. See *Chan-kuo ts'e*, SPPY, 17.4b–5a and *Han shih wai-chuan* 4/25. It has been translated by J. J. L. Duyvendak, TP 26 (1929), 89–90; James R. Hightower, *Han Shih Wai Chuan* (Cambridge, 1952), pp. 151–2; J. I. Crump, *Chuan-Kuo Ts'e* (London, 1970), p. 269; Hellmut Wilhelm, 'The Scholar's Frustration', p. 317.

37. The titles could be puns. For example, *Chen* means both 'needle' and 'admonition'. It is difficult to discover any applicable puns in Cloud (*Yün*) and Silkworm (*Ts'an*), however; see 'The *Fu* Chapter of *Hsün-tzu*'.

38. HS 30.1753.
39. HS 30.1753, n. 2.
40. See Nakashima 1965, pp. 170–2, for a discussion of the similarities between the 'Small Song' and the coda of the *Ch'u tz'u* poems.
41. Cf. Aristotle's definition of rhetoric: 'So let Rhetoric be defined as the faculty [power] of discovering in the particular case what are the available means of persuasion' (*Rhetoric* 1.2, trans. Lane Cooper, *The Rhetoric of Aristotle* [New York, 1932; 1960], p. 7).
42. Kenneth Burke, *A Rhetoric of Motives* (1950; rpt. Berkeley and Los Angeles, 1969), p. 41.
43. There is disagreement about the existence of an oratorical tradition in ancient China; see V. A. Rubin, 'Byl li v istorii kitaiskoi literatury etap oratoskogo istkusstva?' *Narody Azii i Afrikii*, No. 5 (1962), pp. 133–4. On the oratory of the *Book of Documents* see Robert T. Oliver, *Communication and Culture in Ancient India and China* (Syracuse, 1971), pp. 100–20.
44. Even Meng tzu acknowledged the necessity for disputation (see *Meng tzu* 3B.9).
45. See Hellmut Wilhelm, 'The Scholar's Frustration', p. 315. On the *Tsung-heng chia* see J. I. Crump, *Intrigues: Studies of the Chan-kuo Ts'e* (Ann Arbor, 1964), pp. 90–3; Peter Theunissen, *Su Ts'in und die Politik der Längs-und-Quer-Achse im chinesischen Altertum* (Breslau, 1938); Ku Nien-hsien, *Tsung-heng chia yen-chiu* [A study of the Tsung-heng chia] (Taipei, 1969).
46. Ma Kuo-han has collected what he calls the 'lost writings' of the Tsung-heng school; see *Yü-han shan-fang chi yi-shu, ts'e*, 72–3.
47. See 'The Scholar's Frustration', p. 315.
48. Crump, *Intrigues*, p. 101.
49. See Theunissen, p. 13. It has been translated by C. S. Kimm in AM 4 (1927), 108–46. An extensive discussion of *Kuei-ku tzu* is found in Yü Yen, *Chung-kuo cheng-lüeh hsüeh shih* [A history of Chinese political strategy] (Nanking, 1933), pp. 55–93 and the same author's *Kuei-ku tzu hsin-chu* [New commentary on *Kuei-ku tzu*] (Shanghai, 1937).
50. Chung Feng-nien's *Kuo-ts'e k'an-yen*, *Yen-ching hsüeh-pao* Monograph No. 11 (Peiping, 1936), provides a fairly complete list of the different sources in which similar persuasions occur.
51. CKT, SPPY, 3.2a–3a. This passage has also been translated by G. Margouliès, *Le Kou-wen chinois* (Paris, 1926), pp. 13–18; Crump, *Intrigues*, pp. 31–5; Crump, *Chan-Kuo Ts'e*, pp. 55–8.
52. *Institutio Oratoria*, v., xi, 6; trans. H. E. Butler, *Institutio Oratoria* (1920–2; rpt. London, 1960), i, 275.
53. See Derk Bodde, *China's First Unifier* (1938; rpt. Hong Kong, 1967), pp. 223–7.
54. *Anatomy of Criticism* (1957; rpt. New York, 1967), p. 245.
55. *Inst. Or.*, viii, iii, 5–6.
56. See Crump, *Intrigues*, pp. 115–22 and *Chan-Kuo Ts'e*, pp. 17–20. On the use of indirection in Chinese rhetoric see Oliver, pp. 98–9, 266.
57. CKT, 15.1b.
58. There are the *fu* attributed to the pseudo-Sung Yü, but these are of doubtful authenticity, and are impossible to date. On the authenticity of Sung Yü's *fu* see Lu K'an-ju, *Sung Yü* (Shanghai, 1929); Liu Ta-pai, 'Sung Yü fu-p'ien wei' [Forgery of the Sung Yü *fu-p'ien*], *Hsiao-shuo yüeh-pao* 17 (1929), 7 pp.; Yang Yin-tsung, 'Sung Yü fu k'ao' [An investigation of the Sung Yü rhapsodies], *Ta-lu, tsa-chih* 27.3 (1963), 19–24, 27.4 (1963), 26–32; Asano Michiari, 'So Gyoku no sakuhin no shingi ni tsuite' [On the reliability of the works of Sung Yü], *Kambun gakkai kaihô* 12 (April, 1961), 3–12.
59. See Chang Ch'ün, 'Han ch'u te tsung-heng chia ho tz'u-fu chia' [Rhapsodists and the School of Politicians of the early Han], *The Hong Kong Baptist College Journal*, 2.1 (March, 1964), 15–27 and Nakashima Chiaki, *Fu no seiritsu to tenkai*, pp. 158–64.
60. His biography is in SC 97.2697–2701 (trans. *Records*, i, 275–80) and HS 43.2111–16.
61. *Wen-hsin tiao-lung chiao-chu* [Collation notes on The Literary Mind and the Carving of Dragons] (Taipei, 1962), p. 298.
62. Cf. Hervouet, p. 151: 'Nous n'avons pas le texte des trois *fou* qui sont mis sous son nom dans le chapitre bibliographique du *Han chou*, mais il est probable que ces *fou* devaient être encore proches des oeuvres des Diplomatistes.'
63. His biography is in SC 97.2701–5 (trans. *Records*, i, 280–3) and HS 43.2116–18.
64. See T. Bönner, *Übersetzung des zweiten Teiles der 24. Biographie Sseu-ma Ts'iens (Kià-i)* (diss. Berlin, 1908) and *Alte chinesische Gedankenkreise* (Berlin, 1912); *Records*, i, 508–16.
65. The 'Lament' is found in SC 84.2493–5; HS 48.2222–5; WH 60.18b–22a; YWLC 40.729. The WH places it in the *Tiao-wen* (lament) category. It has been translated by Bönner; G. Margouliès, *Le Kou-wen chinois*, pp. 66–7, reprinted in *Anthologie raisonnée de la litterature chinoise* (Paris, 1948), pp. 206–7; Anna Akhmatova, in Kuo Mo-jo and N. T. Federenko, eds., *Antologiia kitaiskoi poezi* (Moscow,

1957), I, 199–201; Burton Watson, *Records*, I, 510–11, reprinted in *Anthology of Chinese Literature*, ed. Cyril Birch and Donald Keene (New York, 1965), pp. 140–1; and D. R. Knechtges, 'Two Studies on the Han *Fu*', *Parerga* 1 (1968), 10–13.

66. See Knechtges, 'Two Studies', pp. 31–2, 38–9, for an analysis of the prosody.
67. Knechtges, 'Two Studies', pp. 10–11.
68. 'The Self as Agent', *The Great Ideas Today 1968*, ed. Robert M. Hutchins and Mortimer J. Adler (Chicago, 1968), pp. 91–7.
69. James R. Hightower, 'Chia Yi's "Owl Fu"', *Asia Major* 8 (December 1959), 125. It is found in SC 84.2497–2500; HS 48.2226–9; WH 13.20b–25b; YWLC 92.1609–10. It has been translated by Hightower, 'Chia Yi's "Owl Fu"', pp. 127–9 and was reprinted in *Anthology of Chinese Literature*, pp. 138–40. Other translations include: H. A. Giles, *Adverseria Sinica* (Shanghai, 1914), pp. 1–10; R. Wilhelm, *Die chinesische Literatur* (Wildpark-Potsdam, 1926), pp. 111–12; *Records*, I, 512–15 reprinted in *Chinese Rhyme-Prose*, pp. 25–8; A. Adolis, *Antologiia*, pp. 202–5.
70. Cf. Hightower, 'Chia Yi's "Owl Fu"', p. 125: 'But "The Owl" is not a prose composition dressed up in the trappings of verse; it is a tightly organized poem in a regular meter.'
71. Chia Yi is attributed (most likely wrongly) with one piece in the *Ch'u tz'u* titled 'Sorrow for Troth Betrayed' (*Hsi shih*) which has been translated by David Hawkes, *Ch'u Tz'u*, pp. 115–18. There is also a fragment of a rhapsody titled 'The Bellstand' (*Chü fu*), which is too brief to evaluate (see KWY-A 1.12b; KWY-B 21.1a; YWLC 44.790; CHC 16.397; PTSC 111.7b). A late source ascribes to him an extremely interesting poem titled 'Dry Clouds Rhapsody' (*Han yün fu*), which seems to be a wrong attribution or a late forgery (see my 'Two Studies', pp. 45–60 for a complete discussion of this piece).
72. *Records*, I, 443.
73. See Hervouet, pp. 25–6.
74. They are contained in his HS biography (HS 51.2359–65) and WH 39.18b–24b. They have been translated by von Zach, II, 729–34.
75. See the title mentioned in Li Shan's *Literary Selections* commentary (WH 27.7b). Two rhapsodies of doubtful authenticity have been attributed to him: 'The Rabbit Garden of the Prince of Liang' (*Liang wang T'u-yüan fu*), which is found no earlier than a T'ang dynasty source (YWLC 65.1162; KWY-A 1.14a–15b; KWY-B 3.5a–7b); 'The willows of the Lodge for Forgetting Troubles' (*Wang-yu kuan liu fu*) contained in HCTC 4.3a, CHC 24.588, and YWLC 65.1162.
76. It is contained in WH 34.1a–17b and YWLC 57.1021–3 (fragment). It has been translated by von Zach, II, 607–17; John Scott, *Love and Protest: Chinese Poems from the Sixth Century B.C. to the Seventeenth Century A.D.* (New York, 1972), pp. 37–48; David R. Knechtges and Jerry Swanson, 'Seven Stimuli for the Prince: the Ch'i-fa of Mei Ch'eng', MS 29 (1970–1), 99–116; and Hans H. Frankel in his forthcoming book *The Flowering Plum and the Palace Lady: Interpretations of Chinese Poetry*.
77. See 'The Great Summons' (*Ta chao*) and 'Summoning the Soul' (*Chao hun*) translated by David Hawkes, *Ch'u Tz'u*, pp. 101–14.
78. For an excellent discussion of the descriptive technique used in the 'Seven Stimuli' see Frankel's book mentioned above.
79. See 'The Squire of Low Degree' 11. 27–60; Chaucer's *Parliament of Fowls* 11. 176–82, 323–64 and *The Knight's Tale* 11. 2919–24 (probably based on *Teseida*, xi, 22–4); Guillaume de Lorris' *Roman de la rose* 11. 605–9; and Spenser's *Faerie Queene*, i, 1, st. 8–9.
80. *Poetria nova* 224–5, in Edmond Faral, *Les Arts poétiques du XIIᵉ et du XIIIᵉ siècle* (Paris, 1924), p. 204. Faral discusses *expolitio* and *interpretatio*, two of the most important means of amplification (pp. 63–7).
81. HS 57B.3575.
82. T. C. Burgess, 'Epideictic Literature', *Studies in Classical Philology*, III (Chicago, 1902), 215.
83. *Early Chinese Literature*, p. 268.
84. *Early Chinese Literature*, p. 268.
85. This point is also made by Frankel; see n. 76.
86. See the definition by Li Shan in WH 7.2a, commentary. Donald Gibbs proposes to render *feng* as 'Suasion', which seems to accord with the word's etymology; see 'Notes on the Wind: The Term "Feng" in Chinese Literary Criticism', *Transition and Permanence: Chinese History and Culture* (Hong Kong, 1972), pp. 285–93.
87. See *Po-hu t'ung te lun* (Comprehensive discussion at White Tiger Lodge), A.51a, *Han Wei ts'ung-shu* (Hsin-hsing shu-chü 1966 rpt.).

88. 'Master Void' is in SC 117.3002–15; HS 57A.2543–5; WH 7.23b–33b and has been translated by Waley, *The Temple*, pp. 41–3 (excerpts); von Zach, I, 103–7; Watson, *Records*, II, 301–7 (reprinted in *Chinese Rhyme-Prose*, pp. 30–7): 'Shang-lin Rhapsody' is in SC 117.3016–43; HS 57A.2547; WH 8.1a–19b and has been translated by von Zach, I, 108–17; Watson, *Records*, II, 307–21 (reprinted in *Chinese Rhyme-Prose*, pp. 37–51 and *Early Chinese Literature*, pp. 273–84). 'Rhapsody Lamenting the Second Emperor of Ch'in' is in SC 117.3055 and HS 57B.2591; it has been translated by Watson, *Records*, II, 331–2. 'The Great Man Rhapsody' is in SC 117.3056–62 and HS 57B.2591; it has been translated by Watson, *Records*, II, 332–5.
89. See Hervouet, pp. 222–3, 259–74 for a detailed discussion and historical account of the Shang-lin Park.
90. Henceforth, the designation 'Shang-lin Rhapsody' refers to the combination of both 'Master Void' and the sequel 'Shang-lin'.
91. HS 57A.2547.
92. See *Sseu-ma Siang-jou*, pp. 260–2.
93. HS 57A.2559, trans. *Records*, II, 113.
94. Charles Rowan Beye, *The Iliad, the Odyssey, and the Epic Tradition* (Garden City, N.Y., 1966), p. 89.
95. *Walt Whitman's Poems*, ed. Gay Wilson Allen and Charles T. Davis (New York, 1959), p. 54.
96. *Sseu-ma Siang-jou*, p. 328.
97. For the meaning of the term see Curtius, p. 135.
98. See Suzuki Torao, *Fushi taiyô*, pp. 46–7.
99. See his review of Hervouet in TP 52 (1965), 167.
100. See Alfred Körte, *Hellenistic Poetry*, trans. Jacob Hammer and Moses Hadas (New York, 1929), p. 271. On the connection between lexicography, glossography, and abstruse language in Lykophron's poetry see Wilhelm von Christ, Otto Stählin, and Wilhelm Schmid, *Geschichte der Griechischen Literatur* (München, 1920), II, 116.
101. 'Archaïsmes de prononciation en chinois vulgaire', TP 40 (1950), 45, n. 3.
102. Wayne Shumaker, *Literature and the Irrational* (New York, 1960), p. 69. For a complete discussion of Ssu-ma Hsiang-ju's use of *impressifs* see Hervouet, pp. 340–59.
103. *Sseu-ma Siang-jou*, p. 338.
104. *Sseu-ma Siang-jou*, p. 297.
105. HS 57B.2596. On Hsi-wang-mu see Homer H. Dubs, 'An Ancient Chinese Mystery Cult', *Harvard Theological Review* 35.4 (1942), 221–40.
106. HS 57B.2598. These lines are patterned on 'Distant Wandering' 11. 87–8.
107. HS 87B.3575. According to Ssu-ma Ch'ien, the emperor upon reading the 'Great Man Rhapsody' was so happy he 'felt like ascending the clouds and travelling Heaven and Earth' (SC 117.3063).
108. *Sseu-ma Siang-jou*, p. 301.
109. *Sseu-ma Siang-jou*, p. 301, n. 4.
110. See HS 51.2365.
111. See HS 51.2367.
112. From *Lun yü* 17.20.
113. HS 64B.2829.
114. See HS 64B.2821–30 for Wang Pao's Biography.
115. See HS 64B.2829.
116. In WH 17.5a–23a. I have done an unpublished translation of this piece.
117. There is a 'Flute Rhapsody' (*Ti fu*) attributed to the pseudo-Sung Yü, which was written most likely in the Six Dynasties period.
118. WH 17.15a–16b.
119. This piece exists only in fragments, which have been collected in CHW 35.1b–2a.
120. This piece is attributed to Liu Hsiang in the 'Chess Discourse' (*Po yi lun*) cited in Li Shan's *Literary Selections* commentary (WH 52.23b). Elsewhere it is attributed to Ma Jung (A.D. 79–166) (see KWY-A 2.17b, KWY-B 5.9b, YWLC 74.1271).
121. See HS 87A.3515.

CHAPTER 3

1. See Appendix I for a discussion of the dating of these pieces.
2. See HS 25A.1218.

3. See HS 25A.1231.
4. See HS 87A,3534–5.
5. See HS 25B.1221–2.
6. See HS 25B.1254. The vote was 50 to 8. See the recent study by Michael Loewe, 'K'uang Heng and the Reform of Religious Practices (31B.C.)', AM 17.1 (1971), 1–27.
7. See HS 25B.1254.
8. See HS 25B.1256.
9. See HS 25B.1258–9.
10. See HS 25B.1259.
11. Wang Pao's 'Ode on Sweet Springs Palace' (*Kan-ch'üan kung sung*) is contained in YWLC 62.1114–15 and CHW 42.10b–11a; Liu Hsin's 'Sweet Springs Palace Rhapsody' (*Kan-ch'üan kung fu*) is found in KWY-A 2.10b–11a; KWY-B 21.3a–b; YWLC 62.1112; CHC 24.569–70.
12. This is the 'Rhapsody on Viewing the Immortals' (*Wang hsien fu*) in YWLC 78.1338 and PTSC 102.3b, 4a. It has been translated by T. Pokora, 'Huan T'an's *Fu* on Looking for the Immortals', AO 28 (1960), 361–6.
13. In HS 87A.3523–34; WH 7.1a–14b. It has been translated by von Zach, I, 93–8, and Elma E. Kopetsky, 'Two *Fu* on Sacrifices by Yang Hsiung, *The Fu on Kan-ch'uan* and *The Fu on Ho-tung*', *Journal of Oriental Studies*, 10 (1972), 104–14.
14. The Ch'eng-ming Hall was where the writing of government documents and other official compositions was done; see Pan Ku's 'Western Capital Rhapsody' (*Hsi-tu fu*), WH 1.13b.
15. HS 87A.3522.
16. On the standard divisions of a rhapsody see Suzuki Torao, pp. 53–4.
17. Yen Shih-ku (HS 87A.3522, n. 1) explains *ming hao* ('bright titles') as 'Praising the emperor by all the accumulated epithets for the Three August Ones and Five Emperors'. Li Chou-han (WH 7.2a) says the term refers to the honorific titles of the sacrificial animals such as those mentioned in *Chou li* 6.32a. An ox was called the 'single head great footprint' and pig, 'stiff bristles'. Either explanation is possible.
18. The exact identity of these legendary rulers is difficult to determine. Fu-hsi and Shen-nung are consistently named as members of the Three August Ones, and the third member has been variously given as Nü-wa, Chu-jung, the Yellow Emperor, or Sui-jen. On this problem see Ku Chieh-kang and Yang Hsiang-k'uei, *San-huang k'ao* [Studies of the Three Emperors], *Yenching Journal of Chinese Studies*, Monograph Series No. 8 (Pei-p'ing, 1936) and Karlgren, *Legends and Cults*, p. 232. For varying versions of the Five Emperors formula see Tjan Tjoe Som, *Po Hu T'ung*, 2 vols. (Leiden, 1949), I, 233–4 and *Ku shih pien* 7, pt. 2, *passim*.
19. Yen Shih-ku (HS 87A.3523, n. 4) explains this line as a reference to the procession which 'spread out like stars and moved like Heaven'. It is difficult to know if a metaphor is implied here. Judging from the following couplet it would seem that astronomical-supernatural activity is being indicated.
20. The Twinkler is Chao-yao (γ Boötis, according to Ho Peng-yoke, *The Astronomical Chapters of the Chin shu* [Paris and The Hague, 1961], p. 81). Chao-yao was also known as the Spear (see SC 27.1294; HS 26.1275; Mh, III, 343). According to the *Star Classic* (*Hsing ching*), *Ts'ung-shu chi-ch'eng* ed., A. 39, it had control over barbarian troops. The Great Yin (β and δ Scorpionis) is the name of a year-marker in Han times, and has other names including Green Dragon and Heavenly Unity (see HNT 3.16a). The Angular Arranger is Kou-chen (δ, ε, ζ, & 6B Ursae Minoris, the Piazzi star viʰ 21 [46 Camelopardis], and 323B Cephei) represents the 'inner palace, the Empress and the abode of the Great Emperor' (Ho Peng Yoke, p. 67).
21. K'an (the cover?) represents Heaven; Yü (the container?), Earth (see HNT 3.14b). K'uei occurs frequently alone as the name of a one-legged monster (see SC 74.1912; Mh, v, 310–11; *Kuo yü* 4.8b; *Shuo yüan* 18.7b; Karlgren, *Legends and Cults*, p. 258). According to the *Shuo wen*, K'uei and Hsü are synonyms, and here they are combined into a binome. See Chang Heng's 'Rhapsody on the Eastern Capital' (*Tung-ching fu*), WH 3.31a for a similar usage. Hsü-k'uang is vaguely identified as a 'rat-ghost' or a 'headless ghost'.
22. The Eight Spirits seem to refer to the Spirits of the eight directions; cf. SC 28.1367; HS 25A.1202; HS 6.191; HS 46.2198.
23. Ch'ih-yu was known as a war-god and inventor of weapons; see *Legends and Cults*, pp. 283–6.
24. Literally 'the imperial carriage', metonymy for 'emperor'.
25. Mount Ch'uan-luan was a mountain south of the Sweet Springs Palace. Ch'ang-ho is the name of the gate to Heaven; cf. 'Li sao' 1. 105 and 'Distant Wandering' 1. 47.
26. The Heaven Penetrating Tower (T'ung-t'ien t'ai) was built in the spring of 109 B.C. by

Emperor Wu as a place for attracting spirits and immortals. See SC 12.479, 28.1400; *Records*, II, 63; HS 6.193; HS 25B.1242; Mh, III, 508, HFHD, II, 90.

27. See *San-fu huang-t'u* (Imperial design of the Three Adjuncts), SPTK, 2.6a for a description of these two viewing towers (Feng-luan and Shih-kuan), which were outside the Sweet Springs Palace. The Stone Gate is also known as the Stone Watchtower (Shih-ch'üeh).

28. Or, following Yen Shih-ku (HS 87A.3527, n. 1): 'Piled up precipitously it creates a shape.'

29. According to the *Story of Emperor Wu* (*Wu-ti ku-shih*) cited in YWLC 83.1428 Emperor Wu planted artificial trees, making the branches of coral and leaves of jade. The *San-fu huang-t'u* 2.5b attempts to identify some 320 locust trees on the north bank of Sweet Springs Valley as the 'jade trees' mentioned in this poem. Undoubtedly, these trees are artificial.

30. The 'bronze men' (*chin jen*) are statues over ten-feet tall that the Chinese captured from the Hsiung-nu in 120 B.C. Later sources claim they were Buddhist images. See Hatani Ryôtei, 'Kyûto-ô no kinjin ni tsuite' (On the metal statues of King Hsiu-ch'u), *Shirin*, 3 (1918), 31–46; Shiratori Kurakichi, 'On the Territory of the Hsiung-nu Prince Hsiu-t'u Wang and His Metal Statues for Heaven-Worship', MTB, 5 (1930), 1–77 (esp. 25–71); H. H. Dubs, 'The "Golden Man" of Former Han Times', TP, 33 (1937), 1–14; 191–2; J. R. Ware, 'Once More the "Golden Man"', TP, 34 (1938), 174–8.

31. The Hanging Garden (Hsüan-p'u) is a famous *locus amoenus* located in the K'un-lun Mountains and is known in Chinese mythology as the above of spirits and immortals.

32. Chang Yi cites the *Luminary Classic* (*Ming ching*, HS 57B.2599, n. 5) which explains the 'falling sunlight' as an 'ether four-thousand miles from the earth. All of its light falls down below.' Chin Cho explains the 'flying bridge' as 'a bridge on a floating road' (HS 87A.3528, n. 14). Lü Hsiang (WH 7.6b) glosses it as the asterism Ke-tao, said to be the road used by the spirits in climbing to Heaven. According to *Erh ya* C.8b, the 'gnats' are 'insects smaller than mosquitoes'. It is apparent that the identification of all of these objects is less than certain, but undoubtedly they are astronomical phenomena.

33. Hsüan-ming is god of the north and winter; see *Legends and Cults*, pp. 222, 239, 243–4, and 246.

34. The Dark City (Yu tu), or according to some commentators (see K'ung Ying-ta, *Shang shu*, 1.3a) 'Gathering of Darkness', was a place in the remote north where the *yin* ether collected.

35. The white tiger is the guardian spirit of the west.

36. On the Kao-kuang Palace see *San-fu huang-t'u*, 2.6a.

37. The Jade Building (Hsüan-shih) was built by Chieh, last of the Hsia rulers. The Jasper Palace (Ch'iung kung), also called the Hundred *Mou* Palace (Ch'ing kung), was built by Chou (some sources say Chieh), last of the Shang rulers (see LSCC, 23.10b).

38. Or: 'the *mu* and *yü* notes all in harmony', after Kao Pu-ying, *Wen hsüan Li chu yi-shu* (Notes on Li Shan's *Literary Selections* commentary), 7.23b.

39. K'uei was the name of Emperor Shun's music master; see BD 1016. Po-ya was a famous lute player; see BD 1662.

40. Kung-shu Pan was a famous artisan of Lu, known in later times as the god of carpenters; see *Meng tzu* 4.4 and *Mo tzu* 13.12a ff. Ch'ui was the master of the artisans under Emperor Yao; see *Legends and Cults*, pp. 256–7. Wang Erh was the name of another craftsman; see HNT 8.2a.

41. Cheng Ch'iao is the name of an immortal; see Ssu-ma Hsiang-ju, 'Rhapsody on the Great Man', HS 57B.2595. Wo Chüan, another immortal, has a biography in *Lieh-hsien chuan* [Biographies of the Immortals], *Ku-chin yi-shih* ed., A.3a–b.

42. The spirits of Heaven, Earth, and Man. The spirits of the mountains are sometimes substituted for Man in this formula.

43. Kao-yao, the famous minister to Shun; see BD 965; Yi Yin, a minister under the Shang ruler Ch'eng T'ang; see BD 913.

44. The title of *Shih* 16, written in praise of the Duke of Shao. Here it is used as metonymy for the Duke.

45. Cf. *Shih* 157: 'The Duke of Chou marched to the east'. This poem was written as an eulogy to the Duke of Chou.

46. The Jo tree was a magic tree on the K'un-lun mountains; see *Shan-hai ching* [Classic of Mountains and Seas], 17.8b, 18.3b; 'Li sao' l. 98; HNT 4.3a.

47. The Armillary Sphere (Hsüan-chi) is the name of a constellation (α, β, γ, δ Ursae Majoris).

48. The San-wei mountains are located in extreme northwestern China.

49. Pu-chou is the northwest mountain where Kung-kung butted the pillar of heaven, which caused the sky to lean toward the northwest, and the rivers to flow toward the southeast (see *Legends and Cults*, pp. 227–8).

50. On the Mother Queen of the West (Hsi-wang-mu) see H. Dubs, 'An Ancient Chinese Mystery Cult', *Harvard Theological Review* 35 (1942), 221–40. The Jade Maiden (Yü nü) has been equated with the goddess of Mount Hua; cf. 'Great Man Rhapsody', HS 57B.2596 and the long note by Pokora in AO 28 (1960), 364, n. 74. Fu-fei is the goddess of the Lo River; see 'Li sao', l. 112; 'Distant Wandering', l. 75.

51. Following the interpretation suggested in the Chung-hua shu-chü edition of HS (p. 3555, n. to p. 3532, l. 10). Some editions of WH give a variant reading, which has led some commentators to claim that the term *chao-yao* ('to shake and agitate') actually is the name of a type of pyre (see Ju Ch'un's commentary in WH 7.12b).

52. The Hung-yi banner is unidentified. The Magic Pennant (*Ling-ch'i*) is conventionally associated with the Great Unity. In the autumn of 113 B.C. an attack was to be made on the southern Yüeh. Prayers were made to the Great Unity. They also made a flag painted with the sun, moon, Northern Dipper, and a soaring dragon as symbols of the Great Unity. This banner was called the Magic Pennant. See SC 28.1395; HS 25A.1231; *Records*, II, 54; Mh. III, 493.

53. The Green Sea (Ts'ang-hai) is another name for the Eastern Sea. The Flowing Sands (Liu-sha) is probably the Gobi in Mongolia.

54. Fu Ch'ien (HS 87A.3533, n. 4) identifies Tan-yai (my 'Cinnabar Cliff') as the 'bank of the Tan River'. There are a number of Tan rivers, none of which is located in the south (see Hervouet, pp. 262–3). Thus I suspect this is a placename associated with a myth that is now lost.

55. The San-luan (Three Peaks) is another name for the Feng-luan (Three Peaks), a viewing tower in Sweet Springs Park. The Pear Palace (T'ang-li) was thirty *li* from Yün-yang.

56. Ch'ang-p'ing was an area where a lodge of the same name was built; see HFHD, II, 259.

57. See *Dai kanwa jiten*, 46671..86, 182, 200.

58. See HFHD, III, 413–14.

59. The colon indicates a following object; words joined by a hyphen are bynomes; / indicates the key word or minor caesura; // indicates the major caesura.

60. Notably Mei Ch'eng's 'Seven Stimuli'. Hans Frankel discusses this aspect of the 'Seven Stimuli' in his forthcoming book on Chinese poetry.

61. See *Shih* 189, 'Preface'.

62. P'an-keng, a Shang dynasty emperor, is famous for moving the Shang capital to Po south of the Yellow River. His speech attempting to persuade his people of the wisdom of the move is contained in the *Book of Documents* (Karlgren, pp. 20–6). See SC 3.102; Mh, III, 193–4.

63. Cf. 'The Discussion of the Six Schools' by Ssu-ma T'an, HS 62.2712: 'The Mohists also honor the ways of the emperors Yao and Shun, saying: "Their halls were three feet high, their earthen stairs were in three steps, their roofs were of untrimmed reeds, and the timbers and rafters were uncut."'

64. Cf. 'Sweet Springs Rhapsody', l. 66.

65. Cf. 'Sweet Springs Rhapsody', l. 79.

66. HS 87A.3535–6.

67. See YWLC 78.1338 and Pokora, 'Fu on Looking for the Immortals', p. 365 for Huan T'an's usage; for Chang Heng see WH 15.17a–18a (von Zach, I, 224).

68. See 'Fu on Looking for the Immortals', p. 364, n. 74.

69. Her behavior should be contrasted with that of Pan Chieh-yü who, when asked by the emperor to ride in the imperial carriage, replied: 'If one looks at the ancient pictures, he sees that sage and worthy rulers had distinguished ministers at their sides. At the end of each of the Three Dynasties the ruler had a favorite girl. Now, if you wish me to ride with you, won't this approach the situation then?' (HS 97B.3983–4).

70. Cf. 'Great Man Rhapsody', HS 57B.2595: 'To the left is Hsüan-ming, on the right Ch'ien-lei.' 'Sweet Springs Rhapsody', 1.46: 'To the left is the Comet, on the right Hsüan-ming.'

71. Cf. 'Shang-lin Rhapsody', HS 57A.2557: 'The Green dragon is coiled around the eastern pavilion.' 'Sweet Springs Rhapsody', l. 47: 'A dragon is coiled around the eastern bank.' Cf. 'Li sao', l. 169: 'I break a jasper branch for my meal.' 'Sweet Springs Rhapsody', l. 71: 'He breaks jasper branches to make perfume.'

72. On Hou-t'u see C. W. Bishop, 'Prefatory Note on the Worship of Earth in Ancient China', *Excavation of a West Han Dynasty Site* (Shanghai, 1932), pp. 1–20 and 'The Worship of Earth in Ancient China', JNCBRAS 64 (1933), 24–43. Sacrifices to Hou-t'u began in 113 B.C. as a complement to the sacrifices to the Lord on High (Shang-ti). The site of these sacrifices has traditionally been located about ten *li* north of Jung-ho *hsien*, Shensi. C. W. Bishop suggests that the actual location may have been north of Wan-ch'üan hsien, Shensi, where a Han sacrificial plot has been found at the southeastern foot of a

mountain called Ku-shan. Since the altar to the Sovereign Earth was near a hill, this location seems more likely than the Jung-ho site, which is now a plain.

73. HS 87A.3536–40. The piece has been translated by Kopetsky, 'Two *Fu* on Sacrifices', pp. 114–18.
74. These mountains are located northeast of Fen-yin.
75. An-yi, the legendary capital of the Great Yü, lay northeast of Chieh *hsien*, Shansi. The Yellow River runs to the south of the city.
76. The Lung-men mountains correspond to the area between modern Ho-chin, Shansi and Han-ch'eng, Shensi. This is the place the Great Yü is said to have bored a hole to make a passage for the Yellow River.
77. The Salt Pond (Yen-ch'ih) lay to the south of An-yi.
78. The Li Viewing-tower (Li kuan) was located on Mount Li, which lay southeast of modern Yung-chi, Shansi.
79. The Western Peak (Hsi yüeh), the highest peak of Hua-shan, is one of the five sacred mountains.
80. T'ang is Yao; Yü is Shun.
81. This proverb was cited by Tung Chung-shu in a memorial addressed to Emperor Wu. There he uses it to persuade the emperor to adopt his reform proposals. 'The ancients have a saying which says: "It is better to go home and make a net than to stand by a pool and admire the fish." Now it would be better to go home and reform than merely stand near one's government and hope to govern well for over seventy years' (HS 56.2506). See also HNT 17.12b.
82. HS 87A.3535.
83. The original text refers more specifically to the burial of sacrificial animals and jade after the sacrifices; see *Erh-ya* 6.8a and HFHD, I, 107, n. 34.8.
84. Yen Shih-ku (HS 87A.3537, n. 4) explains that this carriage was in the shape of a phoenix (*feng*) and decorated with kingfisher plumes.
85. Yen Shih-ku (HS 87A.3537, n. 4) explains that the horses ran so fast they remained ahead of their shadows!
86. The Heavenly Wolf (T'ien-lang) is Sirius in Canus major (Schlegel, I, 430). It is above the Bow Star (Hu hsing), with which it is commonly associated.
87. The *tu* was a large streamer placed on the left side of the imperial carriage.
88. According to *Shang-shu ta-chuan* 2.4a, there were five bells on the right and left of the emperor. Those on the left were sounded when the emperor left court; those on the right were rung when he returned. Yen Shih-ku (HS 87A.3537, n. 8) cites the *Old Ceremony of Han* (*Han chiu-yi*) which says that five flags were placed on the imperial carriage. Each flag represented one of the five directional colors.
89. Hsi-ho is the charioteer of the sun; see *Shang shu*, 'Canon of Yao', 1.1b and 'Li sao' 1.96. Yen Lun is a famous charioteer of antiquity; see *Han shih wai-chuan* 2.6b–7a (Hightower, pp. 48–9).
90. The Ch'in Spirit refers to a deity who appeared in the reign of Duke Wen of Ch'in. In his twenty-seventh year 'They cut down a large catalpa tree on Nan-shan. It appeared in the Feng River as a large bullock' (SC 5.180). The commentators explain that an ox came from inside the tree and became a spirit in the Feng River. A shrine was erected there, and was called the Shrine of the Angry Bullock. Apparently the bullock became known as the Ch'in Spirit.
91. The River Spirit (Ho ling) is the god of the Yellow River, also known as Hu-po.
92. The spirits of the five directions.
93. These mountains were also called Chieh-mei, the Mien, and Fen mountains. According to legend the name is derived from Chieh Chih-t'ui (BD 353), who retired and died here.
94. Chieh Chih-t'ui was a loyal official of Duke Wen of Chin. The subject of this line is ambiguous. The historical fact is that Duke Wen lamented the tragic death of Chieh Chih-t'ui (he died in a fire on a mountain), and this could be the logical subject of the line. However, the grammatical subject seems to be the emperor (understood). Inversion is rare in classical Chinese (reading as such the line would translate: 'Sighed Duke Wen as he lamented T'ui'). For this reason I have made the emperor the subject.
95. Yü bored a hole in Mount Lung-men to make a passage for the Yellow River. The Nine Rivers (Chiu ho) refer to the nine tributaries of the Yellow River (HS 28A.1252, n. 2).
96. According to legend Yü-shih (Shuh) plowed at Mount Li (see *Legends and Cults*, p. 297). There are a number of Mount Lis that compete for the honor of being where Shun set his plow. The one most appropriate for this poem is southeast of Yung-chi, Shansi.
97. Emperor T'ang is another name for Yao. Yang Hsiung may be referring indirectly to *Lün-yü* 8.19: 'Lofty, high – only Heaven is great; only Yao can imitate it.'
98. Kai-hsia (southeast of Ling-pi in Anhwei) was the location of Liu Pang's victory over Hsiang Yü. P'eng-ch'eng (T'ung-shan in Kiangsu) was Hsiang Yü's capital.

99. Nan-ch'ao, northeast of Ch'ao *hsien* in Anhwei. It was here that Ch'eng T'ang, the founder of the Shang dynasty, drove the last of the Hsia rulers. Pin was the home of Kung Liu, the founder of Chou. Ch'i was the old Chou capital.

100. Cf. 'Great Man Rhapsody', HS 57B.2596: 'He summons P'ing-yi, chastizes the Wind Earl, punishes the Rain Master.'

101. 'They' refers to Yao, Shun, the Yin and Chou.

102. Ch'ien (Heaven) is the first hexagram in the *Book of Changes*; K'un (Earth) is the second hexagram. The dragon is the primary image of the Ch'ien hexagram.

103. These are the guardian spirits of the east, west, north, and south respectively.

104. The *Six Classics* are the *Changes, Songs, Documents, Spring and Autumn Annals, Rites* and *Music*. The 'songs of praise' may refer to the Hymns (*sung*) of the *Songs* or perhaps more generally to songs in praise of the greatness of the Han.

105. A reference to *Shih* 265, the first of the 'Hymns of Chou' (*Chou sung*): 'Oh august is the Pure Temple,/Solemn and harmonious are the illustrious attendants.' 'Continuous brightness' is a phrase in *Shih* 271.

CHAPTER 4

1. See pp. 117–18 below for a discussion of this piece.

2. See Appendix I for a discussion of the dating.

3. Cf. Hervouet, p. 50, n. 4: 'Il est difficile de dire si Sseu-ma Siang-jou participa effectivement à une chasse dans le Chang-lin avec l'empereur Wou avant de composer son poème.'

4. HS 10.327 (also trans. in HFHD, II, 412). The *chiao* was a barricade used to enclose the animals held in the park. Some interpret *chiao* as 'contest' (see HFHD, II, 412, n. 14.4).

5. HS 87A.3540–53; WH 8.20a–33a; trans. von Zach, I, 117–25.

6. There are two explanations of the term '*yü lieh*': (a) Fu Ch'ien (HS 87A.3541, n. 1) says that the soldiers carried plumes, hence the name 'plume hunt'; (b) Lü Hsiang (WH 8.20a) says that *yü* (feather, plume) refers to the arrows used by the hunters. The former explanation is more plausible, since the hunters obviously used weapons other than bow and arrow.

7. Yao and Shun, Hsia, Yin, and Chou dynasties.

8. This is the three-fold function of the hunt as formulated in *Li chi* 4.5b.

9. Cf. *Meng tzu* 3B.4.

10. Cf. *Li chi* 7.11a.

11. Cf. *Li chi* 7.11a.

12. See *Shang shu* 1.10b (Karlgren, p. 7).

13. See *Meng tzu* 1B.2.

14. According to *San-fu huang t'u* 4.1a–2a Emperor Wu expanded the Shang-lin Park in 138 B.C. Yi-ch'un was located southeast of Ch'ang-an, east of modern Tu *hsien* (see *San-fu huang t'u* 3.8a). Ting-hu was located below Mount Ching, south of modern Wen-hsiang, Honan (see *San-fu huang t'u* 3.8b, HS 25A.1228, and SC 28.1394). Yü-hsiu was a park south of Ch'ang-an (see *San-fu huang-t'u* 4.2a–b). K'un-wu was northeast of modern Lan-t'ien.

15. The Southern Mountains (Nan-shan) were located west of Ch'ang-an. The Ch'ang-yang Palace was thirty *li* southeast of Chou-chih (see *San-fu huang-t'u* 1.3b). Wu-tso Palace was in the same area as Ch'ang-yang and was named for the five large oak trees planted there (see *San-fu huang-t'u* 3.8b).

16. The Yellow Mountains (Huang-shan) is the name of a mountain range near modern Wu-kung, Shensi. Huang-shan is also the name of a palace located southwest of modern Hsing-p'ing, Shensi (see Hervouet, p. 226, n. 5 and HS 65.2847 and *San-fu huang-t'u* 3.7a).

17. K'un-ming was a small lake built in imitation of Tien Lake, located in modern Yün-nan province. It was used for practicing naval warfare (see HS 6.177; SC 30.1428; Mh, III, 568–9; *Records*, II, 89; HFHD, II, 63, n. 15.10; *San-fu huang t'u* 4.3a–4b).

18. Chien-chang was a palace west of the Wei-yang Palace built in 104 B.C. (see *San-fu huang-t'u* 2.3b–4b and HFHD, II, 99, n. 31.6). Feng-ch'üeh (Phoenix Tower) and Shen-ming were towers near the Chien-chang Palace (see *San-fu huang-t'u* 2.3b–4b). Sa-so is the name of a palace in the same complex.

19. The Chien Tower or Tower of Lapping Water was built in the middle of T'ai-yi Pond, located north of the Chien-chang Palace (see SC 28.1402; HS 25B.1245; *Records*, II, 66; *San-fu huang t'u* 4.5a–6a). The three islands were apparently replicas of the three islands of the immortals in the Eastern Sea.

20. Cf. *Chou yi*, Hexagram 8, 9/5, 1.14b: 'In the hunt the king uses beaters on three sides only/And forgoes game that runs off in front' (Wilhelm/Baynes, I, 40). The expression also refers to the three-fold function of the hunt: providing sacrificial meat, food for guests, and food for the ruler's kitchen.
21. According to *Ch'un-ch'iu*, Wen 16, Duke Wen destroyed the Ch'üan Tower. The Kung-yang commentary condemned the destruction of the tower, saying that all that was necessary was for the duke not to live in it. This presumably is the 'middle course' Yang Hsiung recommends for the Shang-lin Park: since Emperor Ch'eng did not build it, he need not tear it down; but he ought not to enter it.
22. HS 87A.3540–1.
23. For Fu-hsi see BD 585; Shen-nung, BD 1695. They are customarily singled out for the simplicity of their government.
24. Reading 'to deceive' after Kao Pu-ying, 8.62b.
25. For the figure of seventy-two rulers who made sacrifices on Mount T'ai see SC 28.1361. See also Tjan Tjoe Som, I, n. 307, pp. 329–30; and Hervouet, pp. 198, 200.
26. Correctly Duke Chuang of Ch'u. Yen is written for Chuang because of the Eastern Han taboo on Chuang. Both he and Duke Huan were famous Hegemons (*pa*) of the Ch'un-ch'iu period.
27. When the *yin* breath is at its highest peak of intensity.
28. The northwest wind is literally Pu-chou wind or wind from Mount Pu-chou in the northwest. Chuan-hsü and Hsüan-ming are the guardian spirits of the north and winter.
29. Ch'ang-ho is the name of the portal of Heaven, but the Shang-lin Park may have had a gate by this name as an imagined replica of the celestial gate.
30. Mountain located northwest of modern T'un-liu, Shansi. The Ssu-ma or Marshall's Gate was the outer gate of the imperial palace (see HS 9.286, n. 10 and HFHD, II, 316, n. 6.9).
31. Yü yüan: where the sun sets.
32. Po-yang was located east of K'un-ming Lake; see *San-fu huang t'u* 5.9a.
33. Pen is Meng Pen (see BD 1525); Yü is Hsia Yü (see BD 684).
34. Fu Ch'ien (HS 87A.3546, n. 2) identifies Duke Meng as the famous Ch'in general Meng T'ien. Chin Cho identifies him as the star Mao-t'ou (Pleides); see WH 8.25b and Hu Shao-ying, *Wen hsüan chien-cheng* [Notes on The Literary Selections], 11.4a–b.
35. Li Shan (WH 8.26b) claims the Shen-kuang (Supernatural Light) is a palace. Yen Shih-ku (HS 87A.3546, n. 7) says this describes the 'supernatural light' emitted by the ornaments on the chariots.
36. Fu Ch'ien (HS 87A.3548) explains 'huo yi' as 'one who captures the Yi barbarians'. Others claim these are specific names of two warriors: Wu Huo (BD 2334) and Hou Yi (BD 667).
37. Hsiung-erh (Bear's Ears) is a common mountain name. Several of the modern equivalents could apply here.
38. For P'eng Meng see *Meng tzu* 4B.24 and *Legends and Cults*, p. 313.
39. Wang Shu is the legendary charioteer of the moon; Shang-lan Lodge was located inside the Shang-lin Park.
40. The Heavenly Treasure (T'ien pao), also known as the Ch'en Treasure (Ch'en pao), was a stone-like object with the head of a rooster (HS says pheasant). It always appeared at night from the east and emitted a light like shooting stars. It made a loud noise that caused male fowl to crow at night. See HS 25A.1195; SC 28.1359; *Records*, II, 18; Mh, II, 17; and Liu Hsiang's memorial on it in HS 25B.1258–9.
41. The Han nymph or Han Woman (*Han nü*) is the name of a goddess who lived in the Han River. Ying Shao (cited in HS 87A.3551, n. 7) claims the name *Han nü* refers to two nymphs Cheng Chiao-fu met near Han-kao (the bank of the Han River). For an interesting account of this deity in later literature see Edward H. Schafer, *The Divine Woman: Dragon Ladies and Rain Maidens in T'ang Literature* (Berkeley, Los Angeles, and London, 1973), pp. 55–7, 91–3.
42. The Grotto (Tung hsüeh), also known as the Cave of Yü (Yü hsüeh), according to legend was where the Great Yü was buried. The traditional site is on the Kuei-chi mountains in Chekiang (see SC 130.3293). Ts'ang-wu is the legendary burial place of Shun.
43. P'eng-li is the ancient name for P'o-yang Lake in northern Kiangsi. Yu Yü is Shun's title.
44. P'eng Hsien and Wu Tzu-hsü. All of these legendary martyrs were worshipped as water spirits in Han times.
45. The canon of T'ang is the 'Canon of Yao' in the *Book of Documents*; the *Odes* and *Hymns* refer to the last two sections of the *Book of Songs*.
46. The Southern Lin (Nan-lin), also known as Chin-lin, lay to the south of China somewhere near India.
47. Mount Lu was located in the territory of the Hsiung-nu; Meng K'ang locates it near the southern court of the khan (HS 87A.3553).

48. Yang Chu (BD 237) and Mo Ti (BD 1537), two prominent pre-Ch'in philosophers. See the discussion below.
49. The sun, moon, and stars.
50. Yün-meng was the famous Ch'u hunting park celebrated in Ssu-ma hsiang-ju's 'Master Void Rhapsody' (see Hervouet, pp. 244–56). Meng-chu was a hunting preserve in the Chou state of Sung.
51. Chang-hua Tower was built by King Ling of Ch'u; the Ling-t'ai is the famous tower built by King Wen of Chou (see *Shih* 242).
52. The extravagant palace built by the Ch'in dynasty.
53. The Han palace in which most governmental activity was concentrated; see *San-fu huang t'u* 2.2a–4b.
54. SC 117.3017; HS 57A.2548.
55. There are similar examples in Ssu-ma Hsiang-ju; see Hervouet, p. 334.
56. Ch'ü Yüan declares in the 'Li sao' that he aspires to imitate the example of P'eng Hsien (1. 39). Late sources say P'eng Hsien was a Shang dynasty official who committed suicide by drowning, but this may be a later fabrication based on the example of Ch'ü Yüan's own suicide. Wu Tzu-hsü, whose body was thrown into the river after he committed suicide, became known as the bore of the Ch'ien-t'ang River.
57. Liu Hsieh in the *Wen-hsin tiao-lung* seems to read the passage exactly this way: 'They flogged Fu-fei in order to feed Ch'ü Yüan' (*Wen-hsin tiao-lung chiao-chu*, p. 245). For a different interpretation see Shih, *The Literary Mind*, p. 200, n. 19: 'Yang Hsiung here tried to point out the extravagant scale of the emperor's hunting expedition. He disturbed the Lo River in the north, of which Fu-fei was the deity, and reached the banks of the rivers in the south where Ch'ü Yüan, P'eng Hsien, and Wu Tzu-hsü drowned. Flogging and feeding are figures for reaching these rivers.' It is unnecessary to interpret 'flogging and feeding' as 'figures for reaching these rivers'. No special significance should be attributed to the River Lo's northern location, since Fu-fei has been also associated with the south (as in 'Distant Wandering', 1. 75). The context indicates that she is present at P'eng-li Lake. Furthermore, we have seen in the section on Ssu-ma Hsiang-ju that Han rhapsodists are notorious for their geographical inaccuracies.
58. *Meng-tzu* 7A.26.
59. See A. C. Graham, *The Book of Lieh-tzu* (London, 1960), pp. 135–7.
60. See Appendix I for more details on the dating of this poem.
61. In HS 87B.3557–65 and WH 9.1a–11a. It has been translated by von Zach, I, 122–31.
62. Perhaps the year after the 'Barricade Hunt Rhapsody' was presented. See Appendix I for a discussion of this problem.
63. An office established in 104 B.C. by Emperor Wu (see HS 19A.736). It had charge of the area around the capital known as Yu Fu-feng.
64. Pao and Hsieh are two ends of a valley that runs from Ssu-ch'uan to Shensi.
65. Hung-nung was a commandery that included the area west of Lo-yang, Sung, and Nei-hsing in modern Honan and the area west of Shang in Shensi; see Herrmann 14–15 E3.
66. Located west of Nan-cheng, Shensi; see Herrmann, 9 B2.
67. The Bear Shooting Lodge was situated near the gate of the Ch'ang yang Palace; see *San-fu huang-t'u* 5.8a.
68. HS 87B.3557.
69. See n. 20, p. 133.
70. This was a legendary animal shaped like an ox with a red body. It had a human face and feet like a horse. See HNT 8.5a.
71. See HNT 8.5a.
72. The Heavenly Barrier (*T'ien-kuan*) is a term that can refer either to the Pole Star (*Pei-chi, Pei-ch'en*) or the Great Dipper (*Pei-tou*). The ancient Chinese considered the Pole Star a fixed star around which the Dipper rotated. Yang Hsiung seems to be saying the founding Han emperor acted in harmony with astral phenomena in his military campaign against the Ch'in and Hsiang Yü.
73. The Jade Balance (Yü-heng) is another name for the armillary sphere on which the celestial revolutions could be represented. It is also the name of ε Alioth in Ursa Major. The Great Stair (T'ai-chieh) was a constellation with three levels, each with an upper and lower star, representing the hierarchy of classes in the empire from the emperor down to the common people. Both the Jade Balance and the Great Stair are equated with order.
74. In 135 B.C. Tsou Ying, king of Min-yüeh, attacked the Southern Yüeh. The emperor send troops to aid the Southern Yüeh, but before they could arrive, Tsou Ying's younger brother, Tsou Yü-shan, assassinated Tsou Ying and assumed the throne. See SC 114.2981 (*Records*, II, 253–4).
75. The Swift Cavalry General is Huo Ch'ü-ping (BD 645), the famous general who defeated the Hsiung-nu. For the great general Wei Ch'ing see BD2268 and *Records*, II, 193–216.

76. The Yü-wu was a river in the Hsiung-nu territory.
77. In anticipation of execution.
78. Dark City is metonymy for 'north'.
79. I.e., his virtue and grace.
80. Short for Wu-yi shan-li, the Chinese name for Arachosia. In the Han it was considered the western most limit of the empire.
81. Cf. *Shih* 215/1.
82. By constructing an altar on top.
83. By inducing them to pay tribute at court when they attend the hunt.
84. 11. 64–7, 71–2.
85. HS 65.2849–50.
86. *Early Chinese Literature*, p. 267.

CHAPTER 5

1. See Kuo Shao-yü, *Chung-kuo wen-hsüeh p'i-p'ing shih* [History of Chinese literary criticism] (Shanghai, 1934), p. 40.
2. See Kung-sun Hung's memorial requesting the establishment of the imperial university, HS 88.3594, 1. 4.
3. There are other explanations of what *Ch'u tz'u* means, but most of these ignore the basic meaning of *tz'u*.
4. *The Analects of Confucius*, pp. 41–2.
5. *Lun yü* 6.18 (Waley, p. 119).
6. FYYS 4.6b.
7. *T'ai hsüan ching*, SPTK, 7.17a–18a.
8. FYYS 8.2b–3a.
9. FYYS 3.10b.
10. Some have suggested that this refers to two of the six forms of calligraphy learned by young boys in their early education (described in HS 30.1721). See FYYS 3.1b–2a and James R. Hightower's note in HJAS, 22 (1959), n. 5.
11. FYYS 3.1a.
12. FYYS 3.4a. 'To mount the hall...to enter the inner compartments' is an allusion to *Lun yü* 11.14.
13. See Diény, p. 66, n. 2.
14. FYYS 18.8b–9a.
15. 'Literary Theory in the Eastern Han', *Chûgoku bungaku ronshu* (Tokyo, 1968), p. 4.
16. HS 87B.3566–73 and WH 45.7a–16b; it has been translated by von Zach, II, 834–40. There are significant differences between the HS and WH texts which I have been unable to indicate in my notes.
17. This piece is found in SC 126.3206–7 (excerpt); HS 65.2864–7; WH 45.2b–7a.
18. The colors worn by nobility.
19. The Golden Horse Gate (Chin-ma men), located in the Wei-yang Palace, was where scholars waited a summons from the emperor.
20. The Jade Hall (Yü-t'ang) was another section of the imperial palace complex.
21. The terms vertical (*tsung*) and horizontal (*heng*) by this time apply to rhetorical or sophistic argument. It is also possible that Yang Hsiung is referring to the type of argument known as the doubled persuasion.
22. This is a pun on the word *Hsüan* (dark). This means that *The Great Dark* (*T'ai hsüan*) was useless since it failed to bring Yang success in his career at court.
23. This is a pun on *chu-tan* (vermeil cinnabar), the color of the wheel hubs of high officials and nobility, and *ch'ih* (the color of blood). Yang is saying he would endanger his family if he undertook an active political career.
24. A common figure for the lords who set up independent states in late Chou times.
25. A reference to the twelve states of the Ch'un-ch'iu period, which were reduced to six and seven (with the addition of Ch'in) during the Warring States period.
26. 'Hiding in a sack': referring to Wu Tzu-hsü, although Yang Hsiung most likely intended this to refer to Fan Chü (BD 533) judging from the description of Fan given below. The erroneous identification probably stems from the mention of Wu Tzu-hsü's hiding in a bag in a speech by Fan Chü in CKT 3.45a. 'Drilling a hole': a story about Yen Ho, a recluse in the state of Lu. The Duke of Lu sent a messenger inviting Yen Ho to become his minister. Yen bored a hole in a wall and escaped. See HNT 11.13b and *Chuang tzu* 9.21b.

27. On Tsou Yen see BD 2030; Biography in SC 74.2344–6.
28. Commentators have applied this line to different events in Meng tzu's life: (a) Li Shan (WH 45.9b) quotes Chao Ch'i (?–A.D. 201) who says King Wen of T'ang honored Meng tzu with the same reverence a student shows to his teacher; (b) Liu Liang (*ibid.*) says Meng went to Ch'i and Liang and found his advice not heeded. Eventually, he became the teacher of King Wei of Chou (sic); a note in *Liang Han wen-hsüeh shih ts'an-k'ao tzu-liao*, p. 71, n. 10 says that Meng, in spite of his many hardships, was honored by the kings of Liang and Ch'i.
29. Ch'ü-sou: see Herrmann 4 AB2. This was a state in the territory of the Western Jung.
30. P'an-yü: modern Canton (see Herrmann 12 C3). Chiao-t'u: located north of modern Yü-yang around Peking.
31. That is, the border areas are at peace and require little supervision.
32. Ministers under the Emperor Shun.
33. A-heng: another name for Yi Yin, minister of the first Shang emperor, Ch'eng T'ang. Yi-wu; another name for Kuan Chung, the seventh century minister of Duke Huan of Ch'i. Yen Ying (BD 2483; SC 62.2134–5) was a prominent minister in Ch'i during the late fifth century B.C.
34. Following the WH reading of 'bank' rather than the HS reading of 'sparrow'.
35. That is, the court is so large that it makes no difference whether worthy ministers leave or come to court.
36. The Three Humane Ones (*San-jen*) are Wei-tzu, Pi-kan, and Chi-tzu (see *Lun-yü* 18.1). The Two Elders (*Erh-lao*) are Po Yi and T'ai-kung (see *Meng tzu* 4A.13).
37. Wen Chung and Fan Li (BD 540): Wen and Fan devised a strategem that enabled King Kou-chien of Yüeh to defeat Wu. Tzu-hsü is Wu Tzu-hsü.
38. Five Sheepskins: Po-li Hsi (BD 1659) was purchased by Duke Mu of Ch'in for five sheepskins, and was given the nickname of Five Sheepskins. Eventually he became Duke Mu's minister. Yüeh Yi (BD 2502) served under King Chao of Yen and helped him defeat Ch'i. Chao's son, King Hui, assumed the throne and replaced Yüeh Yi with another man. Yüeh, fearing execution, fled to Chao where he was given a high position. King Hui then was afraid Yüeh would work for his enemy. See SC 80 (F. A. Kierman, *Ssu-ma Ch'ien*, pp. 20–5).
39. Fan Chü from Wei was falsely accused of accepting a bribe and suffered a severe beating in which his ribs and teeth were broken. He fled to Ch'in where he eventually persuaded King Chao to expel Wei Jan, Marquis of Jang, who was Chao's minister. Fan then became minister. See SC 79.2401–18. Ts'ai Tse went to the physiognomer T'ang Chü. T'ang, pointing out Ts'ai's ugly features, laughed at him and his request to know his political future. Eventually he went to Ch'in where he became minister in place of Fan Chü. See SC 79.2418.
40. Hsiao: Hsiao Ho (BD 702; biography SC 53, *Records*, I, 125–33); Ts'ao: Ts'ao Shen (BD 2012; biography SC 54, *Records*, I, 421–6); Tzu-fang: Chang Liang (BD 88; biography SC 55, *Records*, I, 134–51); P'ing: Ch'en P'ing (BD 240; biography SC 56, *Records*, I, 152–63); Po: Chou Po (BD 422; biography SC 57, *Records*, I, 427–40); Fan: Fan K'uai (BD 539; biography SC 57, *Records*, I, 255–6); Huo: Huo Kuang (BD 653; see also HFHD II, 143–9. All were important ministers or imperial advisers in the early Han.
41. The term *chang-chü* (paragraphs and phrases) is pejorative to Yang Hsiung. Yang opposed the *chang-chü* school of exegesis which involved lengthy explanations of a passage or even a single character from the classics.
42. Kuan Chung was captured by Ch'i and put in fetters. Later he was released and given a high position (see *Tso chuan*, Chuang 9). 'Took off coarse clothing': possibly a reference to Fu Yüeh (see *Mo tzu* 2.9b). Some commentators say this refers to Ning Ch'i (BD 1568).
43. 'Yi Gate': Hou Ying was a guard at Yi Gate. Wu Chi, the Prince of Wei, wished to employ him but Hou Ying always refused. Wu Chi then personally drove a chariot to his home to fetch him. He then drove through the marketplace with Hou Ying occupying the honored left-hand side (see SC 79. 2378). 'Fished': the famous fisherman with whom Ch'ü Yüan debated (see *Records*, I, 54–5).
44. 'Seventy times': reference to Confucius; the number of rulers that Confucius tried to persuade varies in Chou and Han sources. See *Liang Han wen-hsüeh shih ts'an-k'ao tzu-liao*, p. 75, n. 41. 'Spoke once': Yü Ch'ing (BD 2515) after one audience with King Hsiao-ch'eng of Chao received one hundred ounces of gold and one white jade disc. At the next meeting he was made prime minister (SC 76.2370).
45. 'Humble alley': Duke Huan of Ch'i tried unsuccessfully to summon a low official named Chi. He eventually went to see Chi at his home. See LSCC 13.11a. 'Sweep the road': Duke Chao of Yan received Tsou Yen in this manner. See SC 74.2345.
46. Also the name of an office; Yang Hsiung spent most of his career as a 'Candidate for Appointment'.

47. These are both the names of famous doctors.
48. Ts'ai Tse was able to induce Fan Chü to give up his position as minister. See SC 79.2418–25 and CKT 3.70b.
49. Lou Ching: Biography SC 99 and HS 43 (*Records*, I, 285–91); he persuaded Kao-tsu to establish the capital at Ch'ang-an.
50. Shu-sun T'ung: Biography SC 99 and HS 43 (*Records*, I, 291–8); he composed the court ritual for Kao-tsu.
51. Also known as the *Code of Lü*, it is a chapter in the *Book of Documents* (*Shang shu* 12.6b–12b).
52. When the capital was in Lo-yang.
53. Chin: Chin Mi-ti (BD 382), a favorite of Emperor Wu; Chang: Chang An-shih (BD 19), another of Emperor Wu's favorites; Hsü: Hsü Kuang-han, the father of Empress née Hsü, the wife of Emperor Hsüan (see HS 97.3964): Shih: Shih Kung, the elder brother of Emperor Hsüan's grandmother, Shih Liang-ti, and Shih Kao, Kung's eldest son, who was a favorite of Emperor Hsüan (see HS 82.3375–6).
54. Ts'ao Shen succeeded Hsiao Ho as minister. The Marquis of Liu is Chang Liang. Ch'en P'ing: see BD 240; SC 56 (*Records*, I, 152–63).
55. Lin Hsiang-ju: Ch'in offered fifteen cities in exchange for the Ho jade owned by King Hui of Chao. Lin Hsiang-ju went to Ch'in to handle the transaction. However, Lin suspected Ch'in of bad faith, and he sent the jade back to Chao. He remained in Ch'in to face the wrath of Ch'in's ruler. See BD 1256 and SC 81 (Kierman, *Ssu-ma Ch'ien*, pp. 26–36). The four grey-heads were recluses who remained hidden throughout the reign of Kao-tsu, and appeared only in his last year before his son, the heir apparent.
56. Kung-sun Hung (BD 1030; SC 112; *Records*, II, 219–25) was a prominent Confucian scholar during the reign of Emperor Wu. The Swift Cavalry General (Huo Ch'ü-ping) achieved his first military victory over the Hsiung-nu at Mount Ch'i-lien, located southwest of modern Chang-yi, Kansu.
57. Ssu-ma Hsiang-ju eloped with the daughter of Cho-Wang-sun, one of the richest men in the province of Shu. Later Cho provided the couple with a substantial amount of money (see SC 117, *Records*, II, 297–342). Tung-fang Shuo was invited along with other court officials to the annual summer presentation of the sacrificial meat. When the Chief Butler did not arrive, and it became late in the evening, Tung-fang Shuo went ahead and cut himself a piece and left. Shuo's behavior was reported to the emperor, who was incensed and demanded an explanation. Shuo explained that he took the meat for his wife. See HS 65.2846.
58. YWLC 35.628–9.
59. KWY-A 2.4a–5b; KWY-B 4.3a–4b.
60. See *Shang shu*, 'Huang fan' 34 (B. Karlgren, *The Book of Documents*, p. 35).
61. Cf. *Shih* 211/1: 'Now we go to the southern acres/Sometimes weeding, sometimes hoeing.'
62. Cf. *Shih* 196/1: 'Small is that dove,/It flew and reached the sky.'; 204/7: 'I am not an eagle, not a hawk,/Who fly up and reach the sky.'
63. Cf. *Shih* 3/3: 'I climb that high slope.'
64. Cf. *Shih* 26/1 and 45/1: 'Tossed was that cypress boat.'
65. Cf. *Shih* 176/4: 'Tossed, tossed the willow boat,/Now it sinks, now it floats.'
66. The name of a mountain in north central China (northwest of Lo-ning, Honan) where a strategic pass was located. Yao without the 'mountain' radical means 'meat'.
67. Chieh was the evil last ruler of the Hsia dynasty. Chih was a notorious robber.
68. Po Yi and Shu Ch'i, sons of the Lord of Ku-chu, became hermits on Mount Shou-yang.

CHAPTER 6

1. See Pokora, 'The Life of Huan T'an', p. 543.
2. See Hervouet, *Sseu-ma Siang-jou*, pp. 413–14 and note 1, p. 414.
3. Shih, *The Literary Mind*, pp. 252–3.
4. See his 'Presented to My Elder the Left Coadjutor Wei' (*Feng tseng Wei tso-ch'eng chang erh-shih-erh yün*), *Tu shih Ch'ien chu* [Ch'ien Ch'ien-yi's commentary on Tu Fu's poems] (Taipei, Shih-chieh shu-chü 1962 ed.), 1.1.
5. *Ch'a-t'u pen Chung-kuo wen-hsüeh shih* [An illustrated history of Chinese literature] (Hong Kong, 1961), pp. 96–7.
6. *Chinese Literature: A Historical Introduction* (New York, 1961), p. 124.

7. *Ch'a t'u pen...*, p. 93.
8. James J. Y. Liu, *The Art of Chinese Poetry* (Chicago, 1962), p. 34.
9. Liu Wu-chi, *An Introduction to Chinese Literature* (Bloomington and London, 1966), p. 51.
10. *The Temple*, p. 17.

APPENDIX I

1. See Shih Chih-mien, 'Yang Hsiung tsou "Kan-ch'üan" "Yü-lieh fu" tsai Ch'eng-ti yung-shih san-nien k'ao' [Investigation of whether Yang Hsiung presented 'Sweet Springs" and "Plume Hunt Rhapsodies" in 14 B.C.], *Ta-lu tsa-chih* 4.2 (1952), 45; T'ang Lan, 'Yang Hsiung tsou "Kan-ch'üan", "Ho-tung", "Yü-lieh", "Ch'ang-yang" ssu-fu te nien-tai' [The year Yang Hsiung presented the rhapsodies "Sweet Springs", "Ho-tung", "Yü-lieh", and "Ch'ang-yang"], *Hsüeh yüan* 2.8 (1949), 8; and T. Pokora, 'Huan T'an's Fu on Looking for the Immortals', AO 28 (1960), 357–60.
2. HS 87B.3583.
3. See HS 10.321 and HS 19B.834–5.
4. See Ssu-ma Kuang, *T'ung-chien k'ao-yi* [Collation of variants in the *Comprehensive Mirror*] in *Tzu-chih t'ung-chien* [The Comprehensive Mirror for Aid in Government] (Ku-chi ch'u-pan she, 1957 ed.), p. 1031. Wang Ken's promotion is recorded in HS 19B.839.
5. Chou Shou-ch'ang (1814–84) was the first to propose this theory. See Tung Tso-pin's *Nien-p'u*, pp. 83–4.
6. Tung, *Nien-p'u*, p. 83.
7. See Ch'en Pen-li, *Nien-p'u*, p. 4b.
8. HS 87A.3522.
9. HS 87A.3535.
10. HS 87A.3540.
11. HS 87B.3557.
12. WH 7.2a, Li Shan's commentary.
13. WH 8.22a, Li Shan's commentary.
14. WH 9.1a, Li Shan's commentary.
15. HS 87B.3583.
16. HS 10.304.
17. HS 10.323.
18. HS 25B.1265.
19. HS 10.322.
20. HS 10.324, 326, 327, 329.
21. 'Huan T'an's Fu', p. 359.
22. HS 10.327.
23. Cited in *Han shu pu-chu* 87B.1a.
24. Cited in *Han shu pu-chu* 87B.1a–b.
25. *Fang-yen chu* 13.26a and KWY-A 5.5a–b.

APPENDIX II

1. See WH 28.12b; 39.29b; 44.22a; 56.14a; 58.14a; 58.14a; 58.13a; 27.5b. For an attempted reconstruction of the text see CHW 52.3a.
2. KWY-A 2.5b–6b; KWY-B 4.1a–3a.
3. Cf. 'The Great Dark Rhapsody':
   Thunder drones but suddenly ceases;
   Fire burns but quickly is extinguished.

   'Dissolving Ridicule', 1. 67:
   When a fire is at its hottest point it begins to die down;
   When thunder drones its loudest it begins to die out.

   'The Great Dark Rhapsody':
   But I am different from them.
   I will hold to the *Great Dark*,
   Freely give vent to my feelings.

'Dissolving Ridicule' 1. 113:
I certainly cannot be classed with these men.
Thus, silently and alone I guard my *Great Dark*.

4. KWY-A 2.6b–14a and KWY-B 4.4b–10b. There is some difference between the KWY-A and KWY-B versions. The KWY-A text is badly fragmented. It is possible that the KWY-B text has been touched up by Chang Ch'iao.

5. YWLC 61.1096. PTSC 142.1b, 3a; 144.5b also appear to quote from the piece.

6. See *Wen hsüan chu yin-shu yin-te* (Index to the titles in the commentary on *The Literary Selections*), ed. William Hung, et. al. (Peiping, 1935), p. 101, for a list of the citations in WH commentaries.

7. See WH.4.28a. The 'Three Capitals Rhapsody' is contained in WH 4.17a–34a, and it has been translated by Zach, I, 46–55.

8. If anything, Tso Ssu appears to be the imitator. There are several places in the piece that could be expansions of the Yang Hsiung poem.

Bibliography

WORKS IN CHINESE AND JAPANESE

Asano Michiari 淺野通有. 'Sô Goyku no sakuhin no shingi ni tsuite' 宋玉の作品の眞僞について, *Kambun gakkai kaihô* 漢文學會會報, 12 (April 1961), 3-12.

Chan-kuo ts'e 戰國策. SPTK.

Chang Ch'ang-kung. 張長弓 'Hsün Ch'ing te yün-wen' 荀卿的韻文, *Ling-nan hsüeh-pao* 嶺南學報, 3.2 (April 1934), 145-67.

Chang Ch'ün 章羣. 'Han ch'u te tsung-heng chia ho tz'u-fu chia' 漢初的縱橫家和辭賦家, *The Hong Kong Baptist College Journal*, 2.1 (March 1964), 15-27.

Chang Ping-lin 章炳麟. *Kuo-ku lun-heng* 國故論衡. *Chang-shih ts'ung-shu* 章氏叢書.

Chao Hsing-chih 趙省之, 'Ssu-ma Ch'ien fu tso te p'ing-chia' 司馬遷賦作的評價, *Wen shih che* 文史哲, 2 (1956), 30-4.

Ch'en Pen-li 陳本禮, *T'ai-hsüan ch'an-mi* 太玄闡祕, *Chü hsuëh hsüan ts'ung-shu* 聚學軒叢書, *ts'e* 71-4.

Cheng Chen-to 鄭振鐸. *Ch'a-t'u pen Chung-kuo wen-hsüeh shih* 插圖本中國文學史. Hong Kong: Commercial Press, 1961.

Ch'ien Ch'ien-yi 錢謙益. *Tu shih Ch'ien chu* 杜詩錢注. Taipei: Shih-chieh shu-chü, 1962.

Chiang Liang-fu 姜亮夫. *Ch'u tz'u shu-mu wu chung* 楚辭書目五種. Peking: Chung-hua shu-chü, 1961.

Chin Chü-hsiang 金秬香. *Han tai tz'u-fu chih fa-ta* 漢代詞賦之發達. Shanghai: Commercial Press, 1931.

Chou li 周禮. SPTK.

Chou Tsu-mo 周祖謨 and Lo Ch'ang-pei 羅常培. *Han Wei Chin Nan-pei ch'ao yün-pu yen-pien yen-chiu* 漢魏晉南北朝韻部衍變研究. Peking: K'o-hsüeh ch'u-pan she, 1958.

Chou yi 周易. SPTK.

Chu Chieh-ch'in 朱傑勤. 'Han fu yen-chiu' 漢賦研究, *Kuo-li Chung-shan ta-hsüeh wen-shih-hsüeh yen-chiu so yüeh-k'an* 國立中山大學文史學研究所月刊, 3.1 (March 1934), 113-36.

Chu Tzu-ch'ing 朱自清. *Shih yen chih pien* 詩言志辨. Taipei: Kai-ming, 1964.

Ch'ü Shui-yüan 瞿蛻園. *Han Wei Liu-ch'ao fu hsüan* 漢魏六朝賦選. Peking: Chung-hua shu-chü, 1964.

Chuang tzu 莊子. SPTK.

Chung Feng-nien 鍾鳳年. *Kuo ts'e k'an yen* 國策勘研, *Yenching hsüeh-pao* 燕京學報, Monograph No. 11 (Peiping, 1936).

Erh ya 爾雅. SPTK.

Han Fei tzu 韓非子. SPTK.

Han shih wai chuan 韓詩外傳. SPTK.

Hoshikawa Kiyotaka 星川清孝. *Soji no kenkyû* 楚辭の研究. Kyoto: Yôdokusha, 1961.

Hsi-ching tsa-chi 西京雜記, SPTK.

Hsiao T'ung 蕭統. *Wen hsüan* 文選. SPTK.

Hsin hsü 新序. SPTK.

Hsing ching 星經. *Ts'ung-shu chi-ch'eng* 叢書集成.

Hsü Chien 徐堅, ed. *Ch'u hsüeh chi* 初學記. Peking: Chung-hua shu-chü, 1962.

Hsü Fu-kuan 徐復觀. 'Hsi Han wen-hsüeh lun lüeh' 西漢文學論略, *Hsin-ya shu-yüan hsüeh-shu nien-k'an* 新亞書院學術年刊, 13 (1971), 99–121.

Hsü Shih-ying 許世瑛. 'Lun "Fu-niao fu" te yung yün' 論鵩鳥賦的用韻, *Ta-lu tsa-chih* 大陸雜志, 29.10–11 (1964), 85–91.

Hsün tzu 荀子. SPTK.

Hu Shao-ying 胡紹英. *Wen hsüan chien cheng* 文選箋證. Taipei: Kuang-wen shu-chü, 1965.

Huai-nan tzu 淮南子. SPTK.

Huang Chung-ch'in 黃仲琴. 'Yang Hsiung te hsing' 揚雄的姓, *Ling-nan hsüeh-pao*, 2.1 (July 1931), 13–18.

Hung Hsing-tsu 洪興祖. *Ch'u tz'u pu-chu* 楚辭補注, Hong Kong: Chung-hua shu-chü, 1963.

Itô Tomi 伊藤富雄, 'Ka Gi no "Fukuchô no fu" no tachiba' 賈誼の鵩鳥の賦の立場, *Chûgoku bungaku hô* 中國文學報, 13 (1960), 1–24.

Jao Tsung-yi 饒宗頤. *Ch'u tz'u shu lu* 楚辭書錄, Hong Kong: Tong Nam, 1956.

Kanaya Osamu 金谷治. 'Ka Gi no fu ni tsuite' 賈誼の賦について, *Chûgoku bungaku hô*, 8 (1958), 1–25.

Kao Pu-ying 高步瀛. *Wen hsüan Li chu yi-shu* 文選李注義疏. Taipei: Kuang-wen shu-chü, 1965.

Ku Chieh-kang 顧頡剛 and Yang Hsiang-k'uei 楊向奎. *San-huang k'ao* 三皇考, *Yenching hsüeh-pao*, Monograph Series No. 8 (Peiping, 1936).

Ku Nien-hsien 顧念先. *Tsung-heng chia yen-chiu* 縱橫家研究. Taipei: Chung-kuo hsüeh-shu chu-tso chiang chu wei-yüan hui, 1969.

Ku-wen yüan 古文苑.
  A: *Tai-nan ko ts'ung shu* 岱南閣叢書.
  B: SPTK.

Kuo Shao-yü 郭紹虞. 'Fu tsai Chung-kuo wen-hsüeh shang te wei-chih' 賦在中國文學上的位置, *Hsiao shuo yüeh-pao* 小說月報, 17 (1927), 1–5.
  Chung-kuo wen-hsüeh p'i-p'ing shih 中國文學批評史. Shanghai: Commercial Press, 1934.

Li chi 禮記. SPTK.

Li-tai fu hui 歷代賦彙. Ch'en Yüan-lung 陳元龍 *et al.* ed. 1706 Yang-chou shih-chü.

Liang Han wen-hsüeh shih ts'an-k'ao tzu-liao 兩漢文學史參考資料. Peking: Chung-hua shu chü, 1962.

Lieh-hsien chuan 列先傳. *Ku chin yi shih* 古今逸史.

Liu Hsieh 劉. *Wen hsin tiao-lung chiao-chu* 文心彫龍校注. Yang Ming-chao 楊明照 ed. Taipei: Shih-chieh shu-chü, 1962.

Lu K'an-ju 陸侃如. 'Sung Yü p'ing chuan' 宋玉評傳, *Hsiao-shuo yüeh-pao*, 17 (1927).
  Sung Yü 宋玉. Shanghai: Ya-tung t'u-shu kuan, 1929.

Lü shih ch'un-ch'iu 呂氏春秋. SPTK.

Ma Kuo-han 馬國翰. *Yü-han shan fang chi yi-shu* 玉函山房輯佚書. Ch'ang-sha: Lang-huan kuan, 1883.

Mao shih 毛詩. SPTK.

Mitarashi Masaru 御手洗勝. *Yô Yu to taigen* 揚雄と太玄, *Shinagaku kenkyû* 支那學研究, 18 (October 1957), 23–32.

Mo tzu 墨子. SPTK.

142 *Bibliography*

Morohashi Tetsuji 諸橋轍次. *Dai kanwa jiten* 大漢和辭典. 13 vols. Tokyo: Taishûkan shoten, 1955–60; 2nd printing 1966–1968.

Nakashima Chiaki 中島千秋. 'Saden inyô shi no imi' 左傳引用詩の意味, *Shinagaku kenkyû*, 10 (1953), 43–56.

'Fu no seiritsu ni tsuite' 賦の成立について, *Tôkyô Shinagaku hô* 東京支那學報, 1 (1955), 165–75.

'Shikyo Jôrin no fu no genryû' 子虛上林の源流, *Tôhô gaku* 東方學, 17 (November 1958), 13–26.

Fu no seiritsu to tenkai 賦の成立と展開. Matsuyama: Kan yôshiten, 1963.

Ou-yang Hsün 歐陽詢, ed. *Yi-wen lei-chü* 藝文類聚. Peking: Chung-hua shu-chü, 1965.

Pan Ku 班固. *Han shu* 漢書. 8 vols. Peking: Chung-hua shu-chü, 1962.

P'ei Ch'ing 沛清. 'Lun Han tai te tz'u fu' 論漢代的辭賦, *Kuo-wen chou-k'an* 國文周刊, 11.8 (March 1934), 1–6.

Po-hu t'ung te lun 白虎通德論. *Han Wei ts'ung-shu* ed.

San-fu huang-t'u 三輔黃圖. SPTK.

Shan hai ching 山海經. SPTK.

Shang shu 尚書. SPTK.

Shang shu ta-chuan 尚書大傳. SPTK.

Shih Chih-mien 施之勉. 'Sung Yü wu fu' 宋玉五賦, *Ta-lu tsa-chih*, 22 (1961), 17–22.

'Yang Hsiung tsou "Kan-ch'üan", "Yü-lieh", erh fu tsai Ch'eng-ti yung-shih san-nien k'ao' 揚雄奏甘泉羽獵二賦在成帝永始三年考, *Ta-lu tsa-chih*, 4.2 (1952), 45.

Shuo yüan 說苑. SPTK.

Ssu-ma Ch'ien 馬遷司. *Shih chi* 史記. 10 vols. Peking: Chung-hua shu-chü 1959.

Suzuki Torao 鈴木虎雄. *Fushi taiyô* 賦史太要. Tokyo: Fusanbô, 1936. Chinese trans.: Yin Shih-ch'ü 殷石臞, 1942; rpt. Taipei: Cheng-chung shu-chü, 1966.

Shinagaku kenkyû 支那文學研究. Kyoto: Kôbundô shobô, 1925.

Suzuki Yoshijirô 鈴木由次郎. *Taigen eki no kenkyû* 大玄易の研究. Tokyo: Meitoku shuppansha, 1964.

T'ang Lan 唐蘭. 'Yang Hsiung tsou "Kan-ch'üan", "Ho-tung", "Yü-lieh", "Ch'ang-yang", ssu fu te nien-tai' 揚雄奏甘泉河東羽獵長楊四賦的年代, *Hsüeh yüan*, 2.8 (1949), 8.

T'ang Ping-cheng 湯炳正. 'Yang Tzu-yün nien-p'u' 揚子雲年譜, *Lun hsüeh* 論學 (April 1937), pp. 76–91; (May 1937), pp. 25–44; (June 1937), pp. 59–83.

Tao-te ching 道德經. SPTK.

T'ao Ch'iu-ying 陶秋英. *Han fu chih shih te yen-chiu* 漢賦之史的研究. Shanghai: Chung-hua shu-chü, 1939.

T'ien Ch'ien-chün 田倩君. 'Ssu-ma Hsiang-ju ch'i-fu' 司馬相如及其賦, *Ta-lu tsa-chih*, 15.4 (August 1957), 115–20; 15.5 (September 1957), 154–7; 15.7 (October 1957), 230–7.

Tung Tso-pin 董作賓. 'Fang-yen hsüeh-chia Yang Hsiung nien-p'u' 方言學家揚雄年譜, *Kuo-li Chung-shan ta-hsüeh yü-yen li-shih yen-chiu so chou-k'an*, 8 (June 1928), 82–8.

Wang Hsien-ch'ien 王先謙. *Han shu pu-chu* 漢書補注. Ch'ang-sha: n.p., 1900.

Wang Jung-pao 王榮寶. *Fa-yen yi shu* 法言義疏. rpt. Taipei: Yi-wen, n.d.

Wang Nien-sun 王念孫. *Tu-shu tsa-chih* 讀書雜志. rpt. Taipei: Shih-chieh shu-chü, 1963.

Wu Tse-yü 吳則虞. 'Yang Hsiung ssu-hsiang p'ing-yi' 揚雄思想評議, *Che-hsüeh yen-chiu* 哲學研究, 6 (1957), 123–38.

Yang Hsiang-shih 楊向時. 'Tso chuan fu shih k'ao' 左傳賦詩考, *K'ung Meng hsüeh-pao* 孔孟學報, 13 (April 1967), 89–124; rpt. *Tso chuan fu shih yin shih k'ao* 左傳賦詩引詩考. Taipei: Chung-hua ts'ung-shu wei-yüan hui, 1972.

Yang, Hsiung 雄揚. *T'ai hsüan ching* 太玄經. SPTK.

Yang Yin-tsung 楊胤宗. 'Sung Yü fu k'ao' 宋玉賦考, *Ta-lu tsa-chih*, 27.3 (1963), 19–24.

Yen K'o-chün 嚴可均. *Ch'üan shang-ku San-tai Ch'in Han San-kuo Liu-ch'ao wen* 全上古三代秦漢三國六朝文. rpt. Taipei: Shin-chieh shu-chü, 1963.

Yü Shih-nan 虞世南, ed. *Pei-t'ang shu-ch'ao* 北堂書鈔. rpt. Taipei: Wen-hai ch'u-pan she, 1966.

Yü Yen 兪棪. *Chung-kuo cheng-lüeh hsüeh shih* 中國政略學史. Nanking: Sheng-huo shu-tien, 1933.

Kuei-ku tzu hsin chu 鬼谷子新注. Shanghai: Commercial Press, 1937.

WESTERN SOURCES

Alekseev, V. M. *Kitaiskaia klassicheskaia proza.* Moscow: Akademiia nauk SSSR, 1959.

Allen, Gay Wilson and Charles T. Davis, eds. *Walt Whitman's Poems.* New York: Grove Press, 1959.

Baldwin, Charles S. *Ancient Rhetoric and Poetic.* New York: Macmillan, 1924.

Medieval Rhetoric and Poetic. New York: Macmillan, 1928.

Belpaire, Bruno, trans. *Le Catechisme philosophique de Yang Hiong-tsé.* Brussels: Editions de l'Occident, 1960.

Beye, Charles Rowan. *The Iliad, the Odyssey, and the Epic Tradition.* Garden City, N.Y.: Doubleday, 1966.

Birch, Cyril and Donald Keene, eds. *Anthology of Chinese Literature.* New York and London: Columbia University Press, 1965.

Bishop, C. W. 'Prefatory Note on the Worship of Earth in Ancient China', *Excavation of a West Han Dynasty Site* (Shanghai, 1932), pp. 1–20.

'The Worship of Earth in Ancient China', JNCBRAS, 64 (1933), 24–43.

Bishop, John L., ed. *Studies in Chinese Literature.* Cambridge, Mass.: Harvard University Press, 1965.

Bodde, Derek. *China's First Unifier: A Study of the Ch'in Dynasty as Seen in the Life of Li Ssŭ 280?–208 B.C.* Leiden: E. J. Brill, 1938; rpt. Hong Kong: Hong Kong University Press, 1967.

Burgess, Theodore C. 'Epideictic Literature', *Studies in Classical Philology*, 3 (Chicago: University of Chicago Press, 1902), 89–261.

Burke, Kenneth. *A Rhetoric of Motives.* 1950; rpt. Berkeley and Los Angeles: University of California Press, 1969.

Buxbaum, David C. and Frederick W. Mote, eds. *Transition and Permanence: Chinese History and Culture A Festschrift in Honor of Dr. Hsiao Kung-ch'üan.* Hong Kong: Cathay Press, 1972.

Chao Yuen-ren. 'Tone, Intonation, Singsong, Chanting, Recitative, Tonal Compositon and Atonal Composition in Chinese', *For Roman Jakobsen, Essays on the Occasion of his Sixtieth Birthday* (The Hague: Mouton, 1956), pp. 52–9.

Chen Shih-hsiang. 'On Structural Analysis of the Ch'u Tz'u Nine Songs', *Tamkang Review*, 2 (April 1971), 3–14.

Christ, Wilhelm von and Otto Stählin. *Geschichte der griechischen litteratur.* 6 vols. Wilhelm Schmid, ed. München: C. H. Beck, 1920.

Ch'ü T'ung-tsu. *Han Social Structure*. Jack L. Dull, ed. Seattle and London: University of Washington Press, 1972.

Cicero ad. C. Herennium, de ratione dicendi, Rhetorica ad Herennium, with an English translation. Harry Caplan, ed. and trans. London: Heinemann, 1954.

Clark, Donald L. *Rhetoric in Greco-Roman Education*. New York: Columbia University Press, 1957.

Cooper, Lane, trans. *The Rhetoric of Aristotle*. New York: Appleton-Century-Crofts, 1932.

Corbett, Edward P. J. *Rhetorical Analyses of Literary Works*. New York, London, and Toronto: Oxford University Press, 1969.

Crump, J. I. 'The Chan-Kuo Ts'e and Its Fiction', TP, 47 (1960), 305–75.

Intrigues: Studies of the Chan-Kuo Ts'e. Ann Arbor: University of Michigan Press, 1964.

trans. *Chan-Kuo Ts'e*. Oxford: The Clarendon Press, 1970.

Curtius, Ernst R. *European Literature and the Latin Middle Ages*. Willard R. Trask, trans. New York: Bollingen, 1953.

Demiéville, Paul. 'Archaïsmes de prononciation en chinois vulgaire', TP, 40 (1950), 1–59.

Dickey, James. 'The Self as Agent', *The Great Ideas Today/1968*. Robert M. Hutchins and Mortimer Adler, eds. (Chicago: Encyclopaedia Britannica, 1968), pp. 90–7.

Diény, Jean-Pierre. *Aux Origines de la poésie classique en Chine: étude sur la poésie à l'époque des Han*. Leiden: E. J. Brill, 1968.

Doeringer, F. M. 'Yang Hsiung and his Formulation of a Classicism', Diss. Columbia University 1971.

Dubs, Homer, H. 'The "Golden Man" of Former Han Times', TP 33 (1937), 1–14; 191–2.

The History of the Former Han Dynasty. 3 vols. Baltimore: Waverly Press, 1938–55.

Dull, Jack, L. 'A Historical Introduction to the Apocryphal (Ch'an-wei) Texts of the Han Dynasty', Diss. University of Washington 1966.

Eichhorn, Werner, 'Die Jagd im alten China', *Ostasiatische Rundschau*, 19 (1939), 416–7.

Fang, Achilles. 'A Note on Huang T'ung and Tzu-wu', HJAS, 12 (1949), 207–15.

Faral, Edmond. *Les Arts poétiques du xiie et du xiiie siècle*. Paris: Champion, 1924.

Forke, Alfred. 'The Philosopher Yang Hsiung', JNCBRAS, 66 (1930), 108–10.

'Der Philosoph Yang Hsiung', *Sinica*, 7 (1932), 169–78.

Geschichte der mittelalterlichen chinesischen Philosophie. Hamburg: Friederichsen, De Gruyter, & Co., 1934.

Frankel, Hans H. *The Flowering Plum and the Painted Lady: Interpretations of Chinese Poetry*. Forthcoming.

Frye, Northrop. *Anatomy of Criticism: Four Essays*. Princeton, N.J.: Princeton University Press, 1957; New York: Atheneum, 1965.

Gaspardone, Emile. 'Les Deux premières fou de Sseu-ma Siang-jou', JA 146 (1958), 447–52.

Giles, Herbert, A. *A Chinese Biographical Dictionary*. 1898; rpt. Taipei: Literature House, 1964.

Graham, Angus C. *The Book of Lieh-tzu*. London: John Murray, 1960.

'The Prosody of the Sao Poems in the Ch'u Tz'u', AM, 10 (1963), 119–61.

Hawkes, David, trans. *Ch'u Tz'u: The Songs of the South*. London: Oxford University Press, 1959; Boston: Beacon, 1962.

'The Quest of the Goddess', AM 13.1–2 (1967), 71–94.

Herrmann, Albert. *An Historical Atlas of China*. 1935; rev. ed. Chicago: Aldine, 1966.

Hervouet, Yves. *Un Poète de cour sous les Han: Sseu-ma Siang-jou*. Paris: Presses Universitaires de France, 1964.
Le Chapitre 117 du Che-ki (Biographie de Sseu-ma Siang-jou). Paris: Presses Universitaires de France, 1972.
Hightower, James R., trans. *Han Shih Wai Chuan*. Cambridge, Mass.: Harvard University Press, 1952.
Topics in Chinese Literature. Cambridge, Mass.: Harvard University Press, 1953.
'Ch'ü Yüan studies', *Silver Jubilee Volume of the Zinbun-Kagaku Kenkyusyo* (Kyoto, 1954), pp. 192–223.
'The *Fu* of T'ao Ch'ien', HJAS 17 (1954), 169–230; rpt. *Studies in Chinese Literature* (Cambridge, Mass., 1965), pp. 45–106.
'The Wen Hsüan and Genre Theory', HJAS, 20 (1957), 512–33; rpt. *Studies in Chinese Literature*, pp. 142–63.
'Chia Yi's "Owl Fu"', AM, 8 (December 1959), 125–30.
Ho Peng-yoke, *The Astronomical Chapters of the Chin shu*. Paris and the Hague: Mouton, 1961.
Hughes, E. R. *Two Chinese Poets: Vignettes cf Han Life and Thought*. Princeton: Princeton University Press, 1960.
Jäger, Fritz. 'Yang Hiung und Wang Mang', *Sinica-Sonderausgabe* (1937), pp. 14–34.
Karlgren, Bernhard. 'The Early History of the Chou Li and Tso Chuan Texts', BMFEA, 3 (1931), 1–59.
'Legends and Cults in Ancient China', BMFEA, 18 (1946), 199–365.
'Glosses on the Book of Documents', BMFEA, 20 (1948), 39–315; 21 (1949), 63–206.
The Book of Odes. Stockholm: Museum of Far Eastern Antiquities, 1950.
'Loan Characters in Pre-Han Texts', BMFEA, 35 (1963), 1–128; II: 36 (1964), 1–105; III: 37 (1965), 1–136; IV: 38 (1966), 1–82; V: 39 (1967), 1–39.
'Grammata Serica Recensa', BMFEA, 29 (1957), 1–332.
Kimm, C. S. 'Kuèi-kuh-Tzè: Der Philosoph vom Teufelstal', AM, 4.1 (1927), 108–46.
Knechtges, David R. 'Two Studies on the Han *Fu*', *Parerga*, 1 (1968), 5–61.
'Yang Shyong, the *Fuh*, and Hann Rhetoric', Diss. University of Washington 1968.
'Wit, Humor, and Satire in Early Chinese Literature', MS, 29 (1970–1), 79–98.
and Jerry Swanson. 'Seven Stimuli for the Prince: the *Ch'i-fa* of Mei Ch'eng', MS, 29 (1970–1), 99–116.
'Narration, Description, and Rhetoric in Yang Shyong's Yeu-lieh Fuh: An Essay in Form and Function in the Hann Fuh', *Transition and Permanence: Chinese History and Culture* (Hong Kong, 1972), 359–77.
'The *Fu* Chapter of Hsun-tzu', *Wen-lin II*, ed. Chow Tse-tsung, forthcoming.
Kopetsky, Elma E. 'Two *Fu* on Sacrifices by Yang Hsiung, *The Fu on Kan-ch'üan* and *The Fu on Ho-tung*', *Journal of Oriental Studies*, 10 (1972), 85–118.
Körte, Alfred. *Hellenistic Poetry*. Trans. Jacob Hammer and Moses Hadas. New York: Columbia University Press, 1929.
Kuo Mo-jo and N. T. Federenko, eds. *Antologiia kitaiskoi poezi*. 4 vols. Moscow: Gos. izdatel'stvo khudozhestvennoi literatury, 1957–8.
Legge, James, trans. *The Chinese Classics*. 7 vols. London: Oxford University Press, 1865–93; rpt. 5 vols. Hong Kong: Oxford University Press, 1960.
Liu, James J. Y. *The Art of Chinese Poetry*. Chicago: Chicago University Press, 1962.
Liu Wu-chi. *An Introduction to Chinese Literature*. Bloomington and London: University of Indiana Press, 1966.
Loewe, Michael. 'K'uang Heng and the Reform of Religious Practices (31 B.C.)', AM, 17.1 (1971), 1–27.

Malmqvist, N. G. D. *Han Phonology & Textual Criticism*. Centre of Oriental Studies, Australian National University, Occasional Papers No. 1, Canberra, 1963.

Margouliès, Georges. *Le Kou-wen chinois*. Paris: P. Geuthner, 1926.

Le 'Fou' dans le Wen-siuan: études et textes*. Paris: P. Geuthner, 1926.

Anthologie raisonnée de la littérature chinoise. Paris: Payot, 1948.

Histoire de la littérature chinoise. 2 vols. Paris: Payot, 1948.

Nagasawa, Kikuya. *Geschichte der chinesischen Literatur*. Eugen Feifel, trans. Darmstadt: Wissenschaftliche Buchgesellschaft, 1959.

Oliver, Robert T. *Communication and Culture in Ancient India and China*. Syracuse: Syracuse University Press, 1971.

Payne, Robert O. *The Key of Remembrance: A Study of Chaucer's Poetics*. New Haven and London: Yale University Press, 1963.

Pokora, Timoteus. 'The Dates of Huan T'an', AO, 27 (1957), 670–77.

'Once More on the Dates of Huan T'an', AO, 29 (1961), 652–7.

'The Necessity of a More Thorough Study of Philosopher Wang Ch'ung and His Predecessors', AO, 30 (1962), 231–57.

'The Life of Huan T'an', AO, 31 (1963), 1–79; 521–76.

'Two Answers to Professor Moriya Mitsuo', AO, 34 (1966), 494–504.

'Huan T'an's *Fu* on Looking for the Immortals', AO, 28 (1960), 353–67.

'Huan T'an and Yang Hsiung on Ssu-ma Hsiang-ju: Some Desultory Remarks on History and Tradition', JAOS, 91.3 (1971), 431–8.

Quintilianus, Marcus Fabius. *The Institutio Oratoria, with an English Translation*. H. E. Butler, ed. New York: G. P. Putnam's Sons, 1920–2.

Rubin, V. A. 'Byl li v istorii kitaiskoi literatury etap oratorskogo istkusstva?' *Narody Azii i Afriki*, No. 5 (1962), pp. 133–4.

Sargent, Clyde B. *Wang Mang: A Translation of the Official Account of His Rise to Power as Given in the History of the Former Han Dynasty*. Shanghai: Graphic Art Book Co., 1947.

Schindler, Bruno. 'Some Notes on Chia Yi and His "Owl Song"', AM, 7 (1959), 161–4.

Schlegel, Gustav. *Uranographie chinoise*. 2 vols. Leiden: E. J. Brill, 1875.

Schwartz, Joseph and John C. Rycenga, eds. *The Province of Rhetoric*. New York: The Ronald Press, 1965.

Scott, John. *Love and Protest: Chinese Poems from the Sixth Century B.C. to the Seventeenth A.D.* New York: Harper Colophon Books, 1972.

Serruys, Paul L-M. 'Prolegomena to the Study of the Chinese Dialects of Han Time According to *Fang Yen*', Diss. University of California, Berkeley 1956.

The Chinese Dialects of Han Time According to Fang Yen. Berkeley and Los Angeles: University of California Press, 1959.

Shih, Vincent Yu-chung, trans. *The Literary Mind and the Carving of Dragons, by Liu Hsieh*. New York: Columbia University Press, 1959.

Shiratori Kurakichi, 'On the Territory of the Hsiung-nu Prince Hsiu-t'u Wang and His Metal Statues for Heaven Worship', MTB, 5 (1930), 1–77.

Shumaker, Wayne. *Literature and the Irrational: A Study in Anthropological Backgrounds*. New York: Washington Square Press, 1960.

Stange, Hans O. H. 'Die Monographie über Wang Mang', *Abhandlungen für die Kunde des Morgenlandes* (1938), pp. 1–336.

Swann, Nancy Lee. *Pan Chao: Foremost Woman Scholar of China*. New York: The Century Co., 1932.

Theunissen, Peter. *Su Ts'in und die Politik der Längs-und-Quer-Achse im chinesischen Altertum*. Breslau: Antonius Verlag, 1938.

Thern, K. L. *Postface of the Shuo-wen chieh-tzu*. Madison, Wisconsin: Department of East Asian Languages and Literature, University of Wisconsin, 1966.

Tjan Tjoe Som. *Po Hu T'ung*. 2 vols. Leiden: E. J. Brill, 1949.

Tökei, Ferenc. *Naissance de l'élégie chinoise*. Paris: Gallimard, 1967.

Waley, Arthur. *The Temple and Other Poems*. New York: A. A. Knopf, 1923.

The Analects of Confucius. New York and London: George Allen and Unwin, 1938.

Translations from the Chinese. New York: A. A. Knopf, 1941.

Chinese Poems. London: George Allen and Unwin, 1946.

The Nine Songs: A study of Shamanism in Ancient China. London: George Allen and Unwin, 1955.

Wang, C. H. 'Sartorial Emblems and the Quest: A Comparative Study of the *Li Sao* and the *Faerie Queene*', *Tamkang Review*, 2.2, 3.1 (October 1971–April 1972), 309–28.

Ware, James R. 'Once More the "Golden Man"', TP, 34 (1938), 174–8.

Watson, Burton. *Ssu-ma Ch'ien: Grand Historian of China*. New York: Columbia University Press, 1958.

Records of the Grand Historian of China. 2 vols. New York: Columbia University Press, 1961.

Early Chinese Literature. New York and London: Columbia University Press, 1962.

Chinese Rhyme-Prose: Poems in the Fu Form from the Han and Six Dynasties Periods. New York and London: Columbia University Press, 1971.

'Literary Theory in the Eastern Han', *Chûgoku bungaku ronshû* (Tokyo: Tsukuma shobô, 1968), pp. 1–13.

Wellek, René and Austin Warren. *Theory of Literature*. New York: Harcourt, Brace and World, 1956.

Wilbur, Martin. *Slavery in China During the Former Han Dynasty*. Chicago: Field Museum of Natural History, 1943.

Wilhelm, Hellmut. 'The Scholar's Frustration: Notes on a Type of "Fu"', *Chinese Thought and Institutions*. John K. Fairbank, ed. (Chicago: University of Chicago Press, 1957), pp. 310–19, 398–403.

'Das Zusammenwirken von Himmel, Erde, und Mensch', *Eranos Jahrbuch 1962* (Zürich: Rhein-Verlag, 1963), pp. 317–30.

'Notes on Chou Fiction', *Transition and Permanence: Chinese History and Culture* (Hong Kong, 1972), pp. 251–63.

Wilhelm, Richard. *Die chinesische Literatur*. Wildpark-Potsdam: Akademische Verlagsgesselschaft Athenaion M.B.H., 1926.

The I Ching or Book of Changes. Gary F. Baynes, trans. Princeton: Princeton University Press, 1950; 1967.

Yang, Lien-sheng. *Studies in Chinese Institutional History*. Cambridge: Harvard University Press, 1961.

Yü Ying-shih. *Trade and Expansion in Han*. Berkeley and Los Angeles: University California Press, 1967.

Character Glossary

A-heng 阿衡
Ai Ch'in Erh-shih 哀秦二世
An-yi 安邑
*b'wât 跋
Chan-kuo ts'e 戰國策
Chang An-shih 張安世
chang-chü 章句
Chang-hua 章華
Chang Liang 張良
Chang Tzu-ch'iao 張子僑
Ch'ang-p'ing 長平
Ch'ang-yang 長楊
Chao 昭, King of Yen
Chao Chao-yi 趙昭儀
Chao Fei-yen 趙飛燕
Chao-yao 招搖
Chen 箴
Ch'en P'ing 陳平
Cheng Ch'iao 征僑
Ch'eng-ming 承明
Ch'eng ti 成帝
chi-shih huang-men 給事黃門
Chi-tzu 箕子
Ch'i 岐
Ch'i fa 七發
Ch'i-lien 祁連
ch'i-lin 麒麟
Ch'i lüeh 七略
chia 家
Chia Yi 賈誼
Chiao-lieh 校獵
Chiao-t'u 椒塗
Chieh 桀
Chieh-ch'ao 解嘲
Chieh Chih-t'ui 介之推
Chieh nan 解難
Chien-chang 建章
Chien Tower 漸臺
Ch'ien 乾
chih (wisdom) 知
chih (content) 質
ch'ih 赤
Ch'ih-yu 蚩尤
Chin-lin 金鄰
Chin-ma men 金馬門
Chin Mi-ti 金日磾
Ching Ts'o 景差
Ch'ing kung 傾宮
Chiu chang 九章
Chiu chen 酒箴

Chiu ho 九河
Chiu ke 九歌
Ch'iung kung 瓊宮
Cho Wang-sun 卓王孫
chou 州
Chou 紂
Chou Po 周勃
Chu p'in 逐貧
chu-tan 朱丹
Ch'u tz'u 楚辭
Ch'ü-sou 渠搜
Ch'ü Yüan 屈原
Chuan-hsü 顓頊
Ch'uan-luan 椽欒
Chuang 莊, Duke of Ch'u
ch'üan 勸
Ch'üan 荃
Chuang Chi 莊忌
Ch'ui 倕
chün-tzu 君子
*d'ôg 跎
*dz'ar-dz'ar ts'iəm-ts'ia 柴虒參差
*dzəp-dəp 雜沓
erh 而
Erh-lao 二老
fa (to attack) 伐
Fa yen 法言
Fan Chü 范雎
Fan K'uai 樊噲
Fan Li 范蠡
Fan sao 反騷
fang 方
Fang yen 方言
Fen-yin 汾陰
feng 諷
feng-huang chü 鳳皇車
Feng-luan 封巒
feng shan 封禪
fu (good fortune) 福
fu (rhapsody) 賦
Fu-fei 宓妃
Fu-niao 鵩鳥
Fu Yüeh 傅說
*gli̯ông-dz'i̯ông 隆崇
Han-chung 漢中
Han-lin chu-jen 翰林主人
hao wen-hsüeh 好文學
He-ling 黻靈
Ho ling 河靈
Ho po 河伯

Ho-tung 河東
Hou-t'u 后土
Hou Ying 侯嬴
hsi 兮
Hsi-ho 羲和
Hsi-wang-mu 西王母
Hsi yüeh 西岳
Hsia Yü 夏育
Hsiang chün 湘君
Hsiang fu-jen 湘夫人
Hsiang Yü 項羽
Hsiao Ho 蕭何
hsiao ke 小歌
Hsieh 斜
Hsiung-erh 熊耳
Hsiung-nu 匈奴
Hsü 盧
Hsü Kuang-han 許廣漢
Hsü-k'uang 猇狂
hзüan 玄
Hsüan 宣, Emperor
Hsüan-chi 璇璣
Hsüan-ming 玄冥
Hsüan p'u 懸圃
Hsüan-shih 璇室
Hsün tzu 荀子
Hu 胡
hua chih 華芝
hua kai 華蓋
Huan 桓, Duke of Ch'i
Huan T'an 桓譚
Huang-shan 黃山
Hui 惠, King of Yen
Hung-nung 弘農
Hung-yi 洪頤
huo 禍
Huo Ch'ü-ping 霍去病
Huo Kuang 霍光
jo-fu 若夫
Jo mu 若木
Ju-shou 蓐收
Kai-hsia 陔下
Kan-ch'üan 甘泉
k'an 堪
Kao-yao 皋陶
*k'ien 掔
*kịwat 蹶
*klôg-kât 膠葛
Kou-chen 鈎陳
Kou-mang 鈎芒
*ku 鈎
Ku-chu 孤竹
Kuan Chung 管仲
K'uang Heng 匡衡
kuei shih 佹詩

K'uei 夔
K'un 坤
K'un-ming 昆明
K'un-wu 昆吾
Kung-shu Pan 公輸般
Kung-sun Hung 公孫弘
lang 郎
Li 禮
Li-kuan 歷觀
Li sao 離騷
lieh chuan 列傳
*lien 轔
*liər 履
Lin Hsiang-ju 蘭相如
Ling-ch'i 靈旗
Ling hsiu 靈脩
*liôk-liang 陸梁
Liu Hsiang 劉向
Liu Hsin 劉歆
Liu Pang 劉邦
Liu-sha 流沙
Liu Wu 劉武
liu yi 六義
Lou Ching 婁敬
Lu 鹿, Mt.
Lu Chia 陸賈
luan 亂
lun-che 論者
Lun yü 論語
Lung-men 龍門
mao 貌
Mei Ch'eng 枚乘
mei-jen 美人
Mei Kao 枚皋
Meng-chu 孟諸
Meng K'o 孟柯
Meng Pen 孟賁
Meng T'ien 蒙恬
Min-yüeh 閩越
ming hao 明號
Mo Ti 墨翟
Mu 穆, Duke of Ch'in
*mung-ńịung 蒙茸
Nan-ch'ao 南巢
Nan-lin 南鄰
Nan-shan 南山
*nịap 躡
*ngiəm-ngiəm 岑崟
nien-p'u 年譜
Ning Ch'i 甯戚
O-fang 阿房
*pâk 搏
Pan Chieh-yü 班婕妤
P'an-keng 庚盤
P'an-yü 番禺

Pao 襃
Pei-chi 北極
P'eng-ch'eng 彭城
P'eng Hsien 彭咸
P'eng-li 彭蠡
P'eng Meng 逢蒙
Pi-kan 比干
Pien Ch'üeh 扁鵲
Pin 豳
piwo 賦
p'iwo 敷
piwang-ńiang 方攘
Po 亳
Po-li Hsi 百里奚
Po Ya 伯牙
Po-yang 白楊
Po Yi 伯夷
pu 部
Pu-chou 不周
pwo 布
p'wo 鋪
san ch'ü 三驅
San jen 三仁
San-luan 三欒
San-tu 三都
San-wei 三危
Shang-lan 上蘭
Shang-lin 上林
She-hsiung kuan 射熊觀
Shen-kuang 神光
shih 事
Shih fu lüeh 詩賦略
shih jen chih fu 詩人之賦
Shih Kao 史高
Shih Kung 史恭
shih lang 侍郎
Shih Liang-ti 史良娣
Shou-yang 首陽
shu 書
Shu Ch'i 叔齊
Shu-sun T'ung 叔孫通
Shu tu 蜀都
shui 說
ssu 思
Ssu-hsüan 思玄
Ssu-ma Ch'ien 司馬遷
Ssu-ma Hsiang-ju 司馬相如
Ssu-ma T'an 司馬談
Su Ch'in 蘇秦
Sung Yü 宋玉
Ta-jen 大人
Ta k'o nan 答客難
t'â 拖
T'ai-chieh 太階
T'ai chih 泰畤

T'ai-hsüan ching 太玄經
T'ai-kung 太公
T'ai-yi 太一
T'ai-yin 太陰
Tan-yai 丹厓
T'ang 唐
T'ang Chü 唐舉
T'ang Le 唐勒
T'ang-li 棠棃
teng kao 登高
Tiao Ch'ü Yuan 弔屈原
T'ien-lang 天狼
T'ien-pao 天寶
Ting-hu 鼎胡
Ts'ai Tse 蔡則
tsan 贊
Ts'an 蠶
Ts'ang Chieh hsün-tsuan 蒼頡訓纂
Ts'ang-hai 倉海
Ts'ang-wu 蒼梧
Ts'ao Shen 曹參
tse 則
Ts'e 測
tsįak 斮
Tso Ssu 左思
Tsou Yang 鄒陽
Tsou Yen 鄒衍
Tsou Ying 騶郢
Tsou Yü-shan 騶餘善
Tsung heng 縱橫
tsung-tsung tswən-tswən 總總撙撙
Tu Fu 杜甫
Tung Chung-shu 董仲舒
Tung-fang Shuo 東方朔
Tung hsiao 洞簫
Tung hsüeh 洞穴
T'ung-t'ien 通天
Tzu-hsü 子虛
tzu-jan 自然
Tzu-mo k'o-ch'ing 子墨客卿
tz'u fu 此夫
tz'u fu 辭賦
tz'u-jen chih fu 辭人之賦
Wang Erh 王爾
Wang hsien 望仙
Wang Ken 王根
Wang Mang 王莽
Wang Pao 王襃
Wang Shu 望舒
Wang Yin 王音
Wei ch'i 圍棊
Wei Ch'ing 衞青
Wei Jan 魏冉
Wei-tzu 微子
Wei-yang 未央

wen 又
Wen Chung 文種
wen-hsüeh 文學
wen tz'u 文辭
Wo Chüan 偓佺
Wu Chi 無忌
Wu shih kung 亡是公
Wu ti 武帝
Wu Tzu-hsü 伍子胥
Wu-yi shan-li 烏弋山離
Wu-yu hsien-sheng 烏有先生
**xiəp-xăk xmwət-xwăk* 翕赫習霍
*xjung-djung 洶涌
Ya ch'in 雅琴
ya-yu 猰貐
Yang Chu 楊朱
Yang Chuang 楊莊
Yang Hsiung 揚雄
yao yen miao tao 要言妙道
yeh 邪
Yen 嚴, Duke of Ch'u
Yen-ch'ih 鹽池
Yen Ho 顏闔
Yen Lun 顏倫
Yen Shih-ku 顏師古
Yen Ying 晏嬰
Yi-ch'un 宜春
Yi-wu 夷吾

Yi Yin 伊尹
yin (riddle) 隱
yin (unrestrained) 淫
Yu Fu-feng 右扶風
yu shui 遊說
Yu tu 幽都
Yu Yü 有虞
yü (interrogative) 與
yü (carriage) 輿
Yü 禹
Yü Ch'ing 虞卿
Yü Fu 臾跗
Yü-heng 玉衡
Yü-hsiu 御宿
Yü hsueh 禹穴
Yü lieh 羽獵
Yü nü 玉女
Yü shih 虞氏
yü shih 於是
Yü-t'ang 玉堂
yü tzu hu 於茲虖
Yü-wu 余吾
Yü yüan 虞淵
Yüan yu 遠遊
Yüeh Yi 樂毅
Yün 雲
Yün-meng 雲夢
Yün-yang 雲陽

Index

A-heng. *See* Yi Yin
Adynata, 124, n. 29
Ai Ch'in Erh-shih fu, 34, 127, n. 88
An-yi, 58, 131, n. 75, n. 77
Analects, See Lun yü
Angular Arranger. *See* Kou-chen
Annotations on the Ts'ang Chieh. See Ts'ang Chieh hsün tsuan
'Answer to a Guest's Objections'. *See Ta k'o nan*
'Appraisal'. *See Tsan*
Aristotle, 125, n. 41
Armillary Sphere. *See* Hsüan-chi
'Autobiography', by Yang Hsiung, 9, 45, 53, 58, 63, 80, 97, 113–14, 115, 116, 122, n. 47

'Barricade Hunt Rhapsody'. *See Chiao-lieh fu*
Bear Shooting Lodge. *See* She-hsiung kuan
'Bellstand Rhapsody'. *See Chü fu*
Book of Changes. See Yi ching
Book of Documents. See Shang shu
Book of Songs. See Shih ching
Brilliant Companion Chao. *See* Chao Chao-yi
Bronze men (*chin jen*), 48, 53, 129, n. 30

Candidate for Appointment. *See Tai chao*
Catalogue, 36–7, 74–5
Chan-kuo ts'e, 22–3, 33, 124, n. 36, 125, n. 51, n. 56, n. 57
Chang An-shih, 102, 137, n. 53
Chang Ch'iao, 127, n. 56, 139, n. 4
Chang-chü, 136, n. 41
Chang Heng, 55, 128, n. 21, 132, n. 62
Chang-hua Tower, 72, 134, n. 51
Chang Liang, 100, 136, n. 40, 137, n. 54
Chang P'u, 11
Chang T'an, 44–5
Chang Tzu-ch'iao, 42
Ch'ang-an, 3, 26, 29, 34, 113, 116, 119, 132, n. 15, 137, n. 49
Ch'ang-ho Gate, 46, 53, 65, 128, n. 25, 133, n. 29
Ch'ang-p'ing, 51, 130, n. 56

Ch'ang-yang fu: content, 85–8; dating, 113–16; translation, 80–5; mentioned, 4, 96, 107, 109, 111, 119
Ch'ang-yang Palace, 63, 64, 80, 84, 87, 132, n. 15, 134, n. 67
'Ch'ang-yang Rhapsody'. *See Ch'ang-yang fu*
Chao (state), 25
Chao, King of Ch'in, 136, n. 39
Chao, King of Yen, 136, n. 38, n. 45
Chao Chao-yi (Brilliant Companion Chao), 54, 56
Chao Ch'i, 136, n. 28
Chao Chü, 25
Chao Fei-yen, 56
Chao-yao (star), 46, 128, n. 20
Ch'en pao. *See* T'ien pao
Ch'en Pen-li, 122, n. 36
Ch'en P'ing, 100, 102, 136, n. 40, 137, n. 54
Ch'en Shou-yi, 109
Ch'en Yüan-lung, 11
Cheng Chen-to, 109, 110
Cheng Chiao-fu, 133, n. 41
Cheng Ch'iao, 49, 129, n. 41
Ch'eng, Emperor of Han, 3, 43, 44, 45, 54, 73, 78, 114, 115, 133, n. 21
Ch'eng, King of Chou, 71, 102
Ch'eng-ming Hall, 46, 114, 128, n. 14
Ch'eng-tu, 3, 117, 119
'Chess Discourse'. *See Po yi lun*
Chi (Ch'i official), 136, n. 45
Chi (legendary minister), 99
Chi-shih huang-men, 4, 119, 121, n. 17
Chi-tzu, 136, n. 36
Ch'i (Chou territory), 60, 61
Ch'i (state), 34, 136, n. 28, n. 38, n. 42
Ch'i fa, 30–1, 32–3, 35, 126, n. 76, 130, n. 60
Ch'i-lien, 102, 137, n. 56
Ch'i lüeh, 114
Chia Yi, 26–8, 29, 95, 126, n. 71
Ch'iang (foreign tribe), 83
Ch'iang-jung (foreign tribe), 82
Chiao (barricade), 132, n. 3

Chiao-lieh fu: dating, 113–16; description in, 74; indirect criticism, 77–80; narration in, 73–4; translation, 63–73; mentioned, 4, 80, 96, 107, 109, 110, 111, 119, 134, n. 62

Chiao-t'u, 99, 136, n. 30

Chieh, King of Hsia, 54, 106, 129, n. 37, 137, n. 67

Chieh-ch'ao: translation, 97–103; mentioned, 5, 107, 111, 118, 139, n. 3

Chieh Chih-t'ui, 60, 61, 131, n. 93, n. 94

Chieh Mountains, 58, 60, 131, n. 90

Chieh nan, 96, 97

Chien-chang Palace, 64, 132, n. 18

Chien ta-fu, 121, n. 13

Chien Ti, 15

Chien Tower, 64, 132, n. 19

Ch'ien (Heaven), 132, n. 102

Ch'ien-lei, 130, n. 70 .

Ch'ien Ta-hsin, 115

Ch'ien-t'ang River, 134, n. 56

Chih (robber), 106, 137, n. 67

Chih (substance, content), 90

Ch'ih-yu, 22, 46, 67, 128, n. 23

Chin-lin, 133, n. 46

Chin-ma men, 97, 102, 135, n. 19

Chin Mi-ti, 102, 137, n. 53

Ch'in (state), 25, 81, 87, 99, 102, 134, n. 72, 136, n. 39, 137, n. 55

Ch'in Spirit, 59, 131, n. 90

Ching, Emperor of Han, 30

Ching River, 59, 62

Ching Ts'o, 95

Ching-yang, Lord of (younger brother of King Chao of Ch'in), 101

Ch'ing kung, 129, n. 37

Ch'ing Pu, 26

Chiu chang, 17

Chiu chen, 121, n. 22

Chiu ho (Nine Rivers), 60, 131, n. 95

Chiu ke, 14–15, 124, n. 19

Ch'iung kung, 49, 54, 129, n. 37

Cho-lu, 22

Cho Wang-sun, 103, 137, n. 57

Chou, Duke of, 22, 57, 71, 129, n. 45

Chou, King of Shang-Yin, 22, 54

Chou li, 123, n. 11

Chou Po, 100, 136, n. 40

Chou sung, 132, n. 105

Chou yi. See Yi ching

Chu Chien, 26

Chu Hsi, 120, n. 7

Chu-jung, 60

Chu-p'in fu: discussed, 107–8; translation, 104–7; mentioned, 110, 121, n. 23

Ch'u (state), 16, 25, 26, 30, 34, 35

Ch'u-hsüeh chi, 10

Ch'u tz'u, 14, 18, 20, 30, 38, 89, 124, n. 18, 125, n. 40, 126, n. 71, 135, n. 3

Chü Ch'in mei Hsin, 119

Chü fu, 126, n. 71

Ch'ü River, 30

Ch'ü-sou, 99, 136, n. 29

Ch'ü Yüan: Chia Yi on, 27; life, 14; suicide, 16; Yang Hsiung on, 3; mentioned, 3, 55, 71, 73, 76, 96, 123, n. 15, n. 16, 134, n. 56, 134, n. 57, 136, n. 44

Chuan-hsü, 65, 73, 133, n. 28

Ch'uan-luan, 46, 128, n. 25

Ch'üan (Fragrant One), 16

ch'üan (exhortation), 61

Ch'üan Han wen, 11

Ch'üan Tower, 64, 133, n. 21

Chuang, Duke of Ch'u, 65, 78, 133, n. 26

Ch'ui, 49, 129, n. 40

Ch'un-yü K'un, 4, 121, n. 19

Chung-san ta-fu, 119

Ch'ung, 22

Ch'ung-hua. *See* Shun

Cloud Master. *See* Yün-shih

Compendium of Arts and Letters. See Yi-wen lei-chü

Complete Han Prose. See Ch'üan Han wen

Confucian teaching, Yang Hsiung on, 6

'Contra Sao'. *See Fan sao*

'Criticizing Ch'in Praising Hsin'. *See Chü Ch'in mei Hsin*

Crump, James I., 25

Dark. See Hsüan

Dark City Mountain. *See* Yu-tu

Demiéville, Paul, 38

Dickey, James, 27

Dictionary, and rhapsody, 38

'Dissolving Difficulty'. *See Chieh nan*

'Dissolving Ridicule'. *See Chieh ch'ao*

'Distant Wandering'. *See Yüan yu*

Documents of the Northern Hall. See Pei-t'ang shu-ch'ao

Doubled-persuasion. *See* Rhetoric.

'Dry Clouds Rhapsody'. *See Han yün fu*

'Early Spring Rhapsody'. *See Meng ch'un fu*

'Eastern Capital Rhapsody'. *See Tung ching fu*

'Elegant Zither Rhapsody'. *See Ya ch'in fu*

'Embracing the Sand'. *See Huai sha*

'Encirclement Chess Rhapsody'. *See Wei ch'i fu*

Epideictic. *See* Rhapsody, Rhetoric.

Erh-lao (Two Elders), 99, 136, n. 36

'Essay on Bibliography'. *See Yi-wen chih*

Essay on Man, 27

'Examining the Spirit Rhapsody'. *See He ling fu*

'Expelling Poverty Rhapsody'. *See Chu-p'in fu*
Expolitio, 24, 31, 126, n. 80

Fa yen: content of, 7; on literature, 94–5; on rhapsody, 95–6; on *wen*, 93, 119; mentioned, 1
Fan Chü, 100, 101, 102, 135, n. 26, n. 39, 137, n. 48
Fan K'uai, 100, 136, n. 40
Fan Li, 99, 136, n. 37
Fan sao, 3, 119
Fang chang Island, 64
Fang yen, 1, 119, 120, n. 4
Fei-lien, 67, 132, n. 100
Fen-yin, 44, 45, 58, 114, 115, 131, n. 74
Feng (indirect criticism), 4, 34, 53
Feng (sacrifices), 64, 71, 79, 87
Feng-ch'üeh (tower), 64, 132, n. 18
Feng-luan (tower), 40, 47, 129, n. 27, 130, n. 55
Feng-lung, 40
Feng River, 86, 131, n. 90
Fiery Mars. *See* Ying-huo
'Five Sheepskins'. *See* Po-li Hsi
'Flute Rhapsody'. *See Ti fu*
Forke, Alfred, 6
Frye, Northrop, 24
Fu (rhapsody); in *Hsün tzu*, 18–21; meaning of, 12–14, 123, n. 11, 127, n. 1
Fu of 'frustration'. *See* Rhapsody, 'frustration'
Fu-fei, 15, 50, 54, 55–6, 71, 76, 130, n. 50, 134, n. 57
Fu-hsi, 64, 76, 77, 133, n. 23
Fu hsing, 102. *See also* Lü hsing
Fu-niao fu, 28, 30, 126, n. 69, n. 70
Fu shih, 12
Fu Yüeh, 136, n. 42

Garden of Ancient Literature. See Ku-wen yüan
Gentleman. *See Lang*
Gold Horse Gate. *See* Chin-ma men
Grandee Remonstrant. *See Chien ta-fu*
Great Altar. *See* T'ai chih
Great Dark Classic. See T'ai-hsüan ching
'Great Dark Rhapsody'. *See T'ai-hsüan fu*
Great Dipper. *See Pei-tou*
'Great Man Rhapsody'. *See Ta-jen fu*
Great Unity. *See* T'ai-yi
Great Yin. *See* T'ai-yin

Han-chung, 80
Han-kao, 133, n. 41
Han nymph (Han nü), 70, 133, n. 41
Han shu, 9, 104

Han Yüan-chi, 122, n. 56
Han yün fu, 126, n. 71
Hao River, 86
Hawkes, David, 16, 17
He ling fu, 117
Heavenly Bow. *See* Hu hsing
Hervouet, Yves, 6, 36, 37
Hightower, J. R., 6
Historical example. *See* Rhetoric
History of the Former Han. See Han shu
Ho ling (River spirit), 59, 131, n. 91
Ho po, 131, n. 91
Ho-tung fu: dating, 113–16; translation, 58–61; mentioned, 4, 44, 63, 110, 119
'Ho-tung Rhapsody'. *See Ho-tung fu*
Hou-t'u, 4, 44, 46, 58, 130, n. 72
Hou Ying, 136, n. 43
Hsi-ching tsa-chi, 10, 120, n. 6
Hsi-ho, 59, 131, n. 89
Hsi shih, 126, n. 71
Hsi tu fu, 128, n. 14
Hsi-wang-mu, 39, 50, 55, 127, n. 105, 130, n. 50
Hsi yüeh (Western Peak), 58, 60, 61, 131, n. 79. *See also* Mount Hua
Hsia Yü, 66, 133, n. 33
Hsiang chün, 15
Hsiang fu-jen, 15
'Hsiang Lady'. *See Hsiang fu-jen*
'Hsiang Princess'. *See Hsiang chün*
Hsiang River, 27
Hsiang Yü, 61, 131, n. 98, 134, n. 72
Hsiao, Prince of Liang. *See* Liu Wu
Hsiao Ho, 100, 102, 136, n. 40
Hsiao ke, 18, 125, n. 40
Hsiao T'ung, 10, 62
Hsieh (minister), 99
Hsieh (valley), 80, 134, n. 64
Hsiung-erh Mountain, 68, 133, n. 37
Hsiung-nu, 87, 88, 129, n. 30, 133, n. 47, 134, n. 75, 135, n. 76, 137, n. 56
Hsü Kuang-han, 102, 137, n. 53
Hsü-k'uang (demon), 46, 128, n. 21
Hsüan, Emperor of Han: on rhapsody, 41; mentioned, 121, n. 13, 137, n. 53
Hsüan, King of Chou, 54
Hsüan, King of Ch'i, 64, 77
Hsüan (dark), 8, 98, 101, 103
Hsüan-chi (Armillary Sphere), 50, 129, n. 47
Hsüan-ming, 48, 60, 65, 73, 129, n. 33, 130, n. 70, 133, n. 28
Hsüan-p'u (Hanging Garden), 48, 129, n. 31
Hsüan shih (Jade Building), 49, 54, 129, n. 37
Hsün Ch'ing, 18. *See also* Hsün tzu
Hsün tsuan p'ien, 119, 120, n. 3

Hsün tzu, 27, 28
Hsün-yü, 82
Hu (non-Chinese tribe), 63, 71, 80, 85, 114
Hu hsing (Bow star), 59, 67, 131, n. 86
Hua, Mount, 55, 68, 80, 131, n. 79. *See also* Hsi yüeh
Huai-nan, 26
Huai sha, 17
Huai-yin, 30
Huan, Duke of Ch'i, 22, 65, 78, 133, n. 26, 136, n. 33, n. 45
Huan T'an, 9, 45, 55, 109, 128, n. 12, 130, n. 67
Huan-tou, 22
Huang (Yellow) Mountains, 64, 132, n. 16
Hui, King of Chou, 137, n. 55
Hui, King of Yen, 99, 136, n. 38
Hundred *Mou* Palace. *See* Ch'ing kung
Hung-nung, 80, 134, n. 65
Hung-yi banner, 50
Huo Ch'ü-ping, 82, 87, 102, 134, n. 75, 137, n. 56
Huo Kuang, 100, 136, n. 40
Hyperbole, 36

Impressifs, 38–9, 40, 52, 57, 127, n. 102
Indirect criticism. *See Feng*, Rhetoric, *Kan-ch'üan fu*, *Chiao-lieh fu*
Interpretatio, 24
Intrigues of the Warring States. See Chan-kuo ts'e
Itineraria, 17–18, 117

Jade Hall. *See* Yü t'ang
Jang, Marquis of, 100, 101, 136, n. 39
Jo tree, 50, 129, n. 46
Ju-shou, 60
Jung (non-Chinese tribe), 80

Kai-hsia, 60, 61, 131, n. 98
Kan-chiang (sword), 46
Kan-ch'üan fu: dating, 113–16; description in, 52–3; indirect criticism in, 53; translation, 45–51; mentioned, 4, 63, 74, 75, 76, 107, 109, 110, 119, 130, n. 71
Kan-ch'üan kung fu, 128, n. 11
Kan-ch'üan kung sung, 128, n. 11
K'an (Heaven), 46, 57, 128, n. 21
Kao-kuang Palace, 48, 129, n. 36
Kao-tsu. *See* Liu Pang.
Kao-yao, 49, 55, 99, 129, n. 43
Ke-tao (asterism), 129, n. 32
Kenning, 57
Kou-chen, 46, 128, n. 20
Kou-chien, King of Yüeh, 136, n. 37
Kou-mang, 60
Ku-chu, 107, 137, n. 68

Ku-wen yüan, 10–11, 104, 117, 122, n. 56
Kuan Chung, 99, 136, n. 33, 136, n. 42
Kuang-ling, 30
Kuang sao, 120, n. 11
K'uang Heng, 44–5, 56
Kuei-chi, 76, 133, n. 42
Kuei-ku tzu, 22, 125, n. 49
Kuei shih, 18, 19, 20
K'uei, 49, 129, n. 39
K'uei-hsü (demon), 46, 128, n. 21
K'un (Earth), 132, n. 102
K'un-lun Mountains, 15, 48, 66, 81, 105, 129, n. 31, 129, n. 46
K'un-ming Lake, 64, 65, 66, 132, n. 17
K'un-wu, 64, 132, n. 14
Kung-kung, 22, 129, n. 49
Kung Liu, 132, n. 99
Kung-shu Pan, 49, 129, n. 40
Kung-sun Hung, 102, 135, n. 2, 137, n. 56

'Lament for Ch'ü Yüan'. *See Tiao Ch'ü Yüan fu*
'Lamenting the Second Emperor of Ch'in Rhapsody'. *See Ai Ch'in Erh-shih fu*
Lang, 4, 121, n. 17. *See also Shih-lang*
Lao tzu, 28
Lautbild, 38
Leaves of Grass, 37
'Letter to Jen An'. *See Pao Jen An shu*
Li kuan (viewing tower), 58, 60
Li Lou, 85
Li, Mount, 131, n. 96
Li Sao, 3, 14–18, 55, 57, 124, n. 24, 134, n. 56
Li Shan, 10, 42, 126, n. 75, n. 86, 133, n. 35
Li Ssu, 120, n. 3
Li-tai fu-hui, 11
Liang (Chou state), 136, n. 28
Liang (Han kingdom), 29–30, 34
Liang, Mount, 71, 85. *See also* Shan (sacrifice)
Liang wang t'u-yüan fu, 126, n. 75
Lieh tzu, 79
Lin Hsiang-ju, 102, 137, n. 55
Ling, King of Ch'u, 134, n. 51
Ling ch'i (Magic Pennant), 50, 130, n. 52
Ling fen (shaman), 16
Ling hsiu (divine Beauty), 16
Ling-t'ai, 72, 134, n. 51
Literary Selections. See Wen hsüan
Liu, Marquis of. *See* Chang Liang
Liu Hsiang, 18, 19, 22, 43, 45, 56, 124, n. 18, 127, n. 120, 133, n. 40
Liu Hsieh, 26, 45, 109, 134, n. 57
Liu Hsin, 9, 19, 114, 115, 116, 125, n. 11
Liu K'uei, 117, 118

Liu Pang, 26, 61, 87, 131, n. 98, 137, n. 49, n. 50
Liu P'i, 30
Liu-sha, 50, 130, n. 53
Liu Wu, 29, 34
Liu yi (six poetic principles), 123, n. 11
Lo River, 15, 76, 134, n. 57
Lo-yang, 137, n. 52
Lou Ching, 102, 137, n. 49
Lu Chi, 28
Lu Chia, 26
Lu, Mount, 71, 133, n. 47
Lü, hsing, 137, n. 51. *See also Fu hsing*
luan (coda), 20
Lun yü, 6, 90, 123, n. 7, 127, n. 112, 131, n. 97, 135, n. 5, n. 12
Lung-men, 58, 60, 61, 131, n. 76, n. 95
Lykophron, of Chalkis, 38, 127, n. 100

Ma Jung, 127, n. 120
Ma Kuo-han, 120, n. 3, 125, n. 46
Magical journey. *See Itineraria*
Mao Heng, 123, n. 8
Mao-t'ou (Pleides), 133, n. 34
'Master Void Rhapsody'. *See Tzu-hsü fu*
Mei Ch'eng, 29, 30, 38, 41, 77, 78, 95, 130, n. 60
Mei jen (Lovely One), 16
Mei Kao, 41
Men-hsia shih, 122, n. 47
Meng, Duke, 67
Meng-chu, 72, 78, 134, n. 50
Meng ch'un fu, 26
Meng Pen, 66, 133, n. 33
Meng T'ien, 133, n. 34
Meng tzu, 79, 99, 125, n. 44, 136, n. 28
Min-yüeh, 82, 134, n. 74
Ming ching, 129, n. 32
Mo Ti, 71, 79, 134, n. 48
Mo-yeh (sword), 66
Model Sayings. *See Fa yen*
Mother Queen of West. *See Hsi-wang-mu*
Mu, Duke of Ch'in, 99, 136, n. 38

Nakashima Chiaki, 5
Nam-Viet. *See Nan-yüeh*
Nan-ch'ao, 60, 132, n. 99
Nan lin (Southern Lin), 71, 133, n. 46
Nan shan (Southern Mountains), 80, 84, 114, 131, n. 90, 132, n. 15
Nan-yüeh, 26, 83, 134, n. 74
'Nine Declarations'. *See Chiu chang*
Nine Rivers. *See Chiuho*
'Nine Songs'. *See Chiu ke*
Ning Ch'i, 136, n. 42
Northern Dipper. *See Pei-tou*

O-fang Palace, 73, 134, n. 52
Ou-yang Hsün, 10
'Owl Rhapsody'. *See Fu-niao fu*

Pan Chieh-yü, 130, n. 69
Pan Ku, 9, 114, 115
P'an-keng, 54, 130, n. 62
P'an lao-ch'ou, 120, n. 11
P'an-yü, 99, 136, n. 30
Pao (valley), 80, 134, n. 64
Pao Jen An shu, 124, n. 27
Pearl, 111
Pei-ch'en. *See Pei-chi*
Pei-chi (Polaris), 48, 53, 81, 134, n. 72
Pei-t'ang shu-ch'ao, 10
Pei-tou (Ursa major), 134, n. 72
P'eng-ch'eng, 60, 131, n. 98
P'eng Hsien, 16, 71, 73, 76, 133, n. 44, 134, n. 56, n. 57
P'eng-lai (island), 64
P'eng-li, 71, 75, 76, 133, n. 42, n. 57
P'eng Meng, 69, 133, n. 38
Persuasion. *See Rhetoric*
Pi-kan, 136, n. 36
Pien Ch'üeh (doctor), 101, 103
Pin, 60, 61, 132, n. 99
P'ing-lo Lodge, 67
P'ing-yi, 132, n. 100
'Plume Hunt Rhapsody'. *See Chiao-lieh fu*
Po (Shang capital), 83, 130, n. 62
Po-li Hsi, 99, 136, n. 38
Po-ya (musician), 49, 129, n. 39
Po-yang Lodge, 66, 133, n. 32
Po Yi, 136, n. 36, 137, n. 68
Po yi lun, 127, n. 120
'Poem of Anomalies'. *See Kuei shih*
Poetria nova, 32
Pokora, Timoteus, 115
Pole Star. *See Pei-chi*
Pope, Alexander, 28
Prosody: 'Sao-style', 17, 20, 27, 124, n. 26; *Shih ching*, 19, 107
Pu-chou (mountain), 50, 129, n. 49, 138, n. 28
Pu-sui, 22
Purple Palace. *See Tzu-wei*

Quintilian, 23, 24

Rabelais, François, 38
'Rebutting Grief and Sorrow'. *See P'an lao-ch'ou*
Records of the Historian. *See Shih chi*
Regional Words. *See Fang yen*
Revolt of the Seven Kingdoms (154 B.C.), 29

Rhapsody: early Han, 26–8; epideictic, 2, 31–2, 36–40, 41, 42–3, 57–8; frustration, 17, 27–8, 103–4, 107, 117; panegryic, 4, 36, 40; persuasion in, 110–12; as entertainment, 40–3; by Shu poets, 3; sources, 10–11; studies, 5–6; recitation of, 12–14, 17, 42, 111; Yang Hsiung on, 2, 4–5, 95–7
'Rhapsody of the *Song* Writers'. *See Shih-jen chih fu*
'Rhapsody on Literature'. *See Wen fu*
Rhetoric: amplification, 32; doubled-persuasion, 25, 33, 88, 96, 135, n. 21; in early Han, 26; epideictic, 32, 38, 42–3, 56, 79, 110–11; indirect criticism, 25, 35–6; meaning of, 24; ornament, 24–5, persuasion, 5, 21–2, 29, 30, 32–3, 35–6, 79–80, 96; Warring States, 21–5; historical example, 23–4, 103, 117
riddle, 18–19
Rimbaud, Arthur, 2
Rites of Chou. See Chou li

Sa-so Palace, 64, 132, n. 18
San-huang (Three August Ones), 61, 65, 128, n. 18
San jen (Three Humane Ones), 99, 136, n. 36
San-luan (tower), 51, 130, n. 55
San tu fu, 117, 139, n. 6
San-tsung Mountain, 66, 133, n. 30
San wang (Three Kings), 65, 84, 102
San-wei Mountains, 50, 129, n. 48
'Sao Expanded'. *See Kuang sao*
School of Politicians. *See Tsung-heng chia*
Serruys, Paul L-M, 120, n. 4
'Seven Stimuli'. *See Ch'i fa*
Shaman, 15, 16
Shaman Hsien. *See Wu Hsien*
Shan (sacrifices), 71, 79, 85, 87
Shang-lan Lodge, 69, 133, n. 39
Shang-lin fu: compared with *Chiao-lieh fu*, 74; rhetoric of, 35–6; mentioned, 34, 35, 57, 63, 75, 78, 110, 112, 127, n. 88, 130, n. 71
Shang-lin Park: 4, 34, 64, 73, 76, 127, n. 89, 132, n. 14, 133, n. 29
'Shang-lin Rhapsody'. *See Shang-lin fu*
Shang shu, 21, 122, n. 1, 125, n. 43, 130, n. 62, 131, n. 89, 133, n. 45
Shao, Duke of, 57, 129, n. 44
She-hsiung kuan (Bear Shooting Lodge), 80, 114, 134, n. 67
Shen Ch'in-han, 115
Shen-kuang Palace, 67, 133, n. 35
Shen-ming Tower, 64, 132, n. 18
Shen-nung, 22, 64, 133, n. 23

Shih (Han family), 102
Shih chi, 10
Shih ching: Yang Hsiung's poetic ideal, 96; Mao no. 3, 137, n. 63; no. 16, 129, n. 44; no. 26, 137, n. 64; no. 45, 137, n. 64; no. 50, 123, n. 8; no. 157, 129, n. 45; no. 176, 137, n. 65; no. 189, 130, n. 61; no. 196, 137, n. 62; no. 204, 137, n. 62; no. 211, 137, n. 61; no. 215, 135, n. 82; no. 265, 132, n. 105; mentioned, 12, 107, 123, n. 6; 132, n. 104, 133, n. 45
Shih ch'üeh (tower), 129, n. 27
Shih fu lüeh, 12–13, 123, n. 15, 124, n. 18
Shih-jen chih fu, 95–6, 103, 107
Shih Kao, 137, n. 53
Shih Kuang, 137, n. 53
Shih kuan (tower), 47, 129, n. 27
Shih-lang, 4, 119, 121, n. 17
Shih Liang-ti, 137, n. 53
Shou-yang Mountain, 106, 137, n. 68
Shu, 3, 42, 43, 116
'Shu Capital Rhapsody'. *See Shu tu fu*
Shu Ch'i, 137, n. 68
Shu ching. See Shang shu
Shu-sun T'ung, 102, 137, n. 50
Shu tu fu, 57, 63, 117–18
Shuai, Mount, 59
Shui (persuasion), 33
Shun, 15, 22, 58, 60, 64, 71, 75, 76, 102, 129, n. 29, n. 43, 131, n. 80, n. 96, 133, n. 42, 136, n. 32
Sir Gawain and the Green Knight, 111
'Small Song'. *See Hsiao ke*
'Sorrow for Troth Betrayed'. *See Hsi shih*
Southern Lin. *See Nan lin*
Southern Mountains. *See Nan shan*
Southern Yüeh. *See Nan-yüeh*
Sovereign Earth. *See Hou t'u*
Ssu-hsüan fu, 55
Ssu-ma Ch'ien, 10, 29, 124, n. 27, 127, n. 107
Ssu-ma Gate, 133, n. 30
Ssu-ma Hsiang-ju: at Liang, 29; rhapsodies of, 39–40; epideictic rhapsody, 1, 36–40; influence on Yang Hsiung, 1–2, 3, 57, 63, 111–12, 114, 116; Yang Hsiung on, 40, 43, 95, 96; on rhapsody, 120, n. 6; mentioned, 28, 42, 45, 52, 53, 55, 74, 75, 77, 78, 103, 109, 121, n. 13, 134, n. 55, n. 57, 137, n. 57
Ssu-ma Kuang, 138, n. 4
Ssu-ma T'an, 130, n. 63
Staff Clerk. *See Men-hsia shih*
Student's Primer. See Ch'u hsüeh chi
Su Ch'in, 22
'Summary on Songs and Rhapsodies'. *See Shih fu lüeh*

Sung (dynasty), 2
Sung (chanting), 13
Sung Yü, 95, 123, n. 14; 125, n. 58, 127,
    n. 117
Suzuki Torao, 5, 13
'Sweet Springs Palace', Ode on. *See Kan-ch'üan
    kung sung*
Sweet Springs Palace, 44, 45, 46, 52, 56,
    114, 114
'Sweet Springs Palace Rhapsody'. *See
    Kan-ch'üan kung fu*
'Sweet Springs Rhapsody'. *See Kan-ch'üan
    fu*
Swift Cavalry General. *See* Huo Ch'ü-ping
Synonomia, 24

Ta-jen fu, 34, 38–40, 52, 55, 63, 76, 78,
    121, n. 18, 127, n. 88, n. 107, 129, n.
    41, 130, n. 70, 132, n. 100
Ta k'o nan, 97
Tai-chao, 3, 100, 119, 136–7, n. 46
T'ai-chieh (Great Stair), 82, 134, n. 73
T'ai chih, 44, 45, 46, 114
T'ai-hsüan ching: contents, 7–8; on *wen*, 90–3;
    mentioned, 1, 9, 96, 98, 103, 117, 118, 119
T'ai-hsüan fu, 117, 118, 138, n. 3
T'ai-hua, Mount. *See* Mount Hua, Hsi yüeh
T'ai-kung, 136, n. 36
T'ai, Mount, 64, 77, 79, 85, 133, n. 25
T'ai-yi (Great Unity), 39, 44, 50, 56, 128,
    n. 20, 130, n. 52
T'ai-yi (pond), 64
T'ai-yin, 46, 128, n. 20
Tan River, 130, n. 54
Tan-yai (Cinnabar Cliff), 50
T'ang, Ch'eng (Shang ruler), 22, 64, 129,
    n. 43, 132, n. 99, 136, n. 33
T'ang Chü, 100, 136, n. 39
T'ang Le, 95
T'ang-li, 51, 130, n. 55
T'ang Yao. *See* Yao
Taoism, 28, 93
Teng kao, 13
Three August Ones. *See* San-huang
'Three Capitals Rhapsody'. *See San tu fu*
Three Kings. *See* San wang
Three Miao (San miao), 22
Ti fu, 127, n. 117
Tiao Ch'ü Yüan fu, 27, 28
Tien-ho, 64
Tien Lake, 132, n. 17
T'ien kuan (Heavenly Barrier), 81, 134, n.
    72
T'ien-lang (star), 59, 131, n. 86
T'ien-lu Gallery, 119
T'ien-pao (Heavenly Treasure), 69, 73, 77,
    133, n. 40

Ting-hu, 64, 132, n. 14
Tristia, 17
Tökei, Ferenc, 15
Topographia, 36
Topoi: time's fate, 27, 103; world upside
    down, 17, 20, 27, 103
'Tribute of Yü'. *See Yü kung*
Ts'ai Tse, 100, 101, 136, n. 39, 137, n. 48
Tsan (Appraisal), 9, 121, n. 14, n. 17, 122,
    n. 47
Ts'ang Chieh, 120, n. 3
Ts'ang Chieh hsün tsuan, 1
Ts'ang-hai (Green Sea), 50, 130, n. 53
Ts'ang-wu, 15, 71, 75, 133, n. 42
Ts'ao Shen, 100, 102, 136, n. 40, 137, n.
    54
Tso chuan, 12, 123, n. 5, n. 6
Tso Commentary. See Tso chuan
Tso Ssu, 117, 139, n. 8
Tsou Yang, 29
Tsou Yen, 99, 135, n. 27, 136, n. 45
Tsou Ying, 134, n. 74
Tsou Yü-shan, 134, n. 74
Tsung-heng chia, 6, 21, 26, 125, n. 46, 135,
    n. 21
Tu Fu, 109
Tung ching fu, 128, n. 21
Tung Chung-shu, 131, n. 81
Tung-fang Shuo, 41, 86–7, 97, 103, 137, n.
    57
Tung hsiao fu, 42–3
Tung hsüeh (Grotto), 71, 75, 76, 133, n.
    42
Tung Tso-pin, 113
Tung Yi (Eastern Yi), 82
Tung yüeh (Eastern Peak), 71. *See also*
    Mount T'ai
T'ung-t'ien (Heaven Penetrating) Tower, 47,
    128, n. 26
Twinkler. *See* Chao-yao
Tzu-fang. See Chang Liang
Tzu-hsü fu, 31, 34, 127, n. 88, 134, n. 50
Tzu-jan (spontaneity), 93
Tzu-wei (star), 54
Tz'u (words, literature), 89, 93
Tz'u fu (rhapsody), 89
Tz'u jen chih fu, 95–6
Tz'u-yeh Mountains, 80

'Viewing the Immortals', Rhapsody. *See
    Wang hsien fu*
Vinsauf, Geoffrey of, 32

Waley, Arthur, 6, 89, 111
Wang Erh (artisan), 49, 129, n. 40
Wang hsien fu, 128, n. 12, 130, n. 67, n. 68
Wang Jung-pao, 3

Wang Ken, 113, 138, n. 4
Wang Mang; and Yang Hsiung 2, 6–7; mentioned, 119, 120, n. 3
Wang Pao, 3, 42–3, 45, 121, n. 13, 127, n. 114, 128, n. 11
Wang Shu, 69, 133, n. 39
Wang Yi, 14, 124, n. 18
Wang Yin, 113, 114, 116, 122, n. 47
Wang-yu kuan liu fu, 126, n. 75
Watson, Burton, 6, 32, 96
Wei (River), 59, 64, 65
Wei (state), 25
Wei ch'i fu, 43
Wei Ch'ing, 82, 87, 134, n. 75
Wei Hung, 123, n. 11
Wei Jan. *See* Marquis of Jang
Wei-tzu, 136, n. 36
Wei-yang Palace, 73, 132, n. 18, 134, n. 53, 135, n. 18
Wen, Duke of Chin, 60, 131, n. 94
Wen, Duke of Ch'in, 131, n. 90
Wen, Duke of Lu, 133, n. 21
Wen, Emperor of Han, 82, 87
Wen, King of Chou, 22, 61, 64, 134, n. 51, 136, n. 28
Wen, King of T'ang, 136, n. 28
Wen (pattern), 89–90
Wen Chung, 99, 136, n. 37
Wen fu, 28
Wen hsüan, 10, 42, 45, 62, 63, 80, 97, 104, 117, 126, n. 75
Wen hsüeh, 89
Western Capital Miscellany. See Hsi-ching tsa-chi
'Western Capital Rhapsody'. *See Hsi tu fu*
Whitman, Walt
Wilhelm, Hellmut, 2, 6, 17, 18
'Willow of the Lodge for Forgetting Troubles'. *See Wang-yu kuan liu fu*
Wind Earl. *See* Fei-lien
Wo Chüan, 49, 129, n. 41
Wu (Han kingdom), 30
Wu (Chou state), 99
Wu, Emperor, 29, 39, 40, 41, 44, 51, 53, 64, 77, 78, 82, 89, 112, 129, n. 26, 131, n. 81, 132, n. 14, 134, n. 63, 137, n. 53, n. 56
Wu, King of Chou, 22, 84
Wu Chi, 136, n. 43
Wu Huo, 133, n. 36
Wu ti (Five Emperors), 44, 46, 61, 65, 72, 102, 128, n. 18
Wu-ti ku-shih, 129, n. 29
Wu-tso Palace, 64, 84, 132, n. 15
Wu Tzu-hsü, 71, 73, 76, 99, 133, n. 44, 134, n. 56, 57, 135, n. 26, 136, n. 37
Wu-yi, 84
Wu-yi shan-li, 135, n. 80

Ya ch'in fu, 43
Ya-yü (beast), 81, 134, n. 70
Yang Chu, 71, 79, 134, n. 48
Yang Chuang, 116
Yao, 22, 58, 60, 64, 71, 102, 106, 131, n. 80, n. 97
Yao, Mount, 106, 137, n. 66
Yellow Emperor, 22
Yellow Gate, 121, n. 17
Yellow Mountains. *See* Huang Mountains
Yen (state), 25, 99
Yen, Duke of Ch'u. *See* Duke Chuang
Yen ch'ih (Salt Pond), 58, 131, n. 77
Yen Ho, 135, n. 26
Yen K'o-chün, 11
Yen Lun, 59, 131, n. 89
Yen Ying, 99, 136, n. 33
Yi (Forester), 64
Yi, Sir (archer), 69
Yi ching: model for *T'ai-hsüan*, 7; on hunt, 133, n. 20; mentioned, 1, 8, 91, 132, n. 102
Yi-ch'un, 64, 132, n. 14
Yi Gate, 100, 136, n. 43
Yi-wen chih, 19, 26, 34
Yi-wen lei-chü, 10, 104, 117
Yi-wu. *See* Kuan Chung
Yi Yin, 49, 55, 99, 129, n. 43, 136, n. 33
Ying-chou (island), 64
Ying-huo (Mars), 66
Yu Fu-feng, 80, 85, 114, 134, n. 63
Yu Meng, 121, n. 19
Yu shui, 21
Yu-tu, 39, 48, 50, 83, 129, n. 34, 135, n. 78
Yü (Earth), 46, 57, 128, n. 21
Yü (legendary emperor), 22, 60, 61, 64, 131, n. 75, 76, 95, 133, n. 42
Yü, Lord of, 15
Yü Ch'ing, 136, n. 44
Yü Fu (doctor), 101, 103
Yü-heng (Jade Balance), 82, 134, n. 73
Yü-hsiu, 64, 132, n. 14
Yü hsüeh (Cavern of Yü), 133, n. 42. *See also* Tung hsüeh
Yü kung, 122, n. 1
Yü lieh (plume hunt), 132, n. 6
Yü lieh fu. See Chiao lieh fu
Yü nü (Jade Maiden), 50, 54, 55–6, 130, n. 50
Yü Shih-nan, 10
Yü Shun. *See* Shun
Yü t'ang (Jade Hall), 97, 130, n. 50, 135, n. 20
Yü-wu, 83, 135, n. 76
Yü-yüan, 66, 74, 133, n. 31
Yü Yüeh, 7

Yüan yu, 18, 39, 55, 74, 76, 134, n. 57
Yüeh Yi, 99, 136, n. 38
Yün-meng, 34, 35, 72, 78, 134, n. 50
Yün shih, 67

Yün-yang, 44, 45
Yung, 115

Zach, Erwin von, 6